Interpretations
of the
First Amendment

William W. Van Alstyne

Interpretations of the First Amendment

Duke Press Policy Studies
Duke University Press, Durham and London

© Copyright 1984, Duke University Press
Printed in the United States of America on
acid-free paper. ∞
Third printing; first printing in paperback, 1990
Library of Congress Cataloging-in-Publication Data
Van Alstyne, William W.
Interpretations of the First Amendment.
(Duke Press Policy studies)
Includes bibliographical references and index.
1. Freedom of speech — United States. 2. Freedom of
the press — United States. 3. Mass media — Law and
legislation — United States. I. Title. II. Series.
KF4770.V36 1984 342.73'085 84-4030
ISBN 0-8223-0590-9 (cloth) 342.30285
ISBN 0-8223-1037-6 (paperback)
The introduction and chapters are adaptations from the
following previous writings:
The introduction was in fact written for this book, but
with an acknowledgment of that fact it appeared in
35 U. Fla. L. Rev. 209 (1983) as "Interpreting This
Constitution: The Unhelpful Contributions of Special
Theories of Judicial Review."
Chapter 1 is an adaptation of an article previously
appearing in 70 Calif. L. Rev. 107 (1982), "A Graphic
Review of the Free Speech Clause."
Chapter 2 is not an adaptation from a previous article,
but related antecedent articles using some of the same
material were in 9 Hofstra L. Rev. 1 (1980), "The
First Amendment and the Free Press: New Trends and
Old Theories," and in 28 Hastings L. J. 761 (1977),
"The Hazards to the Press of Claiming a 'Preferred'
Position."
Chapter 3 originally appeared in different form in 29
S. Car. L. Rev. 539 (1978), "The Möbius Strip of
the First Amendment: Perspectives on Red Lion."

Contents

Preface

The chapters of this book integrate some previous work on interpretations of the speech and press clause of the first amendment. They are meant to be useful to the general reader. The substantial notes section is intended to be of additional assistance to serious students of the principal case law and professional literature addressed to this subject. Needless to say, I am most grateful to the Duke University Press for its interest in making these revised essays available in this form.

The object of the first chapter is to provide a serial review of standard interpretations that have competed for judicial supremacy during the long history of our first amendment. This presentation integrates a good deal of specific case law and a great deal of academic criticism that has questioned the clarity and adequacy of the Supreme Court's administration of the free speech clause. It is meant to make the nature of constitutional issues in free speech conflicts readily accessible to anyone who may well wonder why these disputes seem to evoke such an astonishing variety of responses and why, even now, we seem to lack a single, succinct statement of "the law."

To sharpen the contrasts among the most dominant interpretations of the free speech clause, I have integrated a series of graphics with the text. These may have several uses. For one thing, they may illustrate quite forcefully why differing interpretations of the first amendment are thought to be so consequential— why one or another interpretation surely *must* be "right," and what a disaster it would be were it otherwise. Fear of the implications of certain interpretations, rather than conviction of the clear correctness of one's own, may in fact explain a great deal in the unstable treatment of the free speech clause. A graphic comparison of the principal interpretations that have competed for judicial fealty during nearly two hundred years of American history may show quite clearly which uncertainties tend most to be feared. Nothing may put the matter quite so well as a good picture. Here, we shall take a look at nearly a dozen different pictures each with its own pregnant implications.

Additionally, if the whole presentation goes well, by the end it may even suggest its own conclusions. Despite their great differences, a number of proposed interpretations may turn out to share more features in common than first met the eye. In the end, as with any well-told tale, they may even yield a somewhat surprising conclusion that nonetheless fits the pieces of the story quite neatly and that, though not perfect (nothing ever is), works. In this case, that conclusion could be captured in some sort of composite statement about the first amendment, responsive to the critical text, not indifferent to the problems that have beset it, and quite congruent with a reasonable notion of constitutional interpretation. I think this is quite possible and indeed it is the very object of the first chapter.

Chapter 2 proceeds to examine an issue deliberately postponed in the first chapter's discussion of the free speech clause and for which that discussion is obviously incomplete as a treatment of the whole clause. This chapter takes a close look at a matter that has generated a great deal of contemporary interest as well as much professional quarreling: whether the "freedom of speech" and the "freedom of the press," both of which are protected by the first amendment, are reiterations of one indivisible freedom or whether they imply separate systems of differing constitutional protection. Who is "the press," it asks, and what difference does it make so far as the first amendment is concerned? Are journalists separated by the phrasing of the first amendment itself ("Congress shall make no law abridging the freedom of speech or of the press")? If they are, in what respects may the press clause yield a separate or distinctive set of first amendment interpretations? The object of our review will be to recapitulate the excellent rival views that still tend to divide scholars and judges, as well as journalists, in interpreting the press clause. The materials may be of particular use to those in journalism, but there is nothing here that cannot also be easily assimilated in a single reading by anyone who has ever experienced the most ordinary kind of ambivalence we have all felt at one time or another about "the press."

Chapter 3 is logically complementary to chapter 2 and takes us to the edge of some of our most modern and difficult first amendment problems. Technically, the subject is the distinction between the familiar "press" of newspapers and other printed materials, and the newer press of the airwaves. The historical press, the press usually dated from Gutenberg's fifteenth-century printing press with its movable typeface, is assuredly the one the drafters and ratifiers of the first amendment already knew much about in 1791. It is surely "the press" as embraced by the first amendment. Whether Marconi's radio and the immense subsequent development of electromagnetic spectrum communications are part of that press as well, however, is less obvious. Whether an answer to that question may make little difference insofar as radio and television would still be fully protected by the speech clause (and the general analysis canvassed in chapter 1), moreover, seems also well worth considering as an alternative possibility. In any event, the immediate object of chapter 3 is to review the comparative first amendment treatment of private commercial publications and the hybridized arrangement imposed upon the airwaves by various acts of Congress. The serious point developed toward the end of the chapter is concerned less with unstable interpretive distinctions that superficially distinguish first amendment disputes over government regulations of the airwaves, however, than with perplexities of understanding the relationship of free speech and private property in the United States. The problem is at least as difficult and as divisive as the philosophical tension between the presuppositions of John Locke and of Karl Marx. It is also very sobering in helping one to understand how it is that persons who are altogether serious in attempting to interpret the first amendment straightforwardly nonetheless concede that the margin of good-faith disagreement can be very considerable.

Finally, a word about the introduction, "Interpreting *This* Constitution." In some respects, it does not fit the balance of the book and many readers may do better to ignore it and to begin at once with chapter I. I have included it in this collection of materials principally in anticipation of criticism that the three principal chapters may appear to pay insufficient credit to works on constitutional law that have developed special theories of judicial review, namely, theories that regard it naive or unsophisticated to carry on discussions about "interpreting" the Constitution without first settling what courts ought to do. The assumption of such theories is that it is erroneous to suppose that courts should address every clause or question arising under the Constitution on the same neutral footing. Rather, the intensity, propriety, and predisposition of judicial review allegedly form an inseparable part of each case that is to be decided and of each clause to be applied or not applied. To put the same matter in different words, the idea of such arguments is that the manner in which a given constitutional clause should be interpreted, not interpreted, or noninterpreted, may in fact have only a little to do with that clause and much more to do with "the role" of the Supreme Court in the relation to that clause. In brief, rightly understood, "the role" of the Court is not one of detached adjudication according to neutral standards. Rather, it is both highly partisan and deliberately instrumental, for example, to provide an imprimatur of constitutional legitimacy to acts of Congress or to advance the political and economic status of unbefriended groups.

The assortment of possible roles under such nonstandard theories of judicial review is limited only by each author's imagination and rhetorical skill. This is so because the stipulation of each such role is itself extraconstitutional or, as some have preferred to describe it, "metaconstitutional." Since the source of each claim as to what that role should be resides almost entirely in the mere excellence of the idea of what different writers think the Supreme Court should do, necessarily the range of such ideas is correspondingly very broad. There are thus nearly as many nonstandard theories of judicial review as there are different people or judges with different instrumental preferences as to which interests or which groups the Supreme Court should favor. The common element shared by all such theories, however, is the view that the one thing the court ought not do is to approach each issue of constitutional law and each clause of the Constitution with the same detachment as it would bring to any other.

For reasons reviewed in the introduction, I have found virtually all of these nonstandard theories of judicial review quite unhelpful. The point of the introduction is to provide the reader with some understanding of the problems associated with such theories generally and to indicate why they may not provide as much relief from the admitted uncertainties of constitutional interpretation as has sometimes been supposed. This way of dealing with the problem is not very satisfactory, especially as it is necessarily more abbreviated than would be appropriate if the subject of this book were itself nonstandard theories of judicial review rather than interpretations of the first amendment. But it seemed better than the alternatives of either omitting any discussion of such matters or of taking account of each special theory all along the way, in each chapter, to indicate exactly how one's interpretations of the first amendment would be affected. The first alternative might have appeared neglectful. The second seemed bound to be more confusing than helpful. Thus I have addressed these approaches separately, solely in the introduction, and more for contrast than for incorporation in the ensuing substantive discussion of the first amendment. Even so, I believe that readers who are persuaded that deus ex machina theories of judicial review do provide answers to first amendment questions that others find perplexing will not be disadvantaged by this treatment. For them, the answer to any first amendment question (as to any other constitutional question) can still be supplied by reference to whatever special theory of judicial review seems most attractive, whether abstracted from the list of such theories as discussed in the introduction or supplied by their own background and imagination. Here it will be enough to share one's own ground for skepticism.

I shall be pleased if the reader gets from these essays some sense of the stimulation I experienced in writing them.

Interpretations of the First Amendment

Introduction

Interpreting *This* Constitution

The United States has an aged Constitution. In fact, among the world's extant constitutions, ours is the oldest of those that are both written and judicially enforceable as supreme law. Most Americans, growing up under the presuppositions of how our own Constitution operates, may well assume that it merely reflects a commonplace feature of government. But that assumption is inaccurate. Even now, the world's general practice is contrary to our own. Indeed, a great deal of our early constitutional law that is so much taken for granted at home is more carefully studied in other countries that have only recently modified their own basic legal arrangements in partial imitation of the American constitutional plan. In India, Japan, and West Germany, for instance, early American Supreme Court decisions (such as *Marbury v. Madison*,[1] which confirmed the authority of the Supreme Court to refuse to apply acts of Congress that in its view are not consistent with the Constitution), are studied with keen interest because somewhat equivalent powers have been vested in their judiciaries only during the last forty years.[2] In England, which even now resists suggestions to entrench a written constitution or a bill of rights,[3] the manner in which the United States Supreme Court has historically exercised its stewardship in constitutional adjudications is also of very modern interest. It fuels the English debate on both sides of controversy;[4] some influential persons utilize certain United States Supreme Court decisions to illustrate the wisdom of providing similar protections in England, while a larger number utilize other decisions that, in their opinion, show the unwisdom and untrustworthiness of such judicial power.

A great deal of the hesitancy in other countries to entrench within their own government an independent judiciary with powers of constitutional superintendence such as those possessed by our Supreme Court reflects an ambivalence still not entirely laid to rest even in the United States. Essentially, it is an ambivalence that such provisions of fundamental law as are worthy of being placed beyond simple majoritarian tampering in a constitution must necessarily be cast in language that nevertheless requires interpretation. But insofar as virtually no amount of editorial precaution can fully ensure against subsequent judicial misconstructions that may grow out of mere judicial hubris (or out of impatience for appropriate constitutional change through amendment), there is an anxiety that entrenching fundamental law is not well advised. The judiciary cannot be trusted. The point is very old and equally new.

In England it takes the form of doubting the wisdom of confiding to judges a power to hem in Parliament by irreversible interpretations of proposed fundamental-law clauses that class-biased judges might construe (or misconstrue) in favor of the propertied classes.[5] It is a concern derived partly from observations about the United States Supreme Court and its uses of the due process clause during the "Lochner" era, namely, that period during which a very large number of state statutes were held invalid as depriving entrepreneurs of "liberty" or "property" without "due" process.[6] In the United States it is equally well represented at the other extreme by the arguments of Alexander Hamilton, who dismissed the desire to include a bill of rights within the proposed constitution of 1787. Here the objection was that the effort would be misleading and insufficient because, however a free speech or free press clause might be framed, the definitional latitude available to courts (as available also to Congress) would tolerate wholesale "evasion":

> What is the liberty of the press? Who can give it any definition which would not leave the utmost latitude for evasion? I hold it to be impracticable; and from this I infer, that its security, whatever fine declarations may be inserted in any constitution respecting it, must altogether depend on public opinion, and on the general spirit of the people and of the government. And here, after all, as intimated upon another occasion, must we seek for the only solid basis of all our rights.[7]

Nonetheless, at the time Hamilton expressed his own skepticism, the more moderate optimism shared by both Thomas Jefferson and James Madison prevailed, although each readily conceded the inconclusiveness of a bill of rights. Indeed, their own observations were extremely measured. Jefferson suggested:

> The declaration of rights, is, like all other human blessings, alloyed with some inconveniences, and not accomplishing fully its object. . . . But though it is not absolutely efficacious under all circumstances, it is of great potency always, and rarely inefficacious. A brace the more will often keep up the building which would have fallen, with that brace the less.[8]

Similarly, writing to Jefferson less than a year before he introduced into Congress his own draft of a bill of rights, Madison quite mildly observed: "I have favored it because I suppose it might be of use, and if properly executed could not be of disservice."[9] Addressing the House of Representatives, Madison reflected the same sensible diffidence:

> I will own that I never considered this provision so essential to the Federal Constitution as to make it improper to ratify it, until such an amendment was added; at the same time, I always conceived, that in a certain form, and to a certain extent, such a provision was neither improper nor altogether useless.[10]

Then, adverting to the expectation of judicial responsibility to apply the proposed Bill of Rights in the normal course of adjudication, Madison noted: "If they are incorporated into the constitution, independent tribunals of justice will consider themselves in a peculiar manner the guardians of these rights."[11] Madison's own notes, jotted down to guide him in this extemporaneous address in Congress, summed up the matter: "Bill of Rights—useful not essential. . . ."[12]

These were modest and quite unexceptionable expectations. They did not dwell upon extraordinary notions of judicial review, but here, as elsewhere (e.g., the *Federalist Papers*),[13] judicial review is treated quite matter-of-factly. The marginal uncertainties of the Bill of Rights were taken for granted. The assumption that judges would nonetheless feel bound to apply its provisions as superior law is seen as no anomaly, but rather as a useful device. The attitudes expressed are those of reasonable optimism and not of either naïveté or fear.

Today, however, things are much changed. Two centuries of constitutional adjudication have produced a greying of the Constitution. They have also produced an uneasiness respecting the interpretive predilections of our own Supreme Court that makes its imitation abroad problematic and amendment here at home discouragingly difficult. One's sense of the ill-fated equal rights amendment,[14] for instance, is that it became a casualty to the apprehensions of persons who frankly feared not what it said but how it might be judicially construed. One's impression of efforts in England to secure an equivalent, enforceable bill of rights in that country is that the task has been made much more difficult, rather than more likely, because of our experience. A great deal of this is due to the judiciary's own excessive ingenuity and to the misplaced wisdom that has urged upon the Supreme Court a variety of utterly remarkable views respecting the interpretation and noninterpretation of the Constitution.

From nearly the beginning, and certainly with the emergence of John Marshall, "special" theories of constitutional interpretation have competed for favor within our Supreme Court. In Marshall's case, it was the innovation of a constitutional jurisprudence pursuant to which acts of Congress (other than those affecting the judiciary)[15] would not be subjected to the same judicial predisposition as acts of the several states. Rather, acts of Congress would be treated as presumptively constitutional; and only in the event that their validity depended upon a manifestly unreasonable or virtually unimaginable interpretation of some clause, might they be successfully impugned.[16] John Marshall, it may be useful to add, had no difficulty concluding that the Alien and Sedition Acts of 1798 (the first pieces of national legislation seriously abridging free speech in the United States) were plainly constitutional. On the other hand, no similar loose construction attended the Marshall Court's review (and invalidation) of state laws in respect to those few constitutional clauses as were addressed to the states.[17]

Still, despite his enormously impressive influence on the Supreme Court and his remarkable thirty-four years of service, John Marshall could not live as long as the Constitution itself. And predictably, the fundamentals of Marshall's double standards of constitutional interpretation would not necessarily be shared by the chief justice (Taney) or the associate justices who would come after him. As the jurisprudence of Marshall's own special theory was not fixed in the Constitution, nor was it by any means otherwise so persuasive that none could give reasons to reject it, it could not last. Thus, it came to be displaced by quite a different theory—one not at all consistent with Marshall's views. For example, it is plain that *Dred Scott v. Sanford*, written by Chief Justice Taney, does not proceed from an interpretive predisposition at all like that reflected in *McCulloch v. Maryland*, in which chief Justice Marshall sustained an act of Congress vesting four-fifths majority control of a national bank in private shareholders and private directors, and a holding that it was immune to the taxation power of any state (despite the absence of any provision in the Bank Act that purported to legislate such immunity).[18]

From that time to this time has, in turn, been quite a long span. And other individuals, holding other strong special theories of judicial role and of constitutional interpretation, have had their own turn on the Court.[19] Each, moreover, has drawn varying measures of extraordinary encouragement from very able and occasionally very zealous American scholars. Some, noting the lack of compunction of their predecessors who presumed to proceed by very different theories than those who preceded them, felt correspondingly at ease in doing likewise. And so things have gone.

Within the span of any one generation, the appearance and the dominance of some special theory need not particularly have mattered. For within a given period, an established judicial predisposition may well become "normal," that is, it may become standard and, in some sense, thus also become correct. Even between two generations, each reflecting quite a different judicial predisposition toward constitutional interpretation, the sense of consternation need not be great. Insofar as the decisional consequences of one Supreme Court's interpretive orientation may well have become politically resented, a shift in the doctrinal vagaries of the next Court, albeit in fact a shift to yet another nonneutral position, would not necessarily be seen as such. Rather, it might be (mis)understood as merely providing a welcome corrective of the perceived hubris or error of the immediately preceding Court.

But it is an inevitable consequence of having an aging constitution that it exhibits these practices over a very long time. And therein is the rub. Over two centuries the precedents of previous adjudications accumulate. The early cases, under John Jay or John Marshall, were not disadvantaged by the geriatrics of accumulated precedent. Increasingly, however, as the detritus of past decisions mass like so many granular mounds, the piles of antecedent case law confront each new justice until the task is principally to account for the prior case law and only incidentally, as it were, to interpret the Constitution.

The early cases arising under the Constitution tended much more strongly to set down a distinctive jurisprudence. They read as one might expect constitutional law to read. The holdings were cast in broad, quite confidently asserted terms. The opinions fastened on principal issues. The Court was infrequently divided, and the resulting doctrines were strong.[20] In reading early cases, whatever else one might think of them, one felt that they had the feel of *constitutional law.* While there was in fact a heavy bias in the interpretive predilections of the Marshall Court, it still had the enormous advantage of not having to answer to the stare decisis legacy of two centuries of shifting schemes of predilection. Now, however, there is such an outstanding exhibition of special interpretive preferences respecting predispositions of constitutional review that it is much more awkward to maintain that it is *this* Constitution that is being interpreted. Rather, it is more widely felt that one must ask: Whose partial jurisprudence is currently being applied?

Among the many varieties of such partial jurisprudence, examples and very elaborate scholarship can be mustered to endorse quite a large number of very different propositions, virtually as though each were itself actually prescribed in article III. The following is by no means an exhaustive list:

1. Acts of Congress shall not be examined for consistency with the Constitution according to the same interpretive predilection as shall be applied to such clauses that may restrict state legislation;[21]
2. *and*, acts of the national government that are challenged merely on the ground that the Constitution confides the power to perform some act to a department other than the department from which it is issued shall not be examined at all;[22]
3. *moreover*, no act of government arising from any source of government, whether national, state, or local, should be seriously examined for consistency with the Constitution except to the extent that it results from a process which the Supreme Court believes to be insufficiently democratic;[23]
4. *but* such laws as may be thought to be representation-reinforcing for neglected minorities shall in any case not be examined for consistency with the Constitution by the same standards as would apply to other legislation;[24]
5. *on the other hand*, such acts of government that, in the Supreme Court's view (as informed by a convincing jurisprudence of moral philosophy), abridge any natural right fundamental to persons shall be examined with sufficient scrutiny as is most likely to determine that they are inconsistent with this Constitution;[25]
6. *and finally*, this Constitution shall be deemed to have enacted all essential principles of justice, despite first impressions to the contrary. Accordingly, the Supreme Court shall hold invalid such legislation as convincing sources of moral philosphy persuade a majority of its members are inconsistent with essential principles of justice, as shall they also employ the judicial power to impose upon all levels of government appropriate enforceable obligations to insure to each person the material conditions of justice.[26]

Of course, not all of these prescriptive interpretive (and noninterpretive)[27] directives could be provided for in article III, even were there a predisposition to do so, for they fit together uncomfortably. It is true, also, that in fact none of them is thus provided for,[28] although each has been enthusiastically endorsed and each, to some extent, has been acted upon by the Supreme Court, albeit to different degrees at different times.

There is, however, a cost to these things. They are those we have adverted to. The American model is difficult to commend abroad when its career at home exhibits such a high degree of unanticipated judicial plasticity. It has become

increasingly difficult to alter, moreover, when the anxiety of even marginal ambiguity in proposed amendments cannot now be answered as Madison was able
to answer Hamilton's concerns. We do not dare now to add the possibility of
new troubles given the troubles we have seen. Time does not always heal all
things. In the aging of our Constitution, time has tended to reveal too many
things.

There is also the misfortune of a negative synergism at work in these matters—a long-term effect that neither the Supreme Court nor a majority of people
would desire if either could control the matter solely by their own action, but an
effect nonetheless that tends to come from their joint reactions. The Constitution
is increasingly difficult to modify by amendment. The difficulty is partly the
consequence of mistrust of uncertainty, a mistrust to which the judiciary has
itself contributed by its endless, shifting quest among special theories of constitutional review. The sheer greater unamendability of the Constitution in turn
reciprocally presses in on the judiciary, so that it must do its best to spin out
additional, mutating "meanings" from existing clauses to maintain the contem-
poraneity of the (now unalterable) Constitution. If, for instance, it is no longer
feasible for an equal rights amendment to be ratified, it becomes even more
legitimate than before for the Supreme Court to construe the fourteenth amendment toward the same end. And yet, since the judiciary tends to take this task
upon itself anyway,[29] what then does it matter that the equal rights amendment
was not ratified, and who, moreover, could be confident of its interpretation were
it to be approved?

It is sometimes observed quite ruefully that were the first amendment or the
entire Bill of Rights to be freshly considered today, as though they were not now
a feature of our Constitution, they could not possibly be accepted. Most often,
the point is offered reproachfully to suggest that Americans do not believe in
these liberties as much as was originally the case. Possibly there is something to
that idea, but possibly it is much oversold. Rather, it may be that we have been
tutored to take proposed constitutional language much more seriously, to parse
each phrase, to imagine every possible nuance of each adjective or noun, and to
treat the matter much more as we would treat the fine print in the exclusionary
clauses of an insurance policy, with apprehension rather than hope. Very little in
the Bill of Rights itself could endure that process and, with all respect, the tendency of the Court to superimpose special, or noninterpretive, predispositions is
certainly part of the difficulty.

To be sure, given a certain view of judges, and given a certain capacity for
philosophic detachment, it may be feasible to dismiss these difficulties as inconsequential. If one imagines that enlightened judges can stay atop matters, one
may also suppose that their own ingenuity may be sufficient to "perfect" the
Constitution, however spare its actual provisions. Surely this view is not merely
remarkably optimistic, however, but considerably silly. A wholly creative Supreme Court could well have made an isolated provision in article IV of the
Constitution (that the United States shall guarantee to each state a "republican"

form of government), an ample text to have outlawed slavery, to have extended the right to vote, and to have protected free speech as well. For is it not obvious that no government can be genuinely republican (i.e., representative) unless it is a government of free people, sharing a common right to vote, and fully protected in their freedom to express their political differences? Thus the bare text of this one clause in article IV can facilitate immense good. A special theory of a constitutional role for courts would endorse it. Accordingly, neither the first amendment,[30] the thirteenth,[31] the fourteenth,[32] the fifteenth,[33] the nineteenth,[34] the twenty-fourth,[35] nor the twenty-sixth[36] was important after all. None needs to have "cluttered" the Constitution. Given suitable ingenuity, perhaps the whole of the Constitution could be reduced to a single paragraph and still not lose any of the judicial glossing it has received!

At the other extreme, there is the very different view that the judiciary ought never invoke the Constitution as an invalidating barrier to legislation unless no amount of ingenuity can plausibly free it from doing so, because judicial review is itself antidemocratic and to that extent objectionable.[37] A recently popular variant of this argument is that the Supreme Court should simply yield the "meaning" of the Constitution in such degree as the legislation under review appears to be the product of democratic processes. In brief, the meaning of the Constitution is generally to be whatever a transient majority declares. One might reject the assumptions of either form of the argument merely on the practical basis that the Court (as well as the Constitution) is on quicksand once it feels impressed by this advice. A majority of people constituting a representative body at one time may be no less genuinely representative at that time than a fully equivalent majority of another time, but with each holding a wholly different view of the power they possess under the Constitution. Depending, then, upon the accident of the substance of the enacted legislation, indistinguishable statutes (indistinguishable, that is, in terms of the degree of representativeness that secures them) are identically "constitutional," though their provisions in fact may be mutually exclusive of one another and mutually exclusive also in terms of their compatibility with the Constitution. In this fashion, judges have little to do other than to be jerked about as manikins, approving the "constitutionality" of whatever is "representatively" enacted and reviewing seriously only "unrepresentative" enactments.

Additionally, the proposition that the Supreme Court should vary the substance of constitutional clauses depending upon its view of the "representativeness" of the particular legislation at issue in the cases is subject to the serious objection that it imputes to the Court an obligation it has no professional competence to discharge. Its "judgments" in this area of political sociology are unlikely to be sophisticated.[38] Its outcomes will be correspondingly eccentric, and its reasoning tends ultimately to exhibit a built-in circularity. Indeed, it may become a mere camouflage for judicial preference of result.

Sometimes, for instance, the object of "representativeness" inquiry is the electoral representativeness of the officeholder or law-making body whose act or practice is in constitutional question.[39] The notion is that the wider the electoral auspices of the immediate source of "law" drawn into question, the greater the demonstration must be of the law's inconsistency with the clause or combination of clauses pursuant to which it is challenged.[40]

At certain other times, however, the focus is not upon the breadth of the electoral base represented by the lawmakers. Rather, it is on the "representativeness" of those who will be most affected by the particular law. The notion here is that if the actual legislative circumstances suggest to the Court that the majority of legislators and those whom they represent may be indifferent to the proposed act (for instance, the act would have no immediate implications for them [except, of course, as a legislative precedent]), then the datum that the act will not in fact have a broad field of application is deemed to undermine the integrity of its "representative" auspices such that a lesser degree of constitutional inconsistency should be sufficient to have the Supreme Court declare that it is unconstitutional.[41]

A variation of this second approach then closes the gap by becoming circular. If, though an act emerges under electorally representative auspices (e.g., Congress rather than an individual police officer), and though it will affect a majority of all persons in all regions of the country alike, to the extent that members of the Court surmise from the content of the act that it cannot be *authentically* representative (because to the Court's satisfaction such an act could not have been passed if it were "authentically" representative), then it is stripped of any presumption of substantive constitutional consistency and, indeed, is presumed not to satisfy the clause invoked to question it.[42]

The circle is closed by generalizing this last analysis: such legislation as certain justices believe to be "unjust" can *never* be representative since by definition authentically representative bodies would not have enacted it had they been *duly considerate* of what they were doing (i.e., duly representative).[43] Thus, every "unjust" law carries no presumption of representativeness and, correspondingly, no presumption of substantive constitutional consistency attaches such that the court should defer in the absence of litigation demonstrating a "clear error" (rather than a mere error) in the constitutional premises of the enacting body.

The denouement of "representativeness" jurisprudence may ultimately follow this form:

1. "Truly representative" legislation is not to be held inconsistent with the Constitution merely because the Court is (otherwise) persuaded that it is unauthorized or forbidden by the Constitution. Rather, such legislation must be sustained unless premised upon a manifestly unreasonable interpretation of that clause or combination of clauses that has been brought to bear on the question.

2. "Unjust" legislation, however, is never "truly representative," because legislation that is in fact "unjust" could not have been duly considerate (i.e., truly representative) in respect to those whom it affects.

3. *Therefore*, all legislation that (the Court thinks) is "unjust" is stripped of any presumption of substantive constitutional consistency; indeed, such legislation must be held invalid once shown to be inconsistent with what is itself not a manifestly fanciful interpretation of that clause or combination of clauses that has been brought to bear on the question.

The simpler form is this:

1. Laws a current majority of this Court think are "just" shall (almost) always be held to be constitutional, the Constitution to the contrary notwithstanding.
2. Laws a current majority of this Court think are "unjust" shall (almost) always be held to be unconstitutional, the Constitution to the contrary notwithstanding.[44]

To foreign students of American constitutional government, moreover, the basic objection itself must sound extremely peculiar. The international significance of American constitutional law is precisely that the institution of judicial review *is* "antidemocratic." It is distinguished in exactly that respect. To reveal that it is antidemocratic may sound as though a shameful discovery had been made that therefore needs to be treated apologetically. In fact it is no revelation at all. It is seized upon with the same indicting passion as though one were to read the Constitution for the first time and discover that several of its original clauses actually condoned slavery, which, until the enactment of the thirteenth and fourteenth amendments, was entirely true.[45] Still, just as in the case of the several slave clauses, the anticipated antidemocratic character of judicial review was no secret. Rather, it was treated most matter-of-factly. And, *unlike* the slave clauses in this respect, it was not defended merely as a necessary concession to secure ratification. It was defended as a positive good: the integrity of the Constitution would *not* depend upon mutating impressions in Congress or elsewhere.[46] Judges were *not* expected to "adjust" the meaning of clauses in proportion to the numbers or representativeness of legislative bodies. The difficulty with the objection is, therefore, that while its endless repetition has given it the appearance of profound insight, it may rather be set aside as altogether trivial.

It is also an objection that goes fundamentally to the endorsement of a radically different constitutional order than our own, but in any event *not* our own. In contemplation of law, for instance, the written constitution of the USSR is little else (indeed, it is nothing else) than what its terms are made to mean by the Supreme Soviet—that nation's highest and most representative elected body. The distinction of the American plan is certainly not in its familiar federalism arrangements, as the Russian constitution provides for similar arrangements. It is not even in the provision of a bill of rights. The Russian constitution has a longer, much more impressive bill of rights. The whole distinction is, rather, that the Constitution counts here (as it frankly does not count there) because of its own emphatic removal of its adjudicative stewardship from the vicissitudes of willful "representativeness." Insinuating that kind of interpretive control back into the process, albeit piecemeal rather than wholesale, does not improve the plan. Rather, it defeats the very distinction of the system. It terminates the reliability as well as the integrity of the plan.

Virtually discarded among the many descriptions of constitutional review in the United States, in contrast with the many special theories, is the following description by the unremarkable Justice Owen Roberts:

> When an act of Congress is appropriately challenged in the courts as not conforming to the constitutional mandate, the judicial branch of the Government has only one duty—to lay the article of the Constitution which is invoked beside the statute which is challenged and to decide whether the latter squares with the former.[47]

As a concise summary of the judicial obligation, Justice Roberts's dictum is worthy of consideration despite the sophisticated criticism it obviously invites. To be sure, its comparison of the judicial task with a mere mechanical exercise may be subject to criticism;[48] the thought that the judicial task is as simply done as laying down a T square to see whether one line is perpendicular to another may itself not square even with an ordinary citizen's impression of the difficulty, to say nothing of those professionally involved in constitutional litigation. But the suggestion that the judicial task of constitutional review should be performed with the same undissembling interest in accuracy as one would bring to his or her own workbench is, nonetheless, a proposal of enormous and lasting appeal. In fact, it may capture more accurately than any other single statement exactly what most people would hope for from the Supreme Court.

The idea is indeed to see whether the two things, the statute and the Constitution, square. If they do not, then the judicial task, which is to state the truth, is not less well done on that account. The correction of the line representing a statute that does not square is for those responsible for drawing such lines. It is with Congress, not the Court. Similarly, the correction of the line representing the relevant article in the Constitution is for those to whom the responsibility is given for altering such lines. It is not the Court's business to move it or to misrepresent its location from any presupposition of its own that a different constitutional line might be better. The fact that the alteration of constitutional lines (i.e., the amendment of constitutional clauses) is difficult in no respect bears on the judicial obligation. If the means of altering constitutional lines is thought to be too difficult to tolerate correct decisions, that observation may propose a very good reason to alter the clause in the Constitution that makes amendment so difficult. It proposes no obvious reason, however, for judges to misstate the Constitution. The case to do so is no better than its opposite, namely, justifications for a predispostion to find that a statute and the Constitution do not square (when in fact the Court believes they do) because of antipathy to the statute or because of one's belief that Congress has made an enormous political or moral (but not unconstitutional) mistake.

The Roberts dictum is sometimes brushed aside on the strength of the suggestion that he did not fully appreciate that it is the Constitution the judges are expounding in these cases,[49] not merely some lesser thing such as a statute, an administrative regulation, or a trivial municipal ordinance. But this suggestion is not at all convincing either biographically or in the abstract. Explicit in the dictum is the recognition that it is the Constitution being expounded. Explicit as well, however, is the important recognition that it is also *this* Constitution the judges are expounding, not some other.

If the Constitution contains clauses not the most noble (as of course it may), clauses that may weigh too heavily upon a judge's conscience, he or she may reassess the personal acceptability of the judicial task. If the task of this Constitution's scrupulous construction and application sometimes seems trivial, demeaning, or even pernicious, the private conviction provides a thoroughly decent reason to find a career in something one believes to be less compromising and more ennobling. Short of entangling considerations that may sometimes excuse personal acts of civil disobedience[50] (in which case, however, one does not pretend to do one's duty but rather declares why one will *not* do so under the circumstances), it provides no reason to refabricate the Constitution or to misrepresent the statute. Because it is the Constitution being expounded, one should be especially conscientious about its determination—should have an exceptional willingness to listen, to consider, and to be very careful.[51] However, that judges should therefore feel more free than otherwise to fudge interpretation because it is the Constitution being expounded is a proposition that, though argued often, has never been argued convincingly.

Despite the straightforwardness of the judicial duty described by Justice Roberts, headway against it has also been directed from quite a different quarter than those suggesting the Supreme Court should simply "adjust" the Constitution to make it better. The Roberts metaphor, as already noted, does imagine something like a T square that judges simply lay down to see whether a statute squares with the Constitution. If not that, at least it must assume that "the line" representing the constitutional clause with which a statute is being compared is reasonably obvious. (It may also imagine that the line is not merely discernible but that it is also fixed, i.e., that it does not move from time to time, though the latter assumption is not critical to all arguments of this type.) In either case, "the line" representing the constitutional clause must at least be reasonably discernible. Otherwise, whether with the aid of a T square or merely with one's own, unaided eyesight, it is impossible to perform the judicial duty, to say whether the statute "squares" with that line. In any event, this much is fairly certain: the less discernible the constitutional line, the less possible the performance of the judicial task even as laid down in the Roberts dictum.

The headway this sort of observation seeks to make against the conventional description of the judicial task now becomes clear. Determining *where* the line represented by a constitutional clause lies is in fact not the same as the mechanical task of seeing *whether* one line "squares" with another. The Roberts dictum takes for granted the obviousness of the line representing the constitutional clause that has been invoked.[52] The task it assumes is solely that of measurement, that is, the determination of whether the two "square." But the problem of judges is not principally that of measurement. It is, rather, that of interpretation. It is the problem of first deciding where does the constitutional line lie? Redundantly, then, the task of judges involves judgment. The Court must determine the meaning of words that in one moment seem plain to one, plain but the opposite to another, marginally uncertain to others, and virtually hopeless to still others.

Between these two critical sentiments, justifications for a great deal of "meta" constitutional law have been proposed. For some, the Constitution is only too clear in certain particulars, but the clarity it yields is extremely disappointing. The actual Constitution does not fulfill one's expectations; it does not exalt what one hopes and it is not commensurate with one's notion of a constitution as ideal norm. "The" judicial duty is therefore to adjust the Constitution by degree, to be guided by a meta-Constitution superimposed upon the inadequate original, to bring it around to normative maturity.[53]

For others, it is quite the opposite point that the Constitution is insufficiently clear in nearly all of its most significant clauses, specifically its most normative clauses such as the due process clause, the equal protection clause, or the ninth amendment virtually in its entirety.[54] Accordingly, "the" judicial duty is to impute some meaning without which the constitutionality of statutes cannot be determined and to impute that meaning according to some notion of what courts might do that neither duplicates legislative processes nor leaves these clauses virtually useless in litigation.[55]

The consequences of these polar objections to the conventional view of the judicial duty (namely, the objection on the one hand that the Constitution is clear but inadequate and on the other that in most essential features it is unclear and thus requires improvisation) nurtures what is perhaps the majority of all academic writing about the Constitution today. I confess that I find very little of it helpful, however, and I do not think we can make any productive use of either point of view. To the contrary, I believe that most of it will eventually be seen at a later date as but the academic residue of yet another period in which American constitutional law records its native propensity for instability and rank politicization.

The first view, that insofar as the Constitution is clear but disappointing the appropriate role of judges is to make it "better" by reconstruction, is not worth further comment. The second view, that in its most interesting features the Constitution is just so indefinite that the Roberts dictum is simply not helpful (because while the preference for a truthful construction of the Constitution is unquestionably alluring, it is frankly also sometimes impossible), is not so lightly dismissed. Indeed, in a large part the following chapters are but a proof of the difficulties. These chapters deal with the speech and press clause of the first amendment, an amendment to the Constitution unquestionably important and, on its face, of exceptional clarity. Yet it is one point of these chapters to induce a wholly sympathetic understanding that conscientious interpretations of the first amendment do differ: that many of the problems of constitutional adjudication are not imagined, that they are not contrived, and that they do not proceed solely from judges who are mere ideologues. Ideologues and persons with hubris have unquestionably served on the United States Supreme Court. But even if one discounts every decision one can dismiss on that basis, other decisions of exquisite difficulty still remain in substantial number. The example of the free speech clause, seemingly the clearest provision we have in the entire Bill of Rights, may paradoxically serve best to make the point.

Even so, while it is surely true that conscientious interpretation of the Constitution is often a more difficult task than the Roberts dictum implied, by no means does its problematic quality lead to a conclusion that failing anything fairly passable as interpretation,[56] courts must improvise meaning according to perceptions of some special judicial role.[57] The dilemma that is sketched that provides a legitimacy for courts to improvise a special role when interpretation fails is not what it seems to be. There is no such duty-at-large and, indeed, certainly no such necessity merely to be able to decide every case appropriately before the court. For in every case, it is not the court who brings the claim and who thus bears the risk of loss. Rather, it is the litigant who brings the claim asserting that there is some "line" (i.e., some article or combination of articles) in the Constitution with which an act does not square. If the location of that line cannot be established, necessarily the claim must fail. If the most one can squeeze from a clause is a mere conjecture, which only if given an improvisational assist by the court, might then fit the claim and protect it from the act, presumably that is insufficient. The decision is that the litigant has failed to show that the act of Congress does not square with the clause that he or she relied upon, and the challenge fails. The burden to show where the constitutional line lies is not with the Court. It is with the party who claims that the act of Congress does not square with that line. The duty of the court is to entertain the claim, to be attentive to it, to require no more of this litigant than would be required of any other, in any other case, to show that "the line lies *here*," so then to see whether the act does not square. Residual uncertainty thus does not impair performance of the judicial function and nothing obliges the court to improvise the line to accommodate the litigant or merely to fill out the Constitution in some abstractly more satisfying way. Indeed, nothing entitles the court to do any of these things. The judicial duty is not less fitly performed because the party raising the challenge fails. Neither was the party raising the challenge necessarily at fault in the sense of having overlooked an approach or a possibility that might have been more helpful. In a certain number of instances, perhaps even a great number of instances, the material necessary to make the case simply may not exist. The case is at an end. The judicial duty is thus to be uniformly fair to those who seek to rely upon the Constitution and neither to disparage those who are successful nor to conjure for the benefit of those who are not.

The point may be briefly illustrated. As sought to be applied to certain claims, it is entirely possible, for instance, that the ninth amendment proves to be difficult to invoke not merely on first impressions but even after one's best efforts to make something of it, though there is no reason, a priori, to take its futility for granted.[57] Similarly, the nature of the United States' obligation to guarantee to each state a "republican" form of government may present a similar difficulty, though again one ought not simply assume that it will.[58] If, then, a state resists application of an act of Congress on the claim that the act does not square with one or the other of these constitutional clauses, of course the state may fail—not because of insufficient effort but because, in the end, the best that could be said was that the "line" representing either clause simply could not be established with sufficient conventional certainty to permit a judgment that the act of Congress failed to square with that line.

It is quite possible, moreover, that some constitutional clauses may turn out to be not merely intractable at their edges but altogether intractable *for litigant use*. If so, it only goes to show in a practical way that such clauses have proved to be unserviceable in litigation before the Supreme Court. They need not, on that account alone, be thought of as unserviceable in legislative debate, unserviceable for executive use, or unserviceable for each citizen's own political or private uses.[59] Rather, it may be merely an unshocking example of nonjusticiability in the most concrete sense. In light of the issue before the Court, the best scholarship the litigant could muster leaves the Court without sufficient basis to hold that the challenged act of Congress does not square with the clause. Indeed, one might suggest that most allegedly "nonjusticiable" clauses are not nonjusticiable in the sense that they may not be a source of litigant reliance. Rather, they are nonjusticiable merely in the practical sense that every effort to invoke them as a means to avoid application of an act of Congress has simply been unsuccessful: in a long list of litigants, none was able sufficiently to show the location of the constitutional line represented by the clause to enable conscientious judges to hold that the line represented by the act of Congress did not square.[60]

Nor is there any peculiarity in this treatment of the matter. To be sure, this description of judicial review does involve a premise that is involved to resolve the putative dilemma, but the premise is neither unconventional nor strained. The premise is merely that when an act of Congress otherwise applies to define a party's rights, it is to be deemed controlling in the Supreme Court unless the litigant is able to show that, as applied, the act fails to square with some clause (or combination of clauses[61]) in the Constitution. The basis of the premise is most immediately the language of the supremacy clause in the Constitution itself: the clause makes an act of Congress the supreme law except insofar as not "pursuant" thereto. The burden of one who claims an act of Congress applies to another is of course to show that the act does so apply. If this demonstration cannot be made with the requisite clarity, that party fails. In turn, the burden of one who claims that an applicable act of Congress nonetheless fails because it does not square with the Constitution is to show that it does not square. If he cannot show what the clause means, he cannot show that the clause helps him and he fails.

Neither does this solution to the alleged interpretive "dilemma" of the courts (i.e., the dilemma that allegedly compels the Court to improvise meanings for constitutional clauses) neglect other observations that may affect how it operates. For instance, one may very well observe that, *depending on the nature of the challenge*, sometimes the burden will be on the party who claims that the act of Congress *does* square. Such an instance would arise when the challenge is not on the basis that the applicable act of Congress is forbidden but rather on the basis that it was not authorized. It notes that only such acts of Congress as the litigant relying upon them is able to show are "pursuant" to the Constitution can be the basis of enforceable claims—enforceable by the government or by anyone else. Moreover, its burden-allocating premise is again quite unexceptionable. The express phraseology in article VI ("This Constitution and the Laws of the United States which shall be made in Pursuance thereof . . . shall be the supreme Law of the Land") straightforwardly supports it.

Indeed, a fuller and relatively complete description, appropriately allocating burdens of uncertainty in respect to constitutional litigation, will itself merely integrate these several observations. First, to the extent that the government or a private litigant claims that an act of Congress does apply to another in the manner alleged, the burden is appropriately the claimant's to show that that is the case. Second, one who claims that an applicable act of Congress nonetheless fails because it does not "square" with the Constitution must indicate in what particular respect the act is alleged not to square. If it is alleged not to square because there is no obvious enumerated power or combination of powers sufficient to sustain the act in question, the burden appropriately becomes that of the party relying upon the act to show that, to the contrary, there is in fact ample authority to sustain it. On the other hand, if the objection is that the act fails not for want of original power to enact it but rather because other constitutional provisions disallow it, the burden of succeeding on that objection is equally clear; it is on the party who so asserts.

Thus, in a particular case the dispute might involve an act of Congress that makes it a federal offense to cross a state line with the intention of inciting others to riot. That the statute applies to the alleged conduct of the accused is for the government to show. Should the act not be challenged as inapplicable but rather as beyond the constitutional competence of Congress, the obligation is again upon the government—to show that the act was within the authority of Congress to enact. Possibly the government may rely upon the commerce clause (the power to "regulate commerce among the several states"), coupled with the famous sweeping clause (i.e., the "necessary and proper" clause), but in any event it is the government's burden to discharge, however easily others may think it can be carried. Separately, however, the party to whom the statute is being applied may object that insofar as the statute means to criminalize interstate travel when undertaken for the purpose of orally inciting certain action by others, it is forbidden by the fifth amendment or by the first amendment; that is, it is an act of Congress that deprives him of "liberty" (the right to travel) without "due" process (i.e., without reasonable consideration of his interests) contrary to the fifth amendment,[62] and it is also an act abridging his freedom of speech and is forbidden by that clause stating that "Congress shall make *no* law abridging the freedom of speech." Of course the burden is upon the defendant to establish that the statute does not "square" with these constitutional provisions and correspondingly to show how each provision fits his case. In this instance, however, that burden may rest upon him quite lightly in the first instance at least in respect to the first amendment, for the language of the clause itself may seem at once to address this case and the government may be appropriately pressed to overcome the weight of his prima facie case.[63]

The Supreme Court thus is *not* bound at all costs to invent some meaning for every word and clause in the Constitution. Rather, it is to measure the adequacy of that meaning or that interpretation tendered by some party to the litigation insofar as that tendered meaning or interpretation is relied upon to show how an act of Congress does or does not "square." Correspondingly, arguments of constitutional meta-interpretation that range beyond the assembly of materials from which reasonable interpretations of constitutional clauses can be derived are of no necessity whatever. Indeed, they are of no propriety. Noninterpreting the only Constitution we are in fact expounding, namely *this* Constitution, whether because one is disgruntled with its limited wisdom or because some provisions are genuinely intractable, is not an impressive enterprise.

We thus return still again to the same observation with which we began. Improvisational interpretations of the Constitution are not required by judicial necessity. Noninterpreting the Constitution has never been a necessity, as no court is obliged to yield to arguments lacking substance in materials reasonably descriptive of *this* Constitution. Similarly, arguments of mere ideological misconstruction (i.e., arguments actually at odds with materials descriptive of *this* Constitution, although quite compatible with that which John Rawls might devise, Karl Marx might approve, or Thomas Hobbes might applaud) are even less interesting professionally. They may possibly frame whole political systems vastly superior to our own and be interesting on that account. They may also stimulate some movement toward amending the Constitution we have in favor of another felt to be substantially better and be interesting also on that account. But precisely to the extent that they are at odds with *this* Constitution, they can play no proper role in its conscientious interpretation in the meantime.

Despite the problems of an aged Constitution, one advantage of having a substantial history is that we may benefit from it by standing aside to see what we think it has produced. In our own history, we have seen the production of a very wide range of nonstandard theories of judicial review. They have ranged from variations on (a), the Supreme Court should regard nearly all constitutional questions as unwelcome and either decline to review them or, failing that, uphold every law it can by ascribing near constitutional finality to legislative discretion, to variations on (z), the Court should engage every dispute that even vaguely resembles a lawsuit to the end of enacting its own preferences through the cellophane wrappers of the Constitution. The intermediate permutations be-tween (a) and (z) have been nearly as numerous as the intervening letters of the alphabet. Other than uncertainty and mistrust, it is not at all clear what they have given us beyond a clutter of embarrassing and contradictory ideas. Neither is it clear that the continuing pursuit of nonstandard theories is nearly as promising as it may once have seemed as a deus ex machina device. As nearly all such advocacy tends to play rather loosely with the remembrance that it is merely *this* Constitution that is being expounded, moreover, it is ultimately rather difficult to take it very seriously.

It remains to be emphasized, however, that the rejection of special theories of judicial review merely reestablishes the legitimate battleground of serious con-stitutional dispute. The fact is, of course, that the materials descriptive of *this* Constitution are actually quite subtle and that they do lend themselves to more than one point of view. Thus, while a rejection of nonstandard theories of judi-cial review delimits the uncertainties of constitutional dispute, it leaves open for consideration the usual hard problems of the law. The ensuing chapters furnish quite solid evidence of these genuine and unimagined hard problems. The dom-inant interpretations of the free speech clause, for instance, are *not* mere inven-tions of wishful thinking. None is neglectful of the text of the first amendment. None flies in the face of an overwhelming history. None attempts to proceed from philosophical premises obviously lacking connections with *this* Constitution. None requires an eccentric appeal to some contrived judicial role. Yet the differences among them are not inconsequential in their effects, and it is no trivial matter to attempt to reconcile them.

The same observation applies equally to chapter 2. As previously foreshad-owed in the preface, this chapter takes up the relationship of the "press" portion of the first amendment and the "speech" portion of the same amendment. With-out hesitating to argue in behalf of what I think professionally represents a better treatment of the matter than I think is produced under the principal alternative choices with which that treatment must withstand comparison, it is nonetheless true that the materials descriptive of this Constitution are not at all on one side and, accordingly, without recourse to novel theories of judicial review, that there is indeed a residual ground of fair choice. An investigation of chapter 3 will discover much the same sort of thing. It reviews the perplexities of applying the first amendment in our increasingly mixed economy, an economy in which the government is increasingly involved in matters that historically were more sub-stantially left to the vicissitudes of the private sector. Here, as well, very able people have argued with great skill in respect to the first amendment's engage-ment, while coming at the matter with strikingly different emphases. For the most part, however, their discussion and the Supreme Court's own analyses have been well within an attitude of judicial review that fits within the spirit of the Roberts dictum.

Indeed, when one may finish with these matters, the net effect may be to find new cause for wonder at the unnecessary expenditure of labored argument devoted to nonstandard theories of judicial review. To an extent more than one might suppose, moderation of judicial role leaves quite enough choice for reasonable people to think about in considering *this* Constitution. One may be surprised that an imperfect, brief, and aged document, even absent those amendments one thinks would significantly improve it, can still speak usefully to our condition, yet I think it still does. The ensuing chapters may make the point quite well.[64]

1

A Graphic Review of the Free
Speech Clause

From its first engagement in the Sedition Act trials of 1798[1] down to the present moment, the free speech clause of the first amendment has been invoked in literally thousands of cases. In the cases handled by the Supreme Court alone, it has been addressed several hundred times. Overall, these adjudicative refinements of the free speech clause present quite an impressive jurisprudence of free speech in America. Even so, there is an awkwardness in this massive case law that makes the discovery of that jurisprudence very hard.

Like so much else about our aging Constitution, the difficulty is partly the consequence of mass and time. The sheer density of precedent is somewhat oppressive, and free speech doctrine has tended to become highly specialized. Contemporary adjudications of the first amendment seem scarcely to reflect the majesty of constitutional law. Judicial review is currently encumbered by such a variety of ramified doctrines that the Supreme Court itself often writes with excessively cautionary disclaimers.

Here, for instance, is how the Court opened its opinion in 1981 in a significant first amendment case.

> Each method of communicating ideas is a "law unto itself" and that law must reflect the "differing natures, values, abuses and dangers" of each method. We deal here with the law of billboards.[2]

In a different case, the Court will "deal" with the law of libel.[3] And so complex has that subspecialty of the free speech clause become that the graphing of a single libel case now requires a chart that may need six to eight "fact categories" running across the top of a page, each to be filled in, opposite five to seven categories running down the edge of the same page.[4]

In another case, the law of obscenity will be constitutionally explicated, wherein a word (*obscene*) that nowhere appears in the first amendment is, nonetheless, deemed so crucial that most of the Court's opinion will be consumed in vexation of that much-abused term. The thought that something has gone astray is itself a thought difficult to avoid when a distinguished associate justice agrees that the first amendment does indeed turn upon whether the speech is "obscene," and then, despairing of his own and his colleagues' lucubrations, concludes as follows: "I shall not today attempt further to define the kinds of material I understand to be embraced within that shorthand description; and perhaps I could never succeed in intelligibly doing so. But I know it when I see it, and the motion picture involved in this case is not that."[5]

Despite the aging of the Constitution, these sorts of disclaimers ("We deal here with the law of billboards." . . . "I know it when I see it") cannot be necessary. Much more generalization must be furnished by the first amendment than technical subspecialities of picayune distinction. However understandable or benign the cautionary instincts of the Supreme Court, there must be larger commonalities that cut across these cases and reduce the field of interesting controversy to more manageable size. And indeed, it turns out that there are. In fact, if one lays aside the Supreme Court's own caveats that suggest the free speech clause merely collects smithereens of technical first amendment subspecialties as in a basket, one may quickly discover that the essential differences among competing ways of formulating basic first amendment questions are not numerous at all. Once one sorts out the basic rival doctrines, they can then be reordered in a sequence that presents all of their fundamental differences very clearly.

What follows here is just that sort of graphic review. The different interpretations of the clause to be reviewed admittedly fall short of exhausting everything that has been tried.[6] Nonetheless, they do include virtually all principal interpretations that have competed most persistently and, treated as they will be here, they may also turn out to be less at odds with one another than one might suppose. In brief, despite the appearance of unbridgeable differences, there may be more coherence and intelligence in the interpretation of the first amendment than first meets the eye.

Especially in view of what was said in the introduction, however, it would be quite inappropriate simply to plunge into the case law and attempt to sort things out from there. Rather, it may make more sense to begin with the first amendment itself.

In comparison with nearly every other provision in the Bill of Rights, the first amendment is of exceptional crispness and clarity. Thus it provides: "Congress shall make *no* law abridging the freedom of speech." Most of the principal affirmative restrictions on government power are far less positive than this. For instance, the fourth amendment protects "the right of the people to be secure in their persons, houses, papers, and effects" only against "*unreasonable* searches and seizures." The fifth amendment assures each person that he or she shall not be deprived of life, liberty, or property without "*due* process." The eighth amendment prohibits only such bail or such fines as are "*excessive*"; it inveighs against only such punishments as are "*cruel and unusual*." From the style of these other amendments, it is quite clear that the rights they secure are qualified and limited. Fines that are not "excessive" are permitted. One may, likewise, even be deprived of life itself, assuming only that the legal process is appropriate, that "due" process is observed. Additionally, the necessary referents of the critical adjectives (*unreasonable, due, excessive, cruel, unusual*) lie outside the words of the Constitution. All of these clauses not only permit interpretation by external reference; they require it.

The first amendment is strikingly different. On its face, it is both unequivocal and absolute. It requires no arcane learning to understand the clear and plain meaning of "Congress," "no law," "abridging," or "speech." To "abridge" means not merely to forbid altogether but to curtail. And the laws forbidden to Congress are not merely such as "unreasonably" abridge speech (cf. the fourth amendment), nor are they laws that are "excessive" abridgments of speech. The imperative is simple, straightforward, complete and absolute: *Congress shall make no law abridging the freedom of speech.*

A literal application of this clause obviously would not make the clause trivial nor would it leave the courts with nothing to do. For consistent with the clause's absolute rejection of laws abridging speech, several difficult questions of interpretation would remain. Those questions, however, would be questions respecting the scope of the clause and not questions respecting the nature or the degree of the protection thus provided. For example, an act of Congress making it a crime to defame the president would be plainly within the scope of the clause and therefore plainly unconstitutional. Whether an act of Congress making it a crime to destroy a draft registration card would also be within the amendment's protection, on the other hand, would still be debatable. The answer would be contingent upon one's willingness to equate the tearing of a pasteboard (a draft card) with "speech."[7] Similarly, an act of Congress making it a crime to criticize any federal judge is plainly within the amendment and accordingly invalid. On the other hand, whether an attempt by a federal judge to silence a witness within the court or speakers outside the court would raise a first amendment issue is a different (and more difficult) question. The amendment says only that *Congress* shall make no law abridging the freedom of speech; on its face, the first amendment is not directed either to the judiciary or to the executive. It does not purport to declare the extent to which the executive or the judiciary is forbidden to abridge speech when acting solely on its own authority, that is, unauthorized or unaided by an act of Congress. Thus, acts of Congress not applicable to "speech," and independent acts of the executive or judiciary that may abridge speech, would continue to raise difficult questions. It is not clear that they would be captured within a literal first amendment. To the contrary, it might appear that they could be captured only by an extended, nonliteral interpretation.[8]

If the source of abridgment is a "law" made by "Congress," however, and if what the law expressly "abridges" is "speech," the amendment itself appears to end the inquiry.[9] What *kind* of speech is involved (e.g., whether political or commercial, private or public, obscene or religious) is, on the face of the amendment, not a question. And equally, whether the speech seems trivial rather than important, reprehensible rather than edifying, fraught with danger rather than insight, are also not questions. For the point, once again, is that while one may always have an appropriate interest in how this amendment to our Constitution came about (e.g., who proposed it, why it was proposed, whether as proposed and ratified it enacted a proposition thoughtful people would find extreme), it is nonetheless *this* amendment that was enacted.[10] If its enactment was a mistake, the means are at hand to alter it. If one finds it too strong (e.g., that it should be

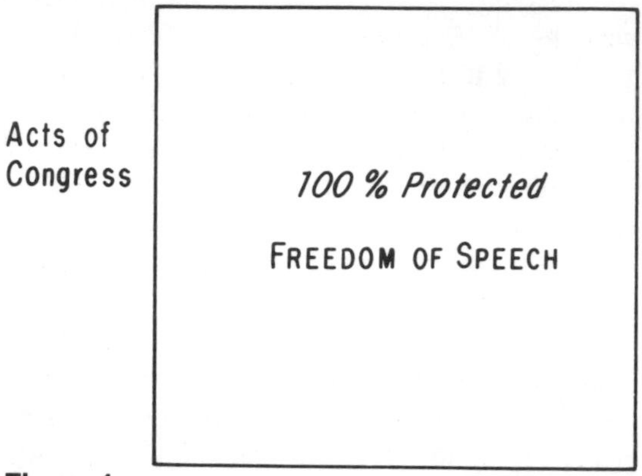

Acts of Congress

100 % Protected

FREEDOM OF SPEECH

Figure 1

recast in terms consistent with the moderation of the fourth, fifth, and eighth amendments), or if one thinks that nothing more than a speech fetishism could account for such a clause, article V of the Constitution provides an amending mechanism for implementing whatever change requisite majorities in Congress and in the states may prefer.[11] In the meantime, we have the free speech clause as it appears; and, as it does appear, it is in *contrast* to, rather than resemblance of, the moderation of other provisions in the Bill of Rights. Accordingly, an accurate depiction of the free speech clause should therefore look like figure 1. There are no lines, no intersecting points, no shaded areas of less protected or unprotected speech. The graphic, though singularly uninteresting, is perfect and inviolate.

Despite the simplicity and considerable logical force of a literal interpretation of the first amendment, it has never commanded a majority of the Supreme Court. Primarily it has succumbed to the buffeting of irresistible counterexamples accommodated both by the first amendment's own uncertain history as well as by its text. An "irresistible counterexample" is merely an instance of speech plainly within the literal protection of the first amendment but an instance nonetheless sufficient to give one pause. One is at once moved to doubt one's own first impression and to move to a position as textually well sustained as the first position but more moderate in its accounting.

Possibly the best-known counterexample is a variation on an instance used by Justice Oliver Wendell Holmes: the case of a person knowingly and falsely shouting "Fire" in a crowded theater for the perverse joy of anticipating the spectacle of others being trampled in a panicky crowd.[12] The counterexample could as well be any of these: an oral statement of one person to another, offering to pay five thousand dollars for the murder of the offerer's spouse; a congressman's bribe solicitation; an interstate manufacturer's false and misleading commercial adver-

Acts of
Congress

Criminal Solicitation
Perjury
Obscenity (?)
Defamation (?)
Commercial Fraud (?)

Figure 2

tisements; a witness committing perjury in the course of a trial; or a member of the public interrupting (by speaking) someone else already speaking at a city council meeting. The counterexample need not be more complicated than a simple, soft statement made to the president—that he will be shot if he fails to veto a particular bill or fails to grant a certain pardon.

Some of these examples may be defensible (i.e., some persons may be willing to defend them as protected by the first amendment), and some may be thought distinguishable (i.e., it will be said that they do not involve speech or that they involve "speech plus").[13] Most of us, however, will recognize that this second response is a mere cavil. Lying on the witness stand is not less speech than lying about the weather (or, for that matter, than telling the truth about the weather), although it may also be perjury. The shout of "Fire!" is not less speech in the Holmes instance than the shout of "Fire!" from the mouth of an actor on the stage of the same theater, a shout spoken as but a word within the play.[14] It is futile to argue that an appropriately tailored law that punishes any or all of these utterances is not a law that abridges speech. It does, it is *meant* to, and one should not take recourse to some verbal subterfuge, for example, that it is "speech-brigaded-with-action" or "conduct alone" that is curtailed by laws reaching these cases. Such ersatz argument proves too much. The recourse to this sort of definitional artifice knows no logical stopping place. It must necessarily operate to demolish the simple, compelling picture of a literal first amendment.[15]

The objection posed by the irresistible counterexample may nonetheless upset one's confidence in an absolute freedom of speech, despite the singular language of the first amendment. And, on closer examination, even the language of the first amendment may provide an *explicit* accommodation (i.e., exclusion) of an indefinite number of these counterexamples. Specifically, it provides merely that Congress shall make no law abridging *the* freedom of speech. In complete fidelity to that language, a graphic depiction of the first amendment might look like figure 2. According to this view,[16] the first amendment is still quite different from several other amendments. When the amendment applies, it applies absolutely. Thus, it still stands in sharp contrast to the fourth amendment ("unreasonable" searches and seizures), the fifth amendment ("due" process), or the eighth amendment ("cruel and unusual" punishments). Consistent with this contrast, however, is the preliminary question of determining whether speech abridged by a given act of Congress is not within "the" freedom of speech that Congress may make no law abridging. And here, admittedly, nothing in the language of the amendment itself is definitive or even helpful. Some external referent must be used to provide the distinction between that speech within "the" freedom of speech and that speech not within it.

It is noteworthy, however, that there is still no balancing or weighing of circumstances so far as the first amendment is concerned, on whichever side of the line particular speech may lie. If it is within "the" freedom of speech, as we have already noted, it is absolutely protected. If it is not within "the" freedom of speech, the first amendment (by its own terms) does not affect it at all.

Figure 2 is thus fundamentally like figure 1 in respect to a common characteristic that continues to distinguish the first amendment from other portions of the Bill of Rights—the quality of absoluteness that makes balancing irrelevant. It differs from figure 1 only with respect to the unsettling uncertainty it introduces by compelling an unspecified external reference to settle the content of "the" freedom of speech. The proper reference is to . . . what? There is obviously no appendix attached to the first amendment that authoritatively lists the varieties of speech within and without "the" freedom of speech. Nor has anyone claimed discovery of such a lucid, uniform, and established consensus respecting "the" freedom of speech in 1789 that, by clear convention, its content was (or is) universally obvious.[17]

To a significant extent, however, figure 2 is reflected in the case law of the first amendment. The Supreme Court has treated speech deemed "obscene" as not within "the" freedom of speech absolutely protected by the first amendment. Rather, the case law neither absolutely protects obscene speech nor even requires *any* first amendment compelled justification for its criminalization.[18] The rationale for its exclusion rests on (rather shaky) historical grounds.[19] And in general, the same holds true for ordinary criminal solicitation,[20] as it once did (although it no longer does) for libel, "fighting words,"[21] and "commercial speech."[22] Since none of these is within the Court's view of "the" freedom of speech that Congress may make no law abridging, Congress has been allowed to abridge these kinds of speech except insofar as *other* kinds of constitutional constraints lying outside the first amendment may affect the problem (e.g., constraints of enumerated powers, due process, or fifth amendment standards of equal protection).

Even if the definitional boundary (between "the" freedom of speech, which may not be abridged, and speech that may be abridged) were the sole uncertainty respecting the first amendment, the picture provided by figure 2 would nonetheless be somewhat incomplete. Since the amendment provides that Congress shall *make no law abridging* "the" freedom of speech, it remains important to secure absolute protection against that which Congress is forbidden to do: the *making* of such laws. In making laws abridging unprotected speech, however, Congress may in fact make a law that also abridges the protected freedom of speech. If it drafts a postal obscenity law too broadly, for instance, the law thus made by Congress may at once "abridge" speech that itself is within "the" freedom of speech, although no one in fact has yet been prosecuted. Or if interstate "criminal solicitation" is outlawed by Congress, the uncertainty of the offense may at once abridge (i.e., curtail) solicitations within the freedom of speech said to be absolutely protected. If, in addition, the sanctions are extremely severe or the procedures attending enforcement of the act of Congress quite summary, then the foreseeable prohibited abridging effects are more obvious and more substantial. In brief, under the view we are now examining, when the first amendment applies, it applies absolutely. And the amendment does not merely provide that no one may be jailed or fined for utterances within "the" freedom of speech. Rather, it provides that Congress shall *make no law abridging the freedom of speech.* The amendment stands violated by the making of a law insofar as the making itself abridges "the" freedom of speech.

One way of enforcing the prohibition (to halt the immediate abridging effects from the mere making of such laws) would be to provide a citizen's right of immediate appeal to the courts, incidental to any bill pending in Congress, assuming only that the bill deals with speech. The function of the appeal, of course, would be to determine at once whether the speech dealt with in the bill is in whole or in part within "the" freedom of speech protected by the first amendment, in which case the law ought at once to be judicially prohibited to Congress. A less perfect procedure will require a longer delay before an act of Congress can come to the Court. By definition, during the delay that occurs after Congress has *made* the law and prior to its authoritative adjudication, the first amendment will stand literally violated. To the extent that other doctrines nonetheless operate to create such delays (e.g., the case or controversy requirement of article III or ancillary requirements of standing), in fact the first amendment will not have been effective.[23] On the other hand, some speech itself not within "the" freedom of speech will go unpunished if the entire law, when finally adjudicated, is held wholly invalid because of the overbreadth or vagueness of only some of its provisions.[24] A modified graphic that takes both of these kinds of effects into account is shown in figure 3. This figure presents a decidedly more discouraging picture of the first amendment, far less perfect and less self-executing than the depiction in figure 1.

Figure 3, like figure 2, admits that there are kinds of speech not within "the" freedom of speech at all. The discouraging aspect of this observation, of course, is that the amendment itself not only fails explicitly to list those excluded kinds of speech but on its face provides no clue as to what they are. Second, because the Constitution itself provides no mechanism to perfect an immediate appeal

Figure 3

from Congress, the literal command of the first amendment prohibiting the *making* of prohibited laws will frequently be violated. The discretion of the judiciary in determining when a case may be brought and who may bring it further commits the actual fate of "the" freedom of speech to judicial vagary.[25] Much of "the" freedom of speech may thus be effectively curtailed by the intimidating presence of the outstanding act of Congress. Judicial sympathy with the unconstitutional objectives of the act may conspire to defeat the command of the amendment by operating to impose severe restrictions on the testing of that law.

On the bright side, however, figure 3 still has much to commend it. So long as an utterance is within "the" freedom of speech contemplated by the amendment and its prohibition is subject to judicial review, it remains fully and unequivocally protected. Passion, deference, and bias in the judiciary may make the line between "the" freedom of speech and unprotected speech discouragingly unstable, but at least they may not operate twice—once to define the boundary and still again to balance away even fully protected speech against some notion of reasonable or necessary abridgments.

The aesthetic appeal of figures 2 and 3 rests in their capacity to accommodate "irresistible counterexamples" and still hold consistent with the complete language of the first amendment. However, there is an alternative perspective that does at least equally well in both respects. Indeed, it may even be superior to both figures 2 and 3 insofar as it eliminates the boundary between "the" freedom of speech (which alone is protected by the amendment) and other speech placed outside the amendment's protection. This alternative view forecloses the risks of judicial necessity to fix that kind of boundary and, to that extent, may constitute a real advance.

This alternative falls back on the language of the first amendment to embrace the commonsense impression with which we started: *all* speech is protected from abridging laws made by Congress without exception. That the speech at issue is a fragment of perjured testimony does not make it any less speech or remove it from the amendment. It stands initially on exactly the same footing as a political candidate's unexceptional campaign remarks or an ordinary citizen's street corner complaints about national economic policy. The instance of the irresistible counterexample is met, moreover, not by question-begging verbal artifices (e.g., by calling it "conduct," "speech-brigaded-with-action," or "speech-acts") but by a different and more general definition of "the freedom of speech" that Congress may make no law abridging. "The freedom of speech" that Congress may make no law abridging is a qualifying phrase, albeit not in the manner suggested in figures 2 or 3. Rather, *the freedom* of speech that Congress may not by law abridge is a reference to some scope of freedom implied by the very term *the freedom* and, logically therefore, a scope of freedom bounded. In short, it stands not as a synonym for complete freedom but in contrast with complete freedom. "The freedom" of speech that Congress may make no law abridging is therefore *that degree*, or that extent, of freedom of speech that Congress may make no law abridging.

This view of the amendment abandons judicial discretion to say what is and what is not the subject matter of speech protected by the amendment, although it necessarily asserts an alternative duty to say what is the scope of "the freedom of speech" within the meaning of "the freedom" as distinct from unlimited or unqualified complete freedom. Again, but unavoidably, it too compels even a conscientious and reluctant judiciary to utilize *some* reference external to the first amendment to determine that scope. Thus, it inevitably reintroduces a measure of uncertainty into the first amendment, although in a different way. But the uncertainty is another instance that cannot be helped; the force of the irresistible counterexample will not go away, the very language of the first amendment contributes to the determination to cope with it in this fashion, and the inconclusive history associated with the amendment is quite compatible with this treatment of the matter. A graphic depiction of the first amendment thus described might look like figure 4.

Note, then, these several features. First, *all* speech is encompassed by the amendment, whether it be talk about the weather, one's choice of elected representatives, or procuring heroin. Second, "the freedom" of speech refers to a latitude, rather than a subject or a kind of speech. Third, the exclusive question in each case is merely whether the utterances were within that latitude of freedom of speech comprising "the freedom" of speech that Congress may make no law abridging. And the irresistible counterexample is accounted for insofar as it may be expected to fall outside the latitude of "the freedom" of speech, albeit the referent for determining whether it does is not provided by the first amendment itself and necessarily, therefore, requires the judiciary to look elsewhere.

To a considerable extent the preceding view of the first amendment has not only characterized a substantial number of Supreme Court decisions but also dominated the entire first amendment case law. Indeed, the main struggle has

"THE FREEDOM" OF SPEECH	SPEECH BEYOND "THE FREEDOM"
100 % *Protected*	*0 %* *Protected*

All Kinds of Speech

Figure 4

been a struggle to choose among contending views respecting the appropriate test according to which speech is held to be either within "the freedom" of speech protected from abridging laws or beyond that freedom and therefore unaffected by the first amendment. A leading example is the following formulation proposed by Judge Learned Hand and approved by a Supreme Court majority in 1951 in *Dennis v. United States*: "In each case [courts] must ask whether the gravity of the 'evil,' discounted by its improbability, justifies such invasion of free speech as is necessary to avoid the danger."[26] Note the discrete elements of this formulation, especially the several determinations that it assigns to the judiciary. Most obviously, it commits to the judiciary a textually unaided directive to rank all possible "evils." Of course, it also implicitly directs the courts to render a determination of what legislatures are constitutionally empowered to define as evil for purposes of criminalizing speech likely to produce that evil. The determination of what may be deemed evils and the rank of their gravities is imperative because the requisite degree of probability sufficient to place particular speech beyond "the freedom" of speech forbidden to be abridged is itself dependent upon the evil's gravity. The greater the evil, the less probable need be its occurrence to forbid speech generating some tendency that the evil might occur. The particular formulation is shown in figure 5.

The vertical axis at the left-hand edge of this figure is graduated from zero probability to absolute certainty. The horizontal axis is graduated from evils of zero gravity to those of absolute gravity. The diagonal line cutting across the figure marks the boundary of that scope of speech within "the freedom" of speech that Congress may make no law abridging. All cases to the left of the line are protected. All cases to the right of the line are unprotected.

Two examples illustrate the apparent objectivity and completeness of the arrangement. The first example of simple trespass is drawn from an opinion by Justice Brandeis.[27] It supposes that a legislature has made it a crime (albeit a

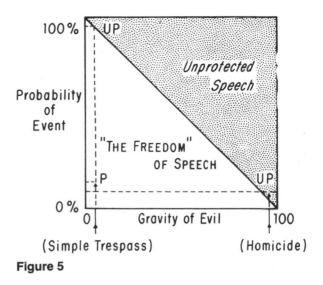

Figure 5

minor one) for persons to go onto the private property of another knowing that the owner does not want them. It is assumed that the trespass law is itself valid (i.e., that the legislature may protect private property in this fashion and deem officious intrusions an "evil" within the police power to prevent). It is assumed also that the trespass is fairly mild, trespassing on a privately owned vacant lot, for instance, as distinct from trespassing upon another's bedroom at night. The case likewise supposes the same legislature adopted a law to discourage the incident of trespass by making it a minor crime for any person to advocate, urge, counsel, incite, or teach to others the desirability of trespassing.

The law thus punishes speech. But it is not on that account either valid or invalid, for its validity requires that as applied *in each case* we discount the gravity of the evil (which is not the speech but rather an act of trespass) by its improbability. Since the evil (simple trespass) is a comparatively trivial evil, nothing less than virtual certainty that it would occur unless the speech were forbidden will suffice to justify proceeding aginst the speaker. So, if an anarchist urges a handful of half-interested citizens to trespass on a posted vacant lot in order to demonstrate their objection to a social order that sanctifies private property, the speaker cannot be convicted when it is plain no one did as the speaker urged, nor was anyone likely to do so. All such trivial evil-inducing speech is within that latitude of "the freedom" of speech protected by the first amendment save that which actually engenders the evil to be avoided or at least very nearly engenders it. Most such cases are thus "P" (protected) cases on the graph. Very few will be "UP"(unprotected).

The converse is true for homicide. The killing of people being a plain instance of what legislatures may rightly consider a grave evil, speech foreseeably engendering a bare possibility of that consequence becomes at once punishable. Virtually all such speech, save perhaps utterances one may make aloud in his bedroom with no one about, is thus "UP" (unprotected). Only a harmless few are "P" (protected). Indeed, given the gravity of this evil, it is likely that in many situations even a post hoc showing of zero likelihood of its occurring will not save it under the first amendment. For example, the prohibition would reach a speaker who solicited another to murder his spouse when, unknown to the speaker, the solicitee was an undercover officer who acknowledged that at no time did he consider acting on the inducement. The origin of figure 5 is taken essentially from the common law of criminal attempts. The effect of the first amendment is to limit the discretion of legislative bodies in punishing such attempts insofar as they involve social advocacy.

One great (although little noted) advantage of the manner in which this particular graphic depiction addresses "the freedom" of speech is its applicability to a number of incidental issues. These are issues conventionally treated separately in the case law of the first amendment, such as those of "reasonable time, place, and manner"[28] and those of so-called indirect effects.[29] In fact, the Learned Hand formulation is quite capable of resolving virtually all free speech adjudications, as a few additional examples may make clear.

"Reasonable time, place, and manner" restrictions do not forbid particular utterances (e.g., advocacy of trespass, incitement of arson or homicide, obscenity, or racial epithets) but merely restrict the time or the place of speech or regulate the manner of speaking.[30] For example, a disorderly conduct law may not apply to one who shouts his message or even amplifies his speech over loudspeakers within an auditorium,[31] but it may apply to one who shouts his message on a street corner downtown or amplifies his speech over loudspeakers carried on a van through residential neighborhoods.[32] The Hand formulation we have been examining is adequate in responding to this problem: merely isolate the evil alleged to arise from the time, place, or manner of speaking; determine initially whether it rests within the legislative prerogative to deem it an evil; identify its relative gravity at the proper point somewhere along the horizontal axis; and finally, ascertain in the particular case the probability that the particular time, place, or manner of the speech will in fact bring about that evil. Having thus located the degree of probability at some point on the vertical axis, it is easy enough as a figurative exercise to draw the proper lines to see whether they intersect in the protected zone or the unprotected zone of the rectangle.

The same is true for controversies conventionally catalogued as instances of "indirect effects." Such a case arises when the regulation in question does not forbid or restrict speech but demands that one speak under pain of punishment for failure to do so. But, paradoxically, it may still be obvious under the circumstances that "the freedom" of speech is threatened and that a straightforward first amendment question is presented.[33] An example is a law that requires a journalist to disclose in a civil or criminal proceeding the name of some person and the exact statements that person may have spoken to the journalist. The occasion for summoning the journalist, moreover, may typically be the occasion of the journalist's own speech, such as a news article that he or she has published. Because the journalist would not have been summoned but for having spoken through the news article, the summons is a plain cost levied by law on his or her speech. Because the anticipation of having to answer under such circumstances may also operate as a disincentive to publish like stories in the future, the law curtails (i.e., abridges) his or her continuing freedom to speak. And because the existence of this coercive process is a law inhibiting third parties from freely speaking to the journalist, it abridges their freedom of speech as well. Certainly, moreover, the journalist is an appropriate party to assert such contingent, third-party free speech objections.

The summoning of the journalist is thus a case arising under the first amendment, but that conclusion does not determine whether the journalist may nevertheless be summoned and made to respond.[34] The answer to that question is provided by Judge Hand's formulation: "In each case [courts] must ask whether the gravity of the 'evil,' discounted by its improbability, justifies such invasion of free speech as is necessary to avoid the danger."[35] Again, the same locational decisions, once made at appropriate points on the vertical and horizontal axes on figure 5, will unerringly permit us to draw the appropriate lines to see whether they intersect at a point that is protected or unprotected. How grave is the evil? In other words, what harm may ensue if the journalist is not made to answer? Is it that murder may go unsolved, a libel plaintiff go uncompensated, a mere parking violation go undetected, or the source of atomic secrets given over to an enemy nation go undetermined? How probable is it that, without the journalist being made to answer questions (which question in particular?), the evil will occur? That question, of course, may be divided into logical lesser questions. What reasons are there for believing the journalist may know a great deal about the matter? What alternative means may be available (and at what cost) to secure that information without the journalist's assistance? Each question is necessary to determine whether summoning the journalist and making him answer is "necessary to avoid the danger." If the evil is very great (the atomic secrets case?), even a minuscule chance that the journalist's compelled testimony might help may be sufficient.

But we have said enough, for the point is not to resolve every hypothetical. It is, rather, to demonstrate the compelling capacity of the Hand formulation to answer an immense number of first amendment disputes. It is, in brief, a very powerful formula for resolving "the freedom" of speech and is used more frequently than is generally acknowledged because its approach figures in time, place, and manner cases and in indirect effects cases as well.

There are nonetheless strongly objectionable features to the Learned Hand formulation quite apart from the quintessential difficulty that it, too, compels even conscientious courts to look outside the first amendment to resolve such imponderables as what evils shall be deemed of more or less greater gravity than others in measuring the scope of "the freedom" of speech. For example, when the evil to be avoided is serious, then, as shown in figure 5, the test virtually dispenses with any probability requirement as a precondition of punishing or preventing speech. Thus, a large (and uncertain) category of speech cases is treated not significantly differently than in figure 2, in which perjury, criminal solicitation, and obscenity were treated as kinds of speech per se not within "the" freedom of speech. While that apparent conformance is exceedingly helpful and comforting in one respect (i.e., it reconciles those cases), in another respect it poses a severe problem.

According to figure 2, "political" speech is not among the outcast kinds of speech. To the contrary, it is altogether within the 100 percent protected field. But the Hand approach precludes this easy (and protective?) definitional address to the first amendment. For the question according to the Hand test is not simply whether the speech in question involves politics or government in some generic, loose sense; rather, the focus is not on the speech at all, it is on the alleged evil to be avoided by outlawing the speech.

The *Dennis* case is itself an example of the resulting problem. Eugene Dennis was prosecuted under the Smith Act[36] for "conspiring" to "organize" a group (the American Communist party) whose purposes included teaching the doctrine of the propriety of force and violence as a means to "overthrow" the government of the United States. Since the deaths of any number of persons rank as a very grave evil, and since Congress has the right to seek to prevent that grave evil, suppression of speech under the formula is permitted by the first amendment on the most meager probability that, unless suppressed, the speech *might* bring about that evil.[37] For all practical purposes, then, the case is treated not much differently from one in which X offers Y five thousand dollars to murder his spouse. X may be punished although Y was never inclined to accept the offer and, indeed, was an undercover agent. The gravity of the evil (of spousal murder) dispenses with the need to show any probability that the danger can be headed off only by punishing the offer.

In the murder solicitation case, doubtless most people are untroubled by the outcome; but we also entertain doubts as to whether (a) such speech was ever imagined to come within the first amendment and, that question aside, (b) why anyone would press to have such speech protected by the first amendment. In the *Dennis* case, however, many *are* troubled. It is not obvious that advocating overthrow of the government contributes *nothing* useful. Nor is it obvious that advocacy of violent overthrow, and not merely of voting to change the form of government, was never imaginably within the first amendment. Rather, so long as there is no discernible prospect of serious harm actually occurring, the freedom to state grievances passionately and angrily, protesting not merely the existing government but expressing a desperate feeling that nothing but violence exists to modify that government, may be important speech. It raises the unspoken questions. It makes visible a despair that may need to be known. It demands attention from others that more genteel suggestions and less threatening discourse may fail to stimulate.[38] It provokes, to be sure, and may well be valuable

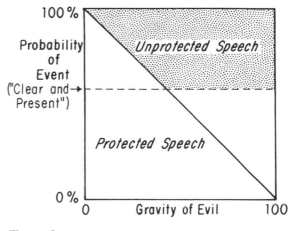

Figure 6

because it does so. But the *Dennis* formulation ignores these central first amendment values because that formulation may permit such utterances to be treated like furtively made offers to hire a murderer. It encourages and sustains their suppression virtually without evidence of any actual or imminent danger. The dissenting opinions in the *Dennis* case made extremely effective use of this point,[39] and the troubling history of prosecutions for political dissent in the United States bears out the complaint.[40]

A formulation to cope with this complaint would set a minimum probability below which the alleged danger feared from this kind of speech would *never* be sufficient to justify punishing the speech. It might, for instance, look like figure 6. Under this view, although violence itself may be passionately advocated, when the feared danger lacks clarity and imminence, such speech remains within the latitude of speech that defines "the freedom" of speech.[41] And this, of course, is the earlier, substantially more protective formula proposed by Justice Holmes in 1919 in *Schenck v. United States*: "The question in every case is whether the words used are used in such circumstances and are of such a nature as to create a *clear and present* danger that they will bring about the substantive evils that Congress has a right to prevent."[42] In a slightly different iteration, it is the formula reasserted quite unanimously by the Court in 1969 in *Brandenburg v. Ohio*: "[T]he constitutional guarantees of free speech and free press do not permit a State to forbid or proscribe advocacy of the use of force or of law violation except where such advocacy is directed to inciting or producing imminent lawless action and is likely to incite or produce such action."[43]

There is, moreover, an addition to the Holmes formulation that may help to alleviate a different kind of problem unresolved in the figure depicting the Learned Hand formulation. Under that formulation, the "gravity" of an evil is traded off against its improbability in measuring the scope of "the freedom" of speech. Speech calculated or likely to produce relatively trivial evils (e.g., trespass on privately owned, vacant lots) would, as we saw, be punishable only in the rare circumstance where it induced such trespasses or at least was virtually certain to do so. Left undetermined by the formula, however, was the extent to which a legislature might add to the legal categories of things deemed evil and, by doing so, provide a sufficient predicate for outlawing or punishing additional forms of speech.

For instance, may not a legislature, acting responsibly within its police power, describe as an evil the infliction of pain and suffering on others? May it not specify mental anguish as one such kind of pain? May it not provide redress (criminal and civil) against those inflicting mental anguish on others? If so, then much speech not hitherto abridged may now be abridged: the speech newly forbidden must merely make the occurrence of the evil highly probable or cause the evil to occur.[44] Frequently, the substantive evil to be avoided (mental anguish) will be not only a clear and present danger under the circumstances, to use Holmes's original formulation, but a fact: Q.E.D., the speech bringing it about can be redressed in both civil and criminal law.

Even the addition of "clear and present danger" to the formulation thus leaves the graphic dramatically incomplete. There remains virtually unlimited elbow-room for legislatures to do in two steps what they might not do in one. If a given kind of detested speech does not generate a constitutionally sufficient danger of one kind of evil to rationalize its abridgment, the legislature may simply describe as an evil something the detested kind of speech *is* likely to bring about. The speech may then constitutionally be abridged. For instance, the street corner distribution of anarchist handbills may be too remote from any likelihood of inducing violence against the government to suppress on that account. But their distribution under the circumstances may nonetheless be very likely to produce litter. Litter in the public streets is assuredly something a legislature may deem an evil. A flat prohibition of any handbill distribution may, under the circumstances, be necessary to avoid the danger of that litter. The result would be no more handbills, anarchist or otherwise.

The Holmes formulation, in its original terms, plainly embraces this outcome since it requires no determination of the gravity of the evil. It is not quite clear whether the Hand formulation does so. It leaves open the possibility that although a complete prohibition of handbills may be necessary to avoid the danger (of litter), the gravity of *that* evil still may be constitutionally insufficient to "justify such invasion of free speech." In brief, is regulation of some evils (e.g., aesthetic blight, mental anguish) otherwise within the capacity of legislatures to avoid nonetheless prohibited when it curtails freedom of speech? In a later and stronger formulation of the Holmes test, the answer was emphatic: yes. The first amendment forbids sanctions against speech except as necessary to avoid "serious" evils. The appropriate graphic appears in figure 7. Thus, Justice Brandeis suggested the following in 1927: "Prohibition of free speech and assembly is a measure so stringent that it would be inappropriate as the means for averting

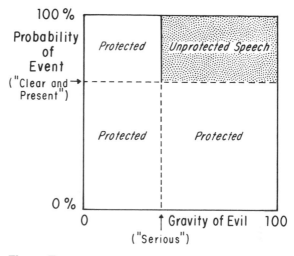

Figure 7

a relatively trivial harm to society."[45] It followed that a certain degree of litter, unwelcome noise, mental perturbation, violated anonymity, and degraded reputation are withdrawn from the general police power to protect against that latitude of free speech contemplated by "the freedom" of speech.[46]

At its zenith, the developed Holmes-Brandeis depiction may be the most sheltering perspective of the first amendment we have had. Its formulation is as readily applicable to "time, place, and manner" abridgments and to "indirect effects" abridgments as to direct abridgments. In this respect, it is as complete as the *Dennis* formulation. Although it demands that the judiciary make a determination for which the first amendment itself supplies no textual assistance (namely, what external and immutable points of reference determine those things legislatures may declare to be serious evils and those they may not so describe),[47] it is no worse than *Dennis* in this respect. And, applied with any degree of tough-minded consistency, it creates a considerably larger field of speech within "the freedom" of speech than the *Dennis* formulation because it demands that a clear and present danger be shown in each case, rather than yielding to speculations of mere calamitous possibility as sufficient to sustain speech abridgments. It thus comes closer than the *Dennis* formulation to the literal text of the first amendment. Moreover, in the face of the irresistible counterexample we confronted earlier in this chapter, we evidently can propose no test for "the freedom" of speech that is free of the criticism that, at bottom, administration of even this test remains subject to an irreducible amount of judicial subjectivism.

The conundrum of the irresistible counterexample is a difficult one, as we have seen. In fact, it is so powerful a device that it has mocked virtually every effort, including even the Holmes-Brandeis graphic, to render the first amend-

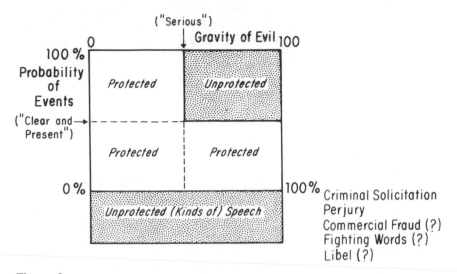

Figure 8

ment foolproof against the risks of judicial discretion. Consider also the following problem. The Holmes-Brandeis graphic demands that in *every* case there be a showing of an actual, clear, and present danger that a serious evil imminently lurks in an utterance punishable by law. That must mean, however, that speech falling literally on deaf ears is never punishable. A villain sadistically, knowingly, and falsely shouting "Fire!" in a crowded theater escapes under cover of the first amendment if, perchance, the theater is crowded only by deaf persons reading subtitles on the screen. An offer of bribery to an honest official who testifies it never entered his mind to accept the offer (and who, rather, at once reported the offer to the police) is not punishable, nor is the act of the lucky person who unwittingly solicits an undercover agent to murder his spouse, rather than a gun-for-hire. No successful prosecution for criminal attempt in any of these cases? That must logically follow unless we cope with the counterexample by pretending that these are not instances of speech at all but rather instances of "conduct" or "speech-brigaded-with-action" (as they are sophistically described), or unless we admit to the nonexclusivity of the developed Holmes formulation.

As it happens, the case law does in fact hedge,[48] even as Holmes tended to do.[49] By combining two graphics we have already set forth, moreover, we can see in figure 8 how the problem might be met straightforwardly. This description is but a composite of figure 2 (certain *kinds* of speech are wholly unprotected), plus the developed Holmes-Brandeis graphic in figure 7. It handles our problem, it has an administrable logic, and it fits the syntax of the first amendment. The language of "the freedom" of speech that Congress may make no law abridging in this view may be a qualifying phrase that communicates two considerations rather than a single distinction. It may mean both a delimitation of *kinds* of speech entitled to that latitude of speech constituting "the freedom" of speech and a certain latitude or *scope* of speech as reported in the *Dennis* formulation or as in the Holmes-Brandeis formulation.[50] As a highly plausible matter, moreover, such an understanding of the first amendment is surely not unimaginable.

Earlier in this review we made passing reference to the controversial history associated with the first amendment's enactment.[51] The reason for doing so is obvious. Despite the exceptionally strong language of the first amendment (i.e., its avoidance of weakening or qualifying adjectives such as *reasonable* or *excessive*), it is nonetheless fairly subject to investigation for the possibility that "the" freedom of speech frames some definite field of reference. The postulation of certain kinds of cases raised that possibility to the level where it warranted more serious investigation. The "irresistible counterexamples" to a literal, first-impression interpretation of the first amendment are too strong and too numerous to dismiss as mere excuses for seeking to weaken the first amendment. It is conceivable of course that they were taken into account when the first amendment was drafted by Madison, revised and proposed by Congress, and ratified by the states, and that they simply did not affect a common resolve. But certainly this is not the sole possibility. It is conceivable as well that the whole matter simply went unnoticed at the time (i.e., that the attention of such debate as there may have been was preoccupied with making the reserved powers of the participating states doubly secure against the possibilities of congressional preemption). In that case the problem would remain: a conscientious court might conclude that the first amendment's exceptional language ought not be compromised on the basis of exceptional cases that those participating in its enactment might have accommodated had they taken them into account, but for which there is no impressive evidence that they either took into account or necessarily would have treated differently had they thought of them.

On the other hand, insofar as there may be impressive evidence that the preoccupying concern of the first amendment was principally to make doubly certain that freedom of speech would generally remain free from congressional interference as a matter of deferring to the states, it would be entirely consistent both with the language of the amendment and with that intention if Congress could adopt at least *some* protective legislation concerned solely with federal interests not usurping the general run of state laws or state constitutional provisions respecting freedom of speech. For instance, the necessary-and-proper clause might vest in Congress a power to protect the life and free movement and public appearances of the president by criminalizing threats upon his life, whether oral or in writing. As such a law would in no way threaten *state* rights generally to protect freedom of speech as much (or as little) as each state otherwise provided, and as it is difficult to suppose that "the" freedom of speech that Congress was meant to be precluded from abridging could conceivably contemplate a general right to intimidate or threaten the president with complete impunity (subject only to such laws as states might or might not see fit to adopt, or subject only to each state's differing common law of crimes), it would be strange and implausible to insist that the Supreme Court should nonetheless interpret the first amendment as forbidding such an act of Congress.

The last graphic we have been examining is not heedless of these matters. While it would be foolish to claim that the associated history of the first amendment is all of a piece (it is certainly not),[52] figure 8 is assuredly not disconnected from that history nor does it rest on views strongly at odds with one's respect for such clarification as that history may provide. Good reasons can be offered to show why certain kinds of speech (e.g., offers of bribes to federal officials) may plainly have been in no one's mind as within "the freedom of speech" that Congress was forbidden to abridge,[53] and why it might also be true that speech well within "the freedom of speech" might sometimes, in some circumstances, also be subject to congressional regulation.[54]

Although figure 8 deals handily with the irresistible counterexample and reflects no insensitivity to the historical roots of the first amendment, it is still assuredly subject to severe hazards of judicial discretion and judicial misapplication. Courts may quite carelessly catalog some kinds of speech as never within the freedom of speech, for example, obscenity, thereby letting the outcome of cases turn on fatally different definitions of "obscene."[55] As to speech that survives that preliminary process of definitional winnowing, courts may also mistakenly presume to catalog degrees of evils or harms to determine whether the harm sought to be avoided is not too trivial to tolerate an abridgment of protected speech when the speech produces that trivial evil. And obviously as well, courts may sometimes err in too weakly superintending the adequacy of legislative fact-findings and of jury adjudicative fact determinations as to whether a serious evil was sufficiently clear and imminent under the circumstances to sustain the punishment of (protected) speech. But these several risks may simply be intrinsic to the kind of constitutional system we have. They do not per se suggest that it is unsound or that a different arrangement would be better.

Despite their evident difficulties, the last several graphics do tend to sum up the principal contending schools of first amendment interpretation during the past several decades. At the same time, there has gradually developed still another view that does not, as did these graphics, make quite so much depend upon which side of one-or-more fixed lines a given kind of case falls. To be sure, this view also does not escape problems of judicial discretion. But by introducing finer gradations of a particular sort, it may appear both more moderate and less rigid in the measuring of protected speech. Interestingly, it complements the graphic (figure 6) we examined in the *Dennis* case.

Dennis defined the principal task of the courts as graduating the kinds and degrees of evil to be balanced against the improbability of their occurrence resulting from particular speech to determine whether the degree of abridgment was unavoidable and therefore permissible. Correspondingly, an increasingly fashionable view holds that it is important to graduate the kind of speech to be

Political
Religious
Philosophic
Economic
Private
Social
Scientific
Aesthetic
Symbolic
Libel
Commercial
Obscene
Criminal

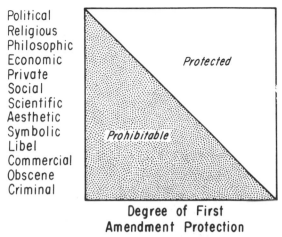

Protected

Prohibitable

Degree of First
Amendment Protection

Figure 9

invaded.[56] If it is political speech (e.g., rhetoric praising or abusing candidates for office, or rhetoric exaggerating the alleged effects, provisions, merits, or demerits of existing laws), the speech is deemed of such central importance to the functions of the first amendment that even the high probability of a reprehensible evil (e.g., that a far more honest and intelligent candidate will lose to a dishonest, manipulative, selfish demagogue) will not justify much recourse against the misrepresentations of the speaker. If it is commercial speech, on the other hand, the evil of consumer deception may be avoided on a lesser probability of fraud than in the political speech case, although commercial speech will not, on that account alone, be treated as 100 percent unprotected,[57] as is obscenity or solicitation of homicide. Graphics carrying these additional views of first amendment priority may look like either figure 9 or figure 10.

These are unquestionably useful and interesting variations, and even our attempt to present them graphically is not quite adequate because it tends to understate their subtlety. The graphics imply a neat, concentric order of speech values, relating the proximity of speech categories to core values of political self-determination, with commensurate first amendment protection contingent upon the distance of an identifiable kind of speech from that first amendment center. Quite obviously, however, a particular speech may in fact cut across these artificial lines, readily embarrassing an attempt to say which kind of speech it was. The libelous may well be related to the political utterance, the aesthetic may be quite inseparable from the allegedly obscene. And in many instances, a criminal conviction based on a statute that aims carefully only at the less protected aspect of a given speech (theoretically leaving unaffected the speaker's prerogative to make his political or aesthetic point in a different way) should not be sustainable because often we will know that the "same" point expressed differently would in fact not be the same point at all. In public places, for instance, many will be

Protection of the First Amendment by Subject

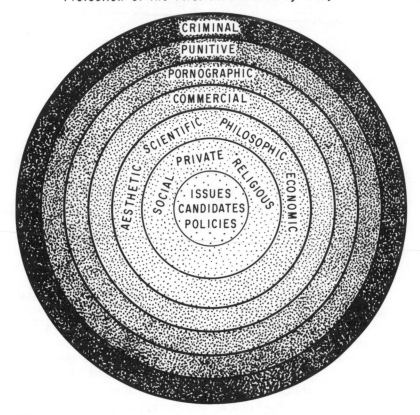

Figure 10

offended by the studied vulgarity of crude expressions made in exception to some important public policy. Still, neither more moderate nor more intellectual discourse may say the same thing, even half as well, as the bluntness of declaring: FUCK THE DRAFT.[58]

In effect, then, figures 9 and 10 illuminate an additional perspective, but they do not reduce the margins of uncertainty, instability, external reference, and elbowroom for judicial administration in the regime of the first amendment. Perhaps, moreover, the point illustrated by these variations is that there is no sure formula for reading the first amendment in any way that (a) copes with the irresistible counterexample, (b) fits with its syntax, *and* (c) enjoys even a plausible congruence with history, to make it foolproof. Which of these graphics seems better (or merely less poor) than the rest is assuredly debatable. More perplexing still, even all the graphics we have examined to this point have left out at least one other consideration. That consideration is the role of "federalism" and free speech. Here is how we reach it.

All along until now we have been carefully scrutinizing the first amendment alone. In figure 1, which treated all acts of *Congress*, we were faithful to that task. In the very first irresistible counterexample of the deliberate false shout of "Fire!" in a crowded theater, however, we tacitly abandoned it. From that point on, the examples and counterexamples were inadvertently both *state* and federal. Indeed, most of them (e.g., an antilitter ordinance) would in fact be typically only state or local. Outside the District of Columbia or the territories of the United States, few would be federal. Congress should have little occasion, and very little power, to adopt run-of-the-mill police power laws. And it may be significant that, numerically, the most telling irresistible counterexamples are predominantly just run-of-the-mill police power counterexamples. Soliciting the murder of one's spouse, for instance, is what *state* governments are designed to discourage. It was certainly not a concern for this kind of problem—or obscenity or libel—that caused a new constitutional convention to be called at Philadelphia in 1787 to amend the Articles of Confederation and to enlarge the enumerated powers of the Continental Congress.

Our graphics have thus been textually (and historically) askew. They have worked exclusively from the text of the first amendment, yet they have propounded analyses indiscriminately inclusive of laws not arising under the first amendment but of state and local origin. But the constitutional directive restricting *state* legislative power in respect to free speech is not on its face even remotely like the first amendment. Indeed, on its face, it acknowledges nothing special in respect to free speech. Rather, the protection of free speech is, at best, just textually subsumed in more general words: as an example of a "privilege or immunity" of national citizenship; as an example of "liberty"; as a subject of legal protection not to be denied "equal protection." In brief, we have indiscriminately mingled examples that typically will not all arise under the first amendment but will more often arise under a later amendment, the fourteenth, which declares:

> No State shall make or enforce any law which shall abridge the privileges or immunities of citizens of the United States; nor shall any State deprive any person of life, liberty, or property without due process of law; nor deny any person within its jurisdiction the equal protection of the laws.[59]

Since 1925 it has been assumed nonetheless that the fourteenth amendment pulls up the first amendment's speech clause into its own provisions.[60] Indeed, it has been held not merely that freedom of speech is incorporated (or selectively absorbed) into the fourteenth amendment but that the standard of judicial review for state or local laws affecting speech is coextensive with the standard that is applicable to acts of Congress. The result is that Supreme Court cases adjudicating state or local laws are now fungible with those adjudicating acts of Congress; each is as valid a source of precedent for the other as it is valid for a case of its own kind.

There was, however, nothing inevitable in this development. The very different texts of the first and the fourteenth amendment do not demand this result. Justice Brandeis expressed serious misgivings in an early case presuming to wed the first and fourteenth amendments in this regard.[61] In an extremely provocative opinion, Justice Harlan did likewise, just thirty years later, suggesting a different latitude of state, vis-à-vis national, authority over obscenity.[62]

Additionally, the equivocal history of the fourteenth amendment is quite compatible with these suggestions.[63] For instance, it may be eminently reasonable to hold (as it has been held) that free speech was meant to be more amply protected against the states than other kinds of "liberty" interests.[64] By itself, however, that proposition does not settle whether state laws affecting speech shall be deemed valid or invalid according to the standards applied to acts of Congress. The special protection of free speech from hostile state legislation has been sought by a number of distinguished justices who nonetheless believed that the latitudes of state and federal speech regulation are not identical. The states, they thought, in some cases should be bound less tightly than Congress.[65] Somewhat divergent regimes respecting freedom of speech were thus readily available under principles of federalism in the United States. A postscript may be appropriate to notice the possibilities of this path not taken.

It may be argued that by refusing to take this path, the Supreme Court has more successfully freed speech in the states by sheltering it against the local passions that local assemblies might translate into laws abridging freedom of speech. By subjecting all local and state laws to the *same* rigor of review as the Court has established for acts of Congress, the courts may have made free speech in the states more robust than it might have been had standards developed under the fourteenth amendment been different from those developed under the first amendment.

But this kind of reasoning cuts both ways. It is equally arguable that had the Supreme Court not tied the review of acts of Congress to the standard applied to state and local laws, the Court might well have protected free speech more resolutely against Congress than it has.[66] In this light, the more serious problem is that at the moment of reviewing an act of Congress, the Court cannot help but be aware that it is simultaneously setting the standard applicable to the states as well. If the Court does not think it appropriate to bind the states very tightly, it must adjudicate acts of Congress with the same looseness it thinks appropriate for diverse state or local laws. It is simply a variation on the familiar homily that what is sauce for the goose is also sauce for the gander. Because acts of Congress reach more widely than state or local laws, however, it may be a great misfortune to treat them in the same way.[67]

There are very few realistic, irresistible counterexamples that can be fielded to embarrass near-absolute construction of the first amendment as applied to acts of Congress. In general, the amendment might therefore be applied to acts of Congress with the vigor of the developed Holmes-Brandeis formulation. In addition, the first amendment may operate collegially with the tenth amendment:

it may be read to restrict the scope of enumerated powers vested in Congress even when, by itself, the tenth amendment would not be deemed to do so. This, in essence, is what Justice Harlan proposed in *Roth v. United States*.[68] In that case, an act of Congress prohibited the mailing of "obscene" matter in the U.S. mails—an instrumentality over which Congress conventionally has an explicit, enumerated plenary power. The invocation of an explicit (postal) power given to Congress under article I did not, for Harlan, end the first amendment inquiry, however. He would have drawn from the first amendment a limiting principle qualifying the power of Congress in respect to the post office, much as the Court subsequently relied on the tenth amendment in *National League of Cities v. Usery*.[69] There, the court employed the tenth amendment to limit the reach of an act of Congress, otherwise valid under the commerce clause, when applied to state and local employees. Although the post office may be a federal instrumentality, the subject of obscenity control is not itself a subject expressly committed to Congress. And the toleration of diverse regulation among states, under a somewhat more permissive reading of the fourteenth amendment,[70] would not present the same nationwide stultification of free speech as would a flat, uniform act of Congress.

In brief, the virtue of a differential first amendment–fourteenth amendment regime might be to read the first amendment for all that it is worth, confining Congress very tightly. Somewhat more (albeit not too much more) play may be left in applying the fourteenth amendment to the processes of state and of local government. If states or local communities presume to enact speech-restricting laws *not* addressed to state or local concerns but, on the other hand, laws penalizing speech deemed contrary to the best national interests or even the best international interest of the United States, then the Court, in its review of such legislation, would have a firm basis for applying a very severe version of the free speech clause through the fourteenth amendment.[71] As a composite of the first and the fourteenth amendments respectively, a suitable graphic that would capture the federalism component of free speech analysis might look like figure II.

The graphic is essentially self-evident. The universe of speech abridgments is divided between two sources: national and state. The basis for division is the Constitution, which separately addresses restrictions on each source: the first amendment and the fourteenth amendment. The Constitution's protection of speech against acts of the national government is more substantial, since the first amendment is far more emphatic and explicit in protecting speech. The propriety of national sources of abridgment is most questionable when the speech subject to such abridgment has no unique or apparent national consequence and thus, drawing from implications of the tenth amendment, Congress's reliance upon enumerated powers may be treated skeptically. A fairly rugged application of the first amendment, however, is still to be expected even when acts of Congress deal with speech generating evils highly appropriate for congressional concern. Insofar as a uniform nationwide restriction must generally operate more suffo-

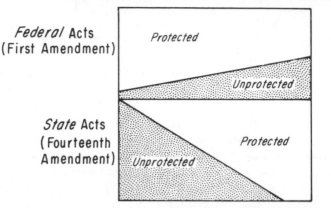

Figure 11

catingly than piecemeal local or diverse state patterns of restriction, moreover, the argument in favor of confining Congress tightly is pragmatically strengthened. A looser regime may be tolerated in respect to state legislation under the looser text (and history) of the fourteenth amendment. Overall, a flat and stale sameness of restrictions is less likely, and the erosion of substantial diversity of expression across the nation is less to be feared. The propriety of state and local abridgments of speech loses its own justification, however, when subjects of national concern are at issue. Such abridgments, if made at all, must be made by Congress and not by a gratuitous gesture of state or local legislatures.

Finally, of course, the federalism graphic in figure 11 is not meant to be indifferent to our previous review. At both the state and national level, for instance, the imminence and seriousness of the evil to be avoided are still issues. And the subject matter of the speech may continue to make a considerable difference. Talk about local political issues, local candidates, and local policies may be as rigorously protected from state or local laws by the fourteenth amendment as talk about national political issues, candidates, and policies shall be protected against abridging acts of Congress by the first amendment. In these and other respects the federalism graphic does not exclude our earlier efforts. Rather, it complements them. Its addition may reflect a more mature treatment of the subject as a whole.

In a dictum featured in the introduction, we noted Justice Roberts's view that

[w]hen an act of Congress is appropriately challenged in the courts as not conforming to the constitutional mandate, the judicial branch of the Government has only one duty—to lay the article of the Constitution which is in-

voked beside the statute which is challenged and to decide whether the latter squares with the former.[72]

It was also very strongly argued that this was an entirely appropriate view. Among the many clauses of the Constitution, moreover, the free speech clause appears to be one of those best suited for this view of the judicial duty. The clause is exceptional in its brevity, its clarity, and its use of concrete terms. Ostensibly, it can be taken literally. And constitutionally, it is worthy of being taken seriously.

Yet, as we have seen, laying the free speech clause beside a particular statute has left even highly conscientious judges doubtful as to whether "the latter squares with the former." We have now traced a number of quite different pictures of the free speech clause. None was at odds with the language of the amendment. Few are foreclosed by any fair assessment of its history or its past judicial exposition. Each, moreover, is fraught with its own problems, and virtually all confide an unavoidable margin of textually uncertain discretion in our courts. What, then, may one conclude?

Perhaps one may conclude that the general cynicism toward written constitutions and judicial review is quite correct, after all. For without attempting to promote any peculiar or nonstandard theory of judicial review and without taking recourse to any extraordinary notions of free speech, we have encountered a number of seemingly vast differences among quite plausible interpretations of a single clause. What has made the exercise even more disconcerting, moreover, is that the clause we have reviewed is probably among the least objectionable for facial ambiguity of any that appear in our written Constitution. If the free speech clause is susceptible to such a variety of dismayingly different interpretations, then presumably the majority of the Constitution will present at least equivalent uncertainties. Insofar as that is true, an insistence that nothing useful has been gained by pressing particular propositions into written constitutions (enforceable in the normal course of adjudication) may appear to be very well taken. It may seem to be especially well taken if, as appears to be true here, even attempts by very careful judges seem to reach such irreconcilable impressions of the Constitution as applied.

Possibly this is the right conclusion, but there is considerable reason to doubt that it is. One reason to doubt such cynicism is that, despite the difficulties the judiciary has experienced administering the first amendment, the free speech clause's good faith administration has nonetheless very probably provided the United States with a greater measure of actually protected free speech than we would otherwise have had. There is in fact an impressive array of case law decisions from the Supreme Court (and a larger number from subordinate courts that have felt bound by the Supreme Court's precedents) that do carry into execution a "strong" version of the free speech clause. Surprisingly, for instance, the comparison of the American experience with the English experience seems quite solidly to endorse the superiority of the former.[73] Despite the deserved reputation of the English for their overall lack of intolerance, it is not true that freedom of speech is equally protected under law in that country as in this country. Indeed, there are a number of American Supreme Court decisions that are without counterpart in England (which of course one would expect insofar as the English have no written, judicially enforceable constitutional guarantees of free speech); rather, there are significant areas where English positive law restricts free speech far more than the first amendment has been interpreted to allow here.[74]

This matter to one side, moreover, there may be less chaos respecting the interpretation of the free speech clause than first meets the eye. In our attempt to be wholly fair to the genuine difficulties of "merely" interpreting the first amendment, we have disaggregated a number of doctrines in order to exhibit their differences. When these several principal competing approaches are pulled apart from one another, and when each is separately ensconced in its own distinctive graphic, they do seem to be dramatically different from one another. Thus, the interpretive exercise, carried through as we have deliberately sought to do here, was calculated to emphasize the consequential differences that tend to characterize these graphic displays. Still, without now reneging on the statement that the particular manner in which a question is framed under the free speech clause can indeed direct a very different answer than the framing of the "same" question in quite different terms, it is also useful to remember that these various graphics are not necessarily mutually exclusive. They tend to agree, for instance, in terms of what are the most troublesome areas. Moreover, they can all be laid aside and still be made to "count" within a more general formulation. Such a more general formulation, the particular elements of which are each informed by the fuller graphic review we have explored, might read this way:

> The question in each case is whether the circumstances were sufficiently compelling to justify the degree of infringement resulting from the law, given the relationship of the speech abridged to the presuppositions of the first amendment, and the relationship of the law to the responsibilities of the level of government that has presumed to act.

The last phrase ("the relationship of the law to the responsibilities of the level of government that has presumed to act") identifies the federalism component of our review. The penultimate phrase of the formulation ("given the relationship of the speech abridged to the presuppositions of the first amendment") takes into account an implied first amendment ranking of speech. In turn, the first phrase ("whether the circumstances were sufficiently compelling to justify the degree of infringement resulting from the law") provides an accommodation for the Holmes-Brandeis standard. It encompasses cases in which the speech is highly protected (and thus may not be abridged save on a showing of clear and present danger of a serious evil) while nonetheless accommodating a lesser standard when the speech is itself far removed from politics and policy (e.g., misleading consumer solicitations redressable in private actions for fraud or restitution). Useful as well is the "degree of infringement resulting from the law," insofar as it may accommodate differences ranging from complete criminalization of certain utterances, through lesser incursions resulting from limited time, place, or manner controls, or limited civil liability to specifically damaged individuals.

Taken in context, that is, given substance, example, and clarity within the context of the discussion we have reviewed, a formulation such as this may work quite well in practice, assuming only a conscientious willingness in the judiciary to try. Much more than this is in any case not to be expected from the Constitution. The diffident optimism of Madison and Jefferson was prematurely crushed in the virulent nationalism of the quasi war with France and the enforcement of the Sedition Act of 1798.[75] But the first amendment has endured and it may well have come around to fulfill their expectations more satisfactorily. There is surely much that we can learn from the mistakes, as well as from the brighter examples, of our own bicentennial history.

In suggesting a general formulation for first amendment questions, incidentally, I have tried only to respond to what do seem to be genuine difficulties of conscientious interpretation, namely, to take into account the most serious problems for which no adequate accommodation can otherwise be made. But it would seriously mistake the main point of this unhurried review to think that the object of the chapter all along has been to have that formulation literally displace the free speech clause. Torn loose from the immediate context of this review, the formulation is much too cumbersome a proposition to withstand comparison with the first amendment's own words, which are so much more powerful and so much less facile. On its face, it unduly lessens the burden for those who are hostile to such speech that they have no interest in defending as against such other interests that they may much more strongly prefer. Precisely for that reason (quite apart from the more obvious reason that personal efforts to "revise" the Constitution are ludicrous), every person may rightly demand that in every case we start with the free speech clause itself. It has its own language, and that language imposes a proper burden of its own; it quite properly throws onto the adversary of speech the whole weight of what ought to be a very heavy burden indeed. If, then, despite its obvious difficulties, the suggested formulation may be useful, it is not as a displacement or substitute for the first amendment. Rather, it is but one way of describing what we should minimally expect to encounter in the course of attempting to discharge the burdens imposed by the first and fourteenth amendments. And that much is the least we should desire in respecting this written Constitution.

2

The Controverted Uses of the Press Clause

The several interpretive modes addressed in the first chapter dealt only with "the freedom of speech" that Congress shall make no law abridging. Nevertheless, the examples drew indiscriminately from cases involving speech-in-print as well as oral speech. For instance, the case in which Justice Holmes tentatively fashioned the clear-and-present-danger test was in fact a case in which the Espionage Act prosecution was directed against a man (Schenck) who urged resistance to the military draft by distributing pamphlets rather than by street-corner oratory.[1] Similarly, the development of that test, which added a subjective element to the objective element (i.e., that the speaker must have reason to know of the condition that would make his presentation wrongful), arose not in the setting of inflammatory rhetoric but in a newspaper libel case: *New York Times v. Sullivan*.[2] Examples of the Hand formulation (gravity of the evil discounted by its improbability) were taken from cases involving antilitter ordinances—ordinances held unconstitutional as applied to printed political handbills.[3] The principal example of an "indirect" abridgement was itself a newspaper case: the instance of a reporter subpoenaed to answer grand jury questions provoked by his published story.[4] Speech-in-print was thus subsumed under "the freedom of speech." The medium of speech, whether sound waves or newsprint, was without per se importance.

Throughout that review, the sole acknowledgment of a clear boundary to the free speech clause was not between oral and printed speech. It was merely the more obvious one: the boundary line defining "speech" in the sense of separating it from activity not within the first amendment at all, for example, the problem of the demonstrative uses of tearing up draft cards or of other acts that may be communicative but that are themselves neither oral nor printed speech.[5] Whether armbands are speech (or should be "deemed" speech) or whether shooting guns at presidents should be deemed speech (because sometimes done to express political objections, or at least to attract someone's attention) are further examples of *that* problem. That problem, however, is merely like the problem of defining "religion," which is also identified in the first amendment: some definitional line must perforce be fashioned, regardless of one's trepidation in fashioning it. In contrast, speech-in-print does not raise that problem. Accordingly, our initial review of the first amendment subsumed its protection under the freedom of speech.

Recurring to the words of the first amendment, however, does raise the question whether speech-in-print and oral speech are protected alike or protected differently, though both are specially protected by the amendment: "Congress shall make no law abridging the freedom of speech or [the freedom] of the press." The obvious question is whether "or of the press" is an expression of precaution or an expression of distinction. Is it meant merely to provide textual fortification against a slight risk that without its express inclusion "the freedom of speech" might be restricted short of the press, or does it suggest something else: for example, that *the* freedom of *the* press is a discernible and separate estate from the freedom of speech? Is there also an additional implication? If the freedom of the press is separate and distinct from the freedom of speech, to whom does this separate system of press freedom extend? To anything in print or, rather, to a distinctive class of businesses and professionals, to members of "*the* press"?[6]

Generally, in the case law of the first amendment, none of these several distinctions have thus far been established. Rather, the full speech-and-press clause has been regarded as expressly precautionary—as an express directive that the press is neither to be excluded from the first amendment nor to be *dis*favored within the full clause. In the latter respect, the clause is regarded as repudiating the Blackstone view that "the liberty of the press . . . consists [only] in laying no previous restraints upon publications and not in freedom from censure for criminal matter when published."[7] As freedom of speech is protected from much more than mere licensing systems, freedom of the press has been more protected than that as well. Thus, the clause has not been regarded as redundant or as trivial, but neither has it been interpreted as much of the press has sometimes wished, as furnishing a *unique* position for journalists and publishers within the first amendment.

In some few cases, however, hints of special protection for "the press" have appeared. For instance, there is an implication in some decisions that certain kinds of licensing systems that are not invalid per se may be invalid if applied to "the press."[8] And in several libel cases, dicta have suggested that "the media" may not be liable without a degree of scienter that nonmedia defendants need not entertain in order to be subjected to civil damages.[9] In an address at the Yale Law School, moreover, Justice Potter Stewart suggested that the press clause might be unique, that it is a clause singling out the publishing business (broadly defined) as a constitutionally favored enterprise.[10] A little later, Justice Douglas crafted a dictum that may furnish a supporting rationale for Potter Stewart's idea:

> The press has a preferred position in our constitutional scheme, not to enable it to make money, not to set newsmen apart as a favored class, but to bring fulfillment to the public's right to know.[11]

The dictum is characteristically cryptic. It may be read to say merely that the press has the same "preferred position" as freedom of speech has a preferred position, that is, "preferred" by force of its inclusion in the first amendment. Still, this is surely not the more likely implication. Rather, the dictum seems to carry a different notion: that newsmen are especially protected within the first amendment in respect to their work as journalists and that their employer-businesses are also specially protected for the same reason. The reason for their special protection (within the first amendment) is not to favor them as a class but rather to enable them to bring fulfillment to "the public's right to know."

If this were the implication, it would not be the first time a member of the Court had introduced into first amendment analysis a component laying particular stress upon the vocational auspices of either speech or writing. In fact, a comparison of these dicta with dicta elsewhere appearing in Supreme Court cases raising issues of "academic" freedom (the teaching, research, and publishing freedoms of professional teachers and scholars) shows a marked similarity.[12] There, too, the rationale for special protection is not based on a desire to favor academics per se. Rather, the justification rests on an observation (or supposition) about the nature of their work: that the essence of the academic profession is the critical examination of received wisdom and that therefore it is essentially the public interest that benefits from the careful protection of an academic's professional liberty. A community that can require the dismissal of a teacher because of the critical content of his or her critical professional utterances frustrates the social usefulness of the academic profession. A community that can restrict the investigations of reporters or levy damages upon their newspaper likewise frustrates the public information function of news personnel. Accordingly, if academic freedom is a "*special* concern" of the first amendment,[13] as the Court says, so also is freedom of the press.

In keeping with that view, taking into account the professional journalist's vocational linkage might indeed furnish *the* difference in certain instances. For example, rules restricting access to certain sources of information on grounds that may be sufficient (as time, place, and manner controls) against unaffiliated citizens might not be adequate against a reporter's special claims: "not to set newsmen apart as a favored class, but to bring fulfillment to the public's right to know."[14] Because, as rephrased by Justice Powell in 1974, "in seeking out the news, the press . . . acts as an agent of the public at large."[15]

The press, then, may be thought to be different institutionally insofar as it is defined by the work of professional reporters who serve the "checking" functions of the first amendment.[16] It is logically and expressly set off within the first amendment on that account. Its distinction is that while each individual's personal freedom of speech may likewise be useful in publicizing public issues (e.g., the speeches of Eugene Debs or of Martin Luther King), the press is regularly and professionally engaged in that pursuit. Moreover, unlike the case of "academic freedom," the claim of "the press" does not rest on mere implications of the first amendment. Rather, it is memorialized on the face of the amendment itself. Indeed, James Madison's original draft of the first amendment, even more than the final version of the first amendment, makes the distinction clearly and emphatically. That draft distinguished one's personal freedom to write and to publish (as well as to speak) from "the freedom of the press." The former, a personal freedom, is subsumed under one's personal freedom of speech. The latter is separated and identified to the press:

> The people shall not be deprived or abridged of their right to speak, to write, or to publish their sentiments; *and* the freedom of the press, as one of the great bulwarks of liberty, shall be inviolable.[17]

The tentative distinction of "the press" may also claim an additional coherence derived from historical usage. Recognition of "the press" institutionally, that is, as a reference to particular identifiable enterprises (and not as a reference merely to anything an individual may have copied on a printing press), was an established and familiar figure of speech well before the formulation of the first amendment. It is very much a part of colloquial recognition even now, whenever newspapers are still spoken of as "the fourth estate."[18] The phrase refers to the fact that newspapers, though privately owned and not formally a part of government at all, nonetheless came to be regarded in England as having nearly as much influence upon public affairs as the recognized estates within the government. Within established government, three estates were represented (estates in Parliament), each providing some measure of countervailing strength to check the tendencies of the other two. Standing apart, outside Parliament, was the fourth estate of newspapers—a powerful external check upon the combination of the three estates. The sense of institutional importance of this press is captured powerfully in a comment by Thomas Jefferson, who, despite his subsequent sense of anger and disappointment with the manner he was treated by the press,[19] observed: "[W]ere it left to me to decide whether we should have a government without newspapers or newspapers without a government, I should not hesitate a moment to prefer the latter."[20]

Definitional closure on "the press" is thus not at all infeasible (obviously it starts with newspapers), and the demarcation of "*the* freedom of *the* press" for purposes of distinctive first amendment analysis is satisfactorily determinable. The tentative case for a distinctive interpretation of the press clause is thus quite appealing. Essentially, it would hold that the press clause is neither redundant nor yet merely precautionary. It means that "the freedom" of "the press" is not to be confused with each person's individual freedom to publish (a freedom subsumed under the speech clause). Neither is it disparaging of that freedom— nothing presented by press attorneys in the Supreme Court needs to be derisive of the general free speech review we canvassed in chapter 1. Rather, the point being advanced is additional to what was said there. The point is that the press clause makes the institutional affiliation of a journalist of separate and compelling weight. Frequently, it must therefore also be dispositive.

The argument we have been reviewing is thus one with quite respectable credentials. At least it is fair to say that the foundations are as good as those which have achieved success in other areas of constitutional doctrine. In effect, it draws together the following elements:

1. a clearly adequate textual basis;
2. a measure of supportive history (i.e., some evidence that "the freedom of the press" was understood to be distinct from "the freedom of speech," and that that distinction was consciously carried into the framing of the first amendment);

3. a measure of analogical reinforcement (i.e., that considerations equivalent to those the Court has deemed sufficient in respect to a special first amendment concern for "academic freedom" are fully present here as well);

4. an adequate measure of coherence and manageability (i.e., it is not infeasible to identify "the press," nor are we without logical stopping places to keep it within sensible boundaries); and

5. a useful foreshadowing of the general principle in sufficient judicial dicta that its more concrete passage into constitutional law can scarcely be objected to as either revolutionary or even as seriously lacking in precedential support.

To be sure, as to this last matter, we are still missing an opinion from the Court that can rightly be labeled as the breakthrough decision. There is nothing yet comparable to the earlier epochal cases that heralded a major shift in judicial thinking about the first amendment—such as Holmes's opinion in *Schenck*[21] (with its clear-and-present-danger formulation), the new assumption in *Gitlow*[22] (applying the free speech clause to the states), or the wholesale revisions in the libel law signaled by *New York Times v. Sullivan*.[23] But a look at one of the Supreme Court's recent adjudications may indicate how very close the issue has become and how very slight is the step that remains to be taken. In fact, the case that brings the matter close to resolution is also significant quite apart from its provocative intimation about "the press" clause. The case of *Richmond Newspapers, Inc. v. Virginia*[24] was epochal in its own right; it extended the first amendment as a sword. Along the way, it also came to the verge of the press clause.

It had been an unsettled question (until *Richmond News*) as to whether the first amendment provides any affirmative leverage to secure information from a reluctant government. Traditionally, the free speech clause has been utilized principally as a defense, that is, as a shield to defend against official attempts to prevent one's speech or to prosecute for one's prior utterances. Increasingly, however, the first amendment has been invoked virtually as though it were a "freedom of information act," namely, as a basis to surmount refusals by government to share information within its possession and to permit access to places under its control.[25] Until *Richmond News*, no such reliance had ever been successful.

To be sure, the law has been settled for at least four decades that government ownership or management of property does not per se exempt the government from the first amendment. At least since the decision in *Hague v. CIO*,[26] overthrowing a state's claim that it was as privileged as a private owner to exclude whom it wished from a public park, the first amendment has been construed to establish some degree of free speech easement in government premises. But though cases such as the *Hague* case quite (rightly) shattered the notion that somehow government was exempt from the first amendment as an owner of property (and therefore constrained by the first amendment only as regulator of private conduct), still the protection thus afforded by the first amendment was for one's own "speech"[27] rather than for access to information. In short, the successful parties in *Hague* relied upon the first amendment to defeat the notion that they could not hold an assembly and make speeches in a public park. Not resolved by *Hague* (nor by any of the cases extending its "time, place, and manner" analysis for determining the extent to which one could communicate to others in a place the government attempted to regulate against such communication), however, was the different issue of first amendment access for information. *Richmond News* is that case. In fact, it was also a "press" case, that is, a suit successfully litigated through the Supreme Court by a newspaper barred (as all members of the public had also been barred) from a portion of a state criminal trial.

The point at issue in *Richmond News* was not whether the trial courtroom could be commandeered for speech purposes. Presumably it could not; that is, a rule, enforceable by contempt, against visitors or others wishing to use the courtroom as a political forum during the course of an ongoing trial would generally be valid. Nor was the point at issue whether someone wishing to be heard by members of the public (or by members of the press) could be kept from having the press or the public present during their testimony; no such claim was made by, or on behalf of, any such "willing" speaker.[28] Rather, the point at issue was whether the first amendment required any special justification for the state trial judge's decision to close the trial, at least when no participant in the proceedings objected to the closing, and the sole interest asserted was that of press "right" to attend the proceedings. As summarized in the concurring opinion by Justice Stevens, the decision establishing such a right made *Richmond News* itself "a watershed case":

> This is a watershed case. Until today the Court has accorded virtually absolute protection to the dissemination of ideas, but never before has it squarely held that the acquisition of newsworthy matter is entitled to any constitutional protection whatsoever. . . . Today, however, for the first time, the court unequivocally holds that an arbitrary interference with access to important information is an abridgement of the freedom of speech and of the press protected by the First Amendment.[29]

To be sure, the several opinions in the case also made quite clear that these third-party access rights are not absolute. Rather, the extent to which the government need give way will hereafter be determined according to a perfectly ordinary first amendment analysis. More specifically, the question will be, in each case, whether the "interference with access to important information" represented by the decision to exclude is "arbitrary" in the ordinary first amendment sense of being inadequately justified by sufficiently compelling, countervailing reasons, in light of the scope of the access restriction.[30] Obviously, then, the access right (including that of the press) is not absolute. It will be examined on the same terms subsumed under the integrative review we previously canvassed in chapter I.

The more intriguing question, not resolved (because not necessary to resolve), was left dangling: whether some contextual justifications sufficient to warrant the exclusion of the public at large might not be sufficient in respect to "the press." But the dicta, tiptoeing to that question, were provocative. Thus Chief Justice Burger suggested:

> Instead of acquiring information about trials by firsthand observation or by word of mouth from those who attended, people now acquire it chiefly through the print and electronic media. In a sense, this validates the media claim of functioning as surrogates of the public. While media representatives enjoy the same right of access as the public, they often are provided special seating and priority of entry so that they may report what people in attendance have seen and heard.[31]

And in a subsequent footnote, the chief justice added:

> [S]ince courtrooms have limited capacity, there may be occasions when not every person who wishes to attend can be accommodated. In such situations, reasonable restrictions on general access are traditionally imposed, including preferential seating for media representatives.[32]

Clearly wanting to guard the chief justice's (plurality) opinion from being misread, Justice Brennan's concurring opinion was both admonitory and provocative:

> A conceptually separate, yet related, question is whether the media should enjoy greater access rights than the general public. [Citations omitted.] But no such contention is at stake here. Since the media's right of access is at least equal to that of the general public . . . this case is resolved by a decision that the state statute unconstitutionally restricts public access to trials. As a practical matter, however, the institutional press is the likely, and fitting, chief beneficiary of a right of access because it serves as the "agent" of interested citizens, and funnels information about trials to a large number of individuals.[33]

The next step, however, is not a very large one conceptually. In an earlier case, involving access to a county jail[34] (rather than a trial courtroom), Justice Stevens had addressed the facts of the case with the same contextual concentration the court finally brought to bear in *Richmond News*. In jail access cases, the proffered justifications for cordoning off access to the jail (other than to attorneys with prisoner-clients and other than to relatives at fixed places and fixed times) were of course quite different from those that might warrant closing a trial. They were reasons of prison security, administrative hardship and expense, and penological judgment, that is, that prisoners may manipulate the press for their own ends and their own exploitative advantage within the prison and inmate population, seriously frustrating good-faith efforts to avoid friction within the jail and to avoid interference with ordinary rehabilitative processes. These were by no means frivolous objections. Jails, moreover, are certainly quite unlike either public parks or even courtrooms, for that matter, in terms of traditional expectations of access. Nonetheless, the presence of other circumstances made the case very close for Justice Stevens, who in fact dissented from the decision sustaining the ban. The record in the case made quite clear that the news reporters seeking access to the jail had not come idly. Inmate suicides had already been reported in the press. Substantial reason evidently existed to question the reasonableness of conditions within the jail. Additionally, there was no pending grand jury investigation of these conditions and no evidence that such interest might be stimulated in the absence of community awareness quickened by investigative reporting. An excellent argument could be made (and was made) that even supposing that unaffiliated individuals or concerned special-interest groups (e.g., the NAACP) could not surmount the exclusionary policy, still professional journalists might do so. Their vocational attachment to news media in the business of such news coverage provided a specific point of distinction from the interests of others. The scope of the exclusion reflected by the ban was not warranted, in Stevens's view, given the auspices under which access was sought and the probable feasibility of accommodating that request without undue strain upon the operation of the jail.

Neither *Richmond News* nor *Houchins* (the jail access case) turned explicitly on "the press" clause per se. Both are thus inconclusive of the special issue, though both also illustrate how close the argument respecting the distinction of that clause has become. Were it to appear, a decision formalizing the transition would be the "epochal" case (in the sense of being *the* case formally marking a significant passage of constitutional doctrine), but it would hardly now come as a surprise.

These access controversies provide merely the most obvious (and thus also the most attractive) example of how the proposed distinction of the press clause would make a difference. But plainly they are not the only context in which journalists could become professionally advantaged by force of the clause. In anticipating the more comprehensive nature of the change that may already be under way, it may be useful to illustrate how the force of the example for preferred press treatment may be readily extended to other areas of recurring controversy.

In chapter 1, we already took account of the relevance of the first amendment to the "indirect effect" of compulsory disclosure demands under law: persons reposing confidence in another may be inhibited from doing so to the uncertain extent that those to whom they speak in confidence can be made to divulge the statement by threat of fine or jail. Though that is true, the general first amendment objection is not conclusive. It raises, but does not automatically decide, the resulting question. The inhibition on such speech arising from its subsequent coerced disclosure may be overcome by the fair trial needs of a criminal defendant, the indictment functions of grand juries, or even the (mere) legislative fact-finding interests of congressional committees.[35] Enter into this calculus, however, significant *additional* weight on one side furnished under the distinct auspices of "the press" clause. The argument is that the explicit, more protective shelter furnished by that clause may well be decisive.[36] When the individual facing subpoena is a journalist and the occasion of the subpoena arose from a confidence entrusted to the journalist in his professional capacity, the press clause (arguably) specially shields it, not necessarily "absolutely" but measurably more than in any other instance.

The example could as well be taken from libel law. In ordinary libel cases, a standard of liability for *negligently* uttered falsehoods defaming another may be the general rule,[37] despite the self-censoring effect such a rule may impose; avoidance of reputational damage is deemed a sufficiently compelling interest to permit redress of such (false) speech as immediately brings about such damage. As to "the press," however, the argument would have it that the reporting function of the press requires an additional margin of protection pursuant to the distinct solicitude of the press clause, lest fear of liability and heavy damages induce such dread that newspapers will simply stay clear of reporting matters likely to precipitate lawsuits against them. Thus, *recklessness* in the publication of damaging statements should be the minimum standard of fault (as required by the press clause) in damage actions brought against journalists in their professional capacity.

Without extrapolating any further, it is quite clear that the advantages for enhanced press freedom under the proposed interpretation of "the press" clause could become both multiple and highly significant in the aggregate. In brief, the proposed interpretation propounds a press clause "system" of superior first amendment rights for (members of) the press. On the logic of the foregoing discussion, even an incomplete list would be inclusive of the following elements:

1. more substantial entitlements of access;
2. more substantial privileges of confidentiality;
3. more substantial immunity from searches and seizures;
4. more substantial immunity from libel actions;
5. more substantial exemptions from injunctions.

Each of these rights is "more," that is, than can be equivalently asserted by other persons who have standing only under the free speech clause and more than can currently be asserted by "the press."

But this cannot be right, can it? A press with superior first amendment rights and immunities in *all* of these respects? To be sure, each separate item in the foregoing list appears to be but a logical example, a mere concrete application of "the press" clause set off from the speech clause and marking a "preferred" set of rights and immunities for those within its special boundaries. Correspondingly, if each item by itself is but one example, surely nothing should strike us differently simply because we have seen fit to look at them again, as a group. Yet, once we have put them together as a group, something may suddenly strike us quite differently than when we had thought of each without connecting the larger implications of what we are about. Is there some basis for this uneasiness, or is it merely a reaction of jealousy? I think there may be ground for such uneasiness. Perhaps we can get at it in the following way.

Once we have strung together the several advantages of "the press," as proposed by the interpretation of the press clause we have been examining, what can it mean to call it "our" press? The press has repeatedly relied upon its usefulness as a vital supplier of needed information in advancing its claim to secure a unique first amendment estate. It has stressed the public interest, rather than its own. It has emphasized its agency function, rather than mere selfish interest. Do the legal implications of the exceptional press privileges and immunities we have outlined fit that explanation, however, or is it not obvious that they fit it very poorly, if at all? There is good reason to think that the fit is highly problematic. Indeed, it may be nonexistent.

The regularly publishing press, even the lesser part purporting to concern itself with straight news, is composed of an immense diversity of very different enterprises. Presumably, most all such commercial publishers will be necessarily included within "the press." In respect to "religion," for instance, a term also requiring a first amendment definition, the term has been rightly construed inclusively rather than exclusively; that is, the special advantages conferred by the free exercise clause in behalf of exemptions asserted on the basis of "religion" have been conferred on nearly any sort of quasi theology that can colorably pass muster.[38] Doubtless this is as it should be. A narrow construction (of "religion") would run risks of imposing a confining conventionality, of limiting itself to "acceptable" or "beneficial" religions, of involving the courts in the odious business of invidious preference among religions. To avoid the equal risk of an equivalent confining narrowness in respect to "the press," certainly the better argument is that that phrase, too, must be generously interpreted. But the specter of a vast, free-wheeling publishing business, sustained principally by advertising revenue linked predominantly to consumer appeal for the "news" of the *National Inquirer* as much as for the "news" of the *New York Times*, with all publishers having significantly greater advantages and significantly less accountability under law than all other individuals, may make one uneasy.

To describe this assortment of journals as "our" press seems seriously misleading. The first amendment protections contemplated for the press are emphatically its own. They are not those of some larger social collectivity. It is quite clear that the system of special position for journalists (and the private enterprises employing them) is not meant to vest rights in the public. To the contrary, several of the specific examples are examples of press rights *against* the public, for example, special degrees of protection from libel actions, special degrees of protection of confidentiality in not having to disclose the source (or lack of source) of a defaming story—just as newspapers have very stoutly resisted the imposition of enforceable statutory duties of publishing material that they prefer not to offer. Even the imposed obligation to publish a reply by a maligned candidate for public office has been successfully opposed on first amendment, "free" press grounds.[39]

To express the expectation that the larger, long-term public interest may benefit from the existence of a ruggedly independent array of commercial publishers in the United States is certainly a reasonable hope, exactly in the same sense that we expect to benefit overall from the special protection that freedom of speech enjoys under the first amendment. But to construct an additional rationale that sets off an entire industry with unique first amendment advantages on the notion that these highly independent businesses are really public agents or public "surrogates" is to mislead and to be misled. Agency is not involved here at all. If it were, then consistent with that view, each agent's principal (i.e., "the public") could presume to set the terms of its agent's obligations: the terms of what its agent must publish, to whom it must account, and the scope of that accountability. That, however, is certainly not contemplated. Indeed, the history of the free press, like the history of free speech, is in this respect a history of the struggle to get free of duties and restrictions that "the public" may seek to impose. But if this much is true, then one may also more readily appreciate why the insistence for still superior rights in "the press" stirs a great deal of resistance. It envisions an exclusive estate inside the first amendment, appropriating to some who publish (members of "the press") strong and unequal advantages against all others (not of "the press") who are confined to the lesser protections of the free speech clause alone. The proposed interpretation may be right, but it is assuredly worth a close second look.

Actually, the idea that "the press" is different is not a new idea at all. But as one turns back to its historical origins, those characteristics that were felt to mark the distinctiveness of the press from other forms of speech were not characteristics that seemed to argue in favor of special protection. To the contrary, they were characteristics that lent themselves forcefully to quite the opposite view. The unequal advantage of the printing press furnished a reason for its special regulation. The damage that might more readily ensue, and the uncontrolled power that printing presses could confer upon their private owners, were not seen as good reasons for loosening the constraints of the common law. Rather, they were seen as compelling reasons for exceptional regulation. And that, of course, is what occurred.

Nearly from the time William Caxton brought the first Gutenberg press to England in 1476, the technical and commercial advantages of the new "technology" became evident. Cheaply producible, multiple copies of printed material, from presses equipped with reusable, movable typeface, quite revolutionized the information business. The advantages of these devices, however, were the ide-ologically indifferent advantages of their owners. They were advantages of mas-sively decreased costs and enhanced broadcast capacity. Whom they might help, whom they might destroy, or what mix of falsehood and profitable defamation might animate the private advantage of these presses was largely a matter of conjecture. Certainly it was not at all obvious that "the press" as such would necessarily serve the public interest.

Unsurprisingly, the reaction of the government to this development was to emphasize the public-interest hazards of this innovation[40] rather than the pos-sible public-interest gains of leaving it unregulated. And thus, in 1557 a select group of London Stationers was granted a royal charter in order to confine the ownership of presses to responsible parties. The preamble of the Stationers' charter recited as one purpose of this regulated monopoly of private owners the appro-priate enforcement of the common law of seditious libel. By 1585 the Stationers' Company was reestablished under the supervision of Star Chamber. A full-scale licensing system was now in place, complete with the generous availability of general warrants and writs of assistance to help ferret out the location of unau-thorized printing presses.[41]

A fair portion of the justification for this regulatory scheme has a peculiarly modern ring to it, much the same ring as is still favored in the United States in respect to the newer media (radio and television), which are licensed and regu-lated by the Federal Communications Commission. Printers capable of influenc-ing mass audiences cheaply and quickly were thought to be appropriate objects of precautionary measures and of fiduciary obligation. The then-existing com-mon law controls were regarded as adequate to redress the abuses of free speech by street-corner orators. These same controls were held to be plainly inadequate, however, against the elusive advantages of unregulated printing presses. The individual speaker is easily identified. The location of the printing press, whose anonymous products are not self-identifying, requires at least a system of press registration. The damage inflicted by a scurrilous statement uttered aloud may typically be neither irreparable nor of overwhelming impact. Private actions for defamation or occasional criminal prosecution might therefore adequately con-tain its harms. But scurrility in widely circulating, mass-copy publications may be more nearly irreparable and overwhelming, as well as more difficult to track down to its source. Prevention, and not merely compensation, was thus more warranted. The special credibility of the printed word, that is, its impressive impersonalism, its sheer graphic authority (vis-à-vis ordinary speech), even now tends to carry greater weight than the spoken word. Thus, licensing and attend-ant precautions in advance of what is printed fall logically into place.[42]

Just so in respect to the fair administration of justice. Threats to fair trials may be tolerable as far as mere pretrial, oral gossip is concerned. But threats to fair trials may be very grave when newspapers publish improper material that quickly penetrates an entire venire or city. Accordingly, the grounds of liability, the form of accountability, the magnitude of damages, and the logic of prior restraint—

all are *more* compelling, not less compelling, in respect to "the press." Vestiges of this thinking persist firmly in modern England. There are extremely strict controls limiting press accounts in advance of trials; the imposition of contempt sanctions and the levying of considerable fines for newspaper contempt is by no means rare.[43]

Viewed from this perspective, the case we have previously examined (which would exempt the press from constraints already applicable to others) seems suddenly quite perverse. The identifying datum of "the press" is simply that its products circulate to mass audiences cheaply and quickly, from machinery itself too expensive for everyone to command. Whether individual owners choose to regard the resulting opportunity as one of private power rather than of "public agency," moreover, is not in any sense predetermined. To elect the rhetoric of treating the press as entitled to exceptional legal rights because the extension of such extra rights must vicariously operate to the public good is entirely to beg an uncertain question. Once one discards the disingenuousness of such rhetoric (e.g., that the press is the public's own agent) and once one registers the full impact of the notion that the regime of exceptional press privilege contemplates extraordinary exemption from standard legal constraints, we are left with a very odd set of propositions. It is as though the rule of the first amendment harbored (in "the press" clause) the following propositions:

1. The greater the circulation of a libel (e.g., by newspaper rather than by word-of-mouth), the more immune is the libeler.
2. The greater the danger of irreparable harm (e.g., by newspaper publication of material prejudicial to a a fair trial), the more absolute the protection of the source from injunction.
3. The greater the incentive for reporting fiction as fact (e.g., anticipated profits by inventing falsehoods that others may not be able to prove were published recklessly without access to the newspaper's own files), the greater protection one has from devices of civil discovery.

From this perspective, it is unclear whether the Supreme Court should even have interpreted the first amendment to repudiate Blackstone's view—that "the freedom of the press" meant merely freedom from the licensing system that was allowed to expire in England in 1694.[44] A different emphasis upon such fashionable rhetoric as "the public right to know" and the description of the press as "agent" of the public could as logically have described a free press clause marking off a separate and unequal estate within the first amendment: separate and unequally inferior. Among its identifiable features, with each quite suitably "explained," would be these:

1. less entitlement (than others) to withhold sources: so that the public may know the source to enable the public rightly to judge the credibility of the story;

2. greater liability (than others) for damaging and false reports upon a lesser showing of fault: so that the measure of redress is in proportion to the magnitude of harm and so that the terms of liability are responsive to the theory of a fiduciary's duty of carefulness;

3. less protection (than others) from varieties of prepublication restraint: in order to avoid the irreparability of harm;

4. less editorial autonomy than either individuals or voluntary associations possess insofar as they assert no special claim to "represent" the public in any sense at all.

The fact of the matter is that neither the communicative efficiency of the modern printing press, its general circulation characteristic, its entrepreneurial or competitive characteristics, not its very mixed history sum up to a strong combination of ingredients for a *favored* estate within the first amendment.

Even the usual pragmatic argument may fall short as well. The practical argument is that a specially favored press may act at least importantly as a champion of everyone else's freedom of speech: that its freedom is a guardian of our freedom. But the evidence of this guardian function is quite mixed. At least one serious author thinks it entirely overstated. Thus, in his recent book-length review of newspaper history in the United States, John Lofton reached the following conclusion:

> One clear impression emerges from this survey of more than 175 years of press reaction to various freedom of expression issues in the United States. It is that, except when their own freedom was discernibly at stake, established general circulation newspapers have tended to go along with efforts to suppress deviations from the prevailing political and social orthodoxies of their time and place rather than to support the right to dissent.[45]

To the extent that Lofton may be correct (and most of what we know of human nature suggests he may be), then it may be continuingly important that "the fourth estate" not be set off via the press clause. The practical realization that we are all threatened when the least among us is threatened is frequently a helpful thought in the law. That the press has much at stake in the first amendment, though no member of "the press" is the particular party struggling for his or her first amendment rights (whether in the Supreme Court or in some county court), may have its own useful instrumentalism. An important insight of this sort is reflected in the following observations of Anthony Lewis (for seven years the principal correspondent for the *New York Times* in the Supreme Court):

> Freedom of the press arose historically as an individual liberty. Eighteenth-century Americans saw it in those terms, and the same view is reflected in the Supreme Court decisions; freedom of speech and of the press, Chief Justice Hughes said, are "fundamental personal rights." To depart from that principle—to adopt a corporate view of the freedom of the press, applying

the press clause of the first amendment on special terms for the "institution" of the news media—would be a drastic and unwelcome change in American constitutional premises. It would read the Constitution as protecting a particular class rather than a common set of values. And we have come to understand, after much struggle, that the Constitution "neither knows nor tolerates classes among citizens."[46]

The elevation of "the press" within the first amendment may thus inure less to the public good than to the undesirable cultivation of an additional hubris within a privileged press. In the absence of more compelling evidence than we have to sustain the idea of that arrangement as the correct interpretation of the first amendment, there seems to be very little warrant to encourage the notion.

In the end, moreover, the attempt to link the freedom of the press with third-party ("public") interests in some distinctive way may simply backfire. On the one hand, to make the distinction meaningful, the press itself is forced into a position that it cannot truly mean and the legal ramifications of which are bound to be threatening. If attorneys for newspapers mean to distinguish their clients as "agents" or "surrogates" for the public in some sense different from the way the public at large may generally profit from each person's own freedom of speech (i.e., that we learn from what people say and that we, as much as they, benefit from their freedom), then they must be speaking of an agency relationship they are prepared to have the public itself take seriously. That would mean, necessarily, a large loss of editorial autonomy and a large increase in institutional accountability: "the public" as entitled to both sides of every story; "the public" as entitled to the "whole" story; the public as entitled to balance and fairness in "its" press, even as the FCC nominally requires of radio and television, which have been subjected to this rationale.[47] But that suggestion would surely be resisted by the newspapers in this country, as indeed it should be resisted.

The regularly reporting press is an unruly anarchy of disparate publications in the United States. No FCC or other public agency can require that each newspaper be "fair," that it grant free space to those in disagreement with its editorial policies, that it not withhold what its editors or owners wish to withhold, or that it conform to agency notions of good taste. To the contrary, the diversity of newspapers and casual journals reflects the capacity of entrepreneurs to profit from every kind of taste in the market, including of course a taste for the lurid, the sensational, and the ideologically biased, as well as the drily instructive news. In certain markets, moreover, certain newspapers are essentially without print competitors in respect to purely local events. Thus, they may very well tip the news quite deliberately to influence the outcome of elections and of legislative proposals well beyond the practical capacity of others, having no newspaper of their own, to offset. Still, despite that consequence, the first amendment has not yet been construed to impress a notion of public agency upon the private press or to force upon its proprietors a restriction of editorial freedom. "Newspapers and the magazines," conceded Justice Douglas, "frequently tip the news one direction or another and even try to turn a public figure into a character of disrepute." Yet, "[t]the standards of . . . newspapers, or magazines—whether of excellence or mediocrity—are beyond the reach of Government."[48] In so concluding, Douglas was merely echoing the observation offered more than a century and a half earlier by Thomas Jefferson:

> I deplore . . . the putrid state into which our newspapers have passed, and the malignity, the vulgarity, and mendacious spirit of those who write them. . . . It is however an evil for which there is no remedy, our liberty depends on the freedom of the press, and that cannot be limited without being lost.[49]

On the other hand, if the contention were meant seriously that the press should be seen as "an agent of the public at large," and on that account should indeed have certain unique prerogatives that others cannot assert equally (e.g., investigative access "rights"), then the logic of the argument leads neither to a press clause wholly favoring "the press" nor to a press clause wholly subjecting "the press" to obligations that cannot be imposed upon others. Rather, it may logically yield a hybrid: a constitutional treatment of "the press" extending to it certain enforceable rights not available to others, offset by a degree of legal accountability not tolerated by the first amendment in respect to others.

If, for instance, only members of the press corps may secure free investigative access to nonpublic places or to official files that unaffiliated individuals or representatives of voluntary associations cannot have, the trade-off may logically entail: (a) an enforceable duty to report what it learns; and (b) a fiduciary standard of care respecting the accuracy of what it publishes. There would thus arise a logical symmetry in the distinction of the press, but not one that we can readily imagine many publishers would find congenial. It may well seem presumptuous, but a good argument can be made that some of the press may need to be "saved" from its own advocacy. Should newspapers succeed in creating special first amendment access privileges that set them uniquely apart, they may thereafter discover that they have also paved the way for the loss of some of their own editorial freedom and for the escalation of their legal liabilities. The model of the airwaves and of the Federal Communications Commission, a model we examine quite closely in the next chapter, is highly suggestive of that possibility.

The press of this country, as we have noted, is characterized by diversity and private ownership. It is as diverse as the tabloids available at check-out counters, the *New York Times*, the house journals of labor unions and corporations, the pronounced partisanship of right- and left-wing subscription magazines, and the boisterous irreverence of the underground press. Some portion of this press aspires to very high professional standards. Its publishers, editors, and reporters care a great deal about the quality of their work. A large portion also operates with far fewer scruples, however, and some plainly pander to whatever seems now profitable.

None of this press, however, "represents" us. Rather, we find our own level in selecting from this blizzard of print what we want, or at worst, we put up with what we think is irritating because we decline to forego other features we think we just cannot do without. But in any case, these newspapers and journals are no more public "agents" than each of us is such an agent. Some of us reflect high personal standards (at least most of the time). Some of us do not care. We sort ourselves out individually, even as the press sorts itself out as well, by being what we choose to be and by taking our chances accordingly.

Within these circumstances, the first amendment is currently generous to the press. It does not provide any special estate, but, significantly, it does not except "the press" from its equal protections. It thus disallows the admissibility of argument that the form of speech, economically unloosed originally in the innovation of movable typeface on a print press, seals off journalism in the United States under a distinct regime of regulation. This interpretation was itself an immense gain for a free press in the United States. It liberated the press. Its assimilation into the interpretation of the first amendment was clearly not an easy, or a foregone, conclusion.

The new form of argument that would now additionally advantage some segment of the press, however, inadvertently threatens the independence of the same press. Those who maintain that they have a special claim to leave the rest behind at the courthouse door, the county commissioners' suite, the prison, or the nuclear plant, and to do so because they are the public's special agency, its surrogate, or its representative, may find themselves prisoners of their own rhetoric. A dissatisfied public may take them very seriously by mounting its own claims to demand a better accounting under law. The manifestations of that demand may go to public rights of access to the newspaper itself, to some public superintendence of its editorial policy, to some enhancement of its liability, some symmetry between agency privileges and fiduciary duties.

There are, moreover, large segments of the American public already eager to press precisely for this end.[50] The institutionalized, corporate newspaper industry, although severely buffeted by newer media competition, remains even now the object of jealousy and resentment. Many groups find themselves "underrepresented" in that press, misreported, and badly treated. The dominant position of particular wire services nationally, and the domination of local news by particular sole newspapers locally, periodically give rise to moves against the press by statute: to force upon it external demands for balance, accountability, and access. The suggestion is seriously put forward even to treat newspapers as mere common carriers, forced by law to carry other people's messages if indeed (as of course they must in order to survive) they agree to carry anyone's message.[51]

Thus far, these efforts have collapsed against the very strong barrier of the first amendment that guards the independence of the private commercial world of journalism. The problem of concentrated economic power is policed by the antitrust laws but not by imposing upon publishers a constricting network of "public-interest" obligations that commandeers their equipment and subordinates their editorial freedom. The struggle to secure that equal freedom under the first amendment was not an easy one. The permanence of its success is not something to be taken for granted. It would be a consummate irony were the press, in seeking certain new advantages framed in terms of serving "the public's right to know," and the press as an agent, surrogate, or fiduciary of the public interest, to embrace a perspective that historically trapped it in a spider web of accountability and regulation.

3

Scarcity, Property, and Government Policy
The First Amendment as a Mobius Strip

> *Möbius strip*. Topology, a one-sided surface that can
> be formed from a rectangular strip by rotating one
> end 180° and attaching it to the other end.
>
> *American Heritage Dictionary*

In chapter 2, several insinuating references were made to radio and television broadcasters, and to the Federal Communications Commission.[1] In each instance, the comparison was one of unflattering contrast with the equal first amendment rights that the (traditional) press shares quite fully with private citizens. The insinuation was that the broadcasting press is more heavily regulated than interpretations of the first amendment have tolerated either for lone pamphleteers or for the *New York Times* and that the critical distinction apparently rests on some notion of public agency peculiar to radio and television. The purpose of this chapter is to examine that distinction more attentively, the better to appreciate its fuller implications.

Following a cursory review of the history of radio regulation (the subject is elaborately presented in many accessible writings),[2] we move at once to a critical comparison of two Supreme Court cases.[3] Decided only five years apart, each case yielded a unanimous decision, and each decision was unanimously the opposite of the other. The first case involved a small radio station. The second involved a highly influential metropolitan newspaper. The unraveling of distinctions thought sufficient to reconcile these cases will bring us into new territory involving presuppositions of private property and government policy. The larger implications for interpreting the first amendment are quite profound. There is an abiding problem here in reconciling property rights and speech rights that none of us may have sufficient wit to solve. The difficulty is one identified in the bemused uncertainty of an able law student. After puzzling through these matters and after attempting quite carefully to give each of the Supreme Court's opinions its due, he submitted what he hoped was a first-rate paper (which it was). Even so, he added a disclaimer at the end:

> Deriving a consistent theory of the First Amendment from the myriad opinions of the Supreme Court represents a task similar to the problem of defining the inside and outside of a Möbius strip; that which appears logical at one point evaporates from another perspective.[4]

And so it does.

The airwaves of this country are governed principally by the Federal Communications Act of 1934.[5] In close imitation of the Radio Act of 1927 that it replaced,[6] the Communications Act prohibits any claim of private property in the airwaves and it vests an exclusive licensing power in a single federal agency, the Federal Communications Commission (the FCC). In its preference for this system, Congress elected a choice that was not altogether different from the manner in which, four centuries earlier, Parliament had dealt with the equivalent novelty of new printing presses in England.[7] Although no such comparison was suggested at the time, the powers vested in the FCC in 1934 were uncomfortably akin to those established in the regulated agency of the London Stationers' Company in the sixteenth century. It, too, had been granted exclusive licensing privileges and unlicensed private publications had been outlawed, exactly as is still true of such broadcasting in the United States.

To be sure, in contrast with the Stationers' monopoly, the standards that fix the licensing discretion of the FCC do not provide that it may grant or withhold licenses on the basis of the political or religious acceptability of an applicant's proposed broadcasts. To the contrary, the Federal Communications Act specifically forbids "censorship."[8] Even so, the meaning of the term has been confined merely to forbid specific attempts to edit proposed broadcasts in advance.[9] The prohibition of censorship does not forbid the FCC to use proposed broadcast content as a reason to withhold a license, and it does not forbid using actual broadcast content to "nonrenew" a license. The commission's principal control arises from the statutory provision that the FCC is to award, renew, suspend, cancel, or nonrenew licenses according to "the public interest, convenience, and necessity,"[10] a licensing standard borrowed altogether casually from the amended language of the Interstate Commerce Act and the licensing power of the Interstate Commerce Commission.[11]

The several reasons leading to this closely superintended regime of the airwaves are themselves a little cloudy,[12] but principal among them were these. First, a half century ago there was still considerable uncertainty in Congress over the nature of the electromagnetic spectrum, its potential uses, its divisibility, and its capacity for development. Second, there was a firm initial impression that for some time the probable usable radio frequencies in various receiving areas, free of congestive signal interference, would not be very numerous. Third, there was also a good deal of industry self-interest in opting for a licensing system; a number of companies first into the broadcasting business were eager to secure government protection of their investments by providing a means that would protect their use of particular frequencies from interference by other broadcasters. In this respect the arrangement also springs from origins that gave rise to the London Stationers' monopoly; there, too, incumbent stationers were quite willing to anticipate the prospect of limited licensing. Fourth, there was a palpable amount of congressional political anxiety, a fear among members of Congress of broadcasters and of their possible influence. (An immediate manifestation of that fear was the enactment of section 315 of the Federal Communications Act;[13] subject to certain limited exceptions, it requires that if any candidate for public office is granted broadcast time by a given licensee, equal time must at once be made available to every other legally qualified candidate for the same office.) And, fifth, there was a general anxiety about the uncertain power of broadcasting as a medium of communication or of speech, namely, its qualitative uniqueness, its credibility, its penetration, and its impact.

Given this legislative background, it was therefore no surprise that the FCC presumed at once to go beyond the determination of each applicant's mere technical competence and financial reliability in awarding or renewing licenses to broadcasters. Nor did the FCC confine itself, beyond these considerations, to such additional regulations as might soundly reflect antitrust interests (an antitrust power sustained by the Supreme Court in 1943[14] and since then extended to special network restrictions and limitations on cross-media ownership).[15] Rather, the FCC began very early also to compare and police the program content of applicants and licensees, and in this additional way to measure their consistency with "the public interest."[16] Again, one may think of this partly in analogy to the Interstate Commerce Commission: the FCC determined whether "the public interest, convenience, and necessity" were best served by the particular cargo or mix of freight a broadcaster would provide,[17] although broadcasters were not designated as common carriers and subsequent attempts to treat them as such have been held to exceed the FCC's statutory authority.[18] One may also think of this, however, with vague misgivings of the history of the Stationers' monopoly as well.

The main features of the FCC's program-content doctrines and regulations have evolved quite unevenly over fifty years, originally with the mere acquiescence of Congress but more recently with its apparent affirmative approval.[19] The history of these on-again, off-again developments is an oft-told tale that need not be repeated in detail still again.[20] We may do better simply to sketch the current principal features.

First, the commission has reserved certain frequencies exclusive of any private use at all. Of those wavelengths otherwise designated as available for private use, moreover, not all are in fact made available. With respect to those that are available (whether for radio or for television), each applicant for a designated frequency has been required to make some survey of "community interests" within the receiving area of the broadcast signal for which it seeks a license and to file with its application a profile of proposed programming according to the percentage of time it proposes to devote to each of fourteen commission-described subject-matter areas. In brief, the programs the broadcaster provides are not to be solely those it wishes to risk. The implication is clear that program profiles more proportioned to "the community," rather than those reflecting the ideological, aesthetic, or economic interests of the broadcaster, will be more likely to be favored by the FCC. A willful failure to conform to the program profile, moreover (even if the departure is to offer programming of viewpoints not otherwise significantly advanced by any other licensee or group in the same community), has been deemed sufficient cause to nonrenew the license.[21] Professional commentary has suggested that one principal result of this constraint is to minimize ideological diversity *among* licensees and to encourage a replicative, uncontroversial "public-interest" fare (e.g., rather standard religious broadcasting on Sunday mornings).[22]

Each licensee is also required to devote a nontrivial portion of broadcast time to the treatment of public issues deemed significant (as determined by the FCC) within the broadcast area—at the licensee's expense if sponsorship is unavailable, whether or not the licensee does not wish to speak to the subject and whether or not the same subject has been prominently featured in other sources.[23] Additionally, any licensee who broadcasts a partisan perspective on any public issue of a controversial nature must also provide a "fair representation" of other views, whether such other views are already well presented over other frequencies in the same market, whether their presentation may be contrary to the broadcaster's own views, and without regard to the unavailability of sponsorship to meet the free-rider expenses of the countervailing presentation.[24] And if within the course of presenting a controversial public issue an identifiable person is referred to in a disparaging fashion (whether or not the disparaging statement is accurate), the licensee must use reasonable effort to contact that person and provide him free time for a personal reply. The broadcaster has this obligation even if the original broadcast was the program of a third party who paid standard rates for the broadcast time and not a presentation by the broadcaster. The reply time must be furnished without charge regardless of the other party's ability to pay.[25]

The Federal Communications Act nominally forbids "censorship," as we have already noted.[26] However, the term does not forbid nonrenewal (and thus complete elimination of the broadcaster) for failing to conform to the program profile, the content of which and submission of which may have controlled the award of the license in the first place.[27] Nor does it forbid utilizing nonconformance to the "fairness" doctrine, the "reply" doctrine, or the candidate's equal time requirement. Nonrenewal of a license, suspension of a license, or the imposition of an administrative fine may also be imposed upon a licensee who broadcasts "indecent" or "vulgar" language, or "drug-oriented" music deemed by the FCC to be contrary to the public interest.[28]

The self-censoring and centripetal tendencies of these various regulations to induce essentially replicative, centrist-oriented, relatively colorless radio and television programming in the United States (in comparison with the starkly greater diversity within the printing press) has frequently been asserted.[29] The extent to which they actually explain the program characteristics of the electronic media (as distinct, for instance, from considerations of network domination or local broadcasters' commercial self-interest), however, is highly uncertain.

Pursuant to its general rule-making power, the FCC also exerts strong indirect program-content controls. The best known of these is the "prime time access" rule.[30] Ostensibly it was meant to encourage a greater diversity of independent productions (vis-à-vis network productions) at peak viewing hours on television. Allegedly, however, its principal effect has been to produce cheap game shows and syndicated reruns ironically for an hour otherwise most likely to attract high viewing interest.[31] A variation of such indirect program-content control has also resulted from informal FCC "eyebrow lifting," that is, censorship pressure to compel broadcasters to agree among themselves not to carry certain programming during "family" viewing hours.[32]

An invited difficulty with the broad, program-content powers of the FCC is that the existence of its powers has generated a litigious demand for their full use, sometimes even against the less intrusive modesty of the commission itself.[33] Judicial review of commission refusal to act *against* a licensee has sometimes made it hazardous for the FCC to permit an experimentalism within the media. In brief, the availability of judicial review to private groups aggrieved by an FCC refusal to intervene against a broadcaster exerts considerable pressure upon the commission to act contrary to its own judgment.

At the same time, the degree of discretion reposed in the FCC equally invites an internal manipulation by the agency itself. In *CBS, Inc. v. FCC*,[34] for instance, a majority of the Supreme Court upheld the disputed power of the commission to require broadcasters to yield time for the airing of a rankly political and one-sided "documentary" on the record of the Carter administration, over the unwillingness of any network to do so. The dispute arose under a 1971 act of congress authorizing the FCC to revoke a broadcaster's license for "willful" failure to allow "reasonable" access to its facilities by a legally qualified candidate for federal elective office.[35] The several networks refused to set aside their regular programming for the Carter show, arguing that the statute was inapplicable insofar as the partisan documentary was pressed against their wishes twelve months prior to the election that might involve Mr. Carter as a candidate. Their position was that "reasonable" access should surely not be interpreted to limit their own programming discretion virtually a year ahead of a given election. The commissioners of the FCC disagreed by the narrowest of majorities, holding 4 to 3 that the networks could be required to yield. Dissenting from the Supreme Court's subsequent acquiescence in this outcome, Justice Stevens noted that the vote within the FCC exactly matched the political party affiliations of its members: the majority consisted of four Democratic commissioners who ruled for the Carter interpretation, the dissenters of three Republican commissioners who ruled for the network interpretation. Justice Stevens did not say that the licensing-with-strings-attached power of the FCC had in fact been abused by a governmental agency to favor a particular political party. Rather, the point of his dissent was that it was dangerous to free speech to contemplate vesting such a power in a federal agency; he was therefore unwilling to interpret the statute as granting such power to the FCC. But of course the Stevens opinion was a mere dissent. The law, overall, is quite settled to the contrary. The FCC possesses very great program-content power over the "other" press of the United States. It is granted that power in the classic form of a government monopoly licensing agency, without whose continuing permission it is a criminal offense to function as a broadcaster.

We have noted that the speech-content requirements issued by Congress and otherwise determined by the FCC have applied to all licensees regardless of the number of broadcast frequencies readily receivable in a given area and regardless also of newspapers and other media already competing in the same area for advertiser dollars and for consumer interest. These requirements have been applied, moreover, whether a particular license issued by the FCC has no ascertainable market value or whether, assuming the license might once have had considerable market value, that value was assumed in the amount already realized (by sale) by the original licensee in an FCC-approved transfer of the license to the current holder. We have noted also that the obligations have applied against the broadcaster whether the broadcast that may trigger some of these duties was sponsored (and the time paid for) by someone or some company other than the broadcaster. By chance, the principal Supreme Court decision sustaining the program-content powers of the FCC involved a case specifically exhibiting many of these features.[36] That case is especially interesting because it provides an unintended contrast with what one might suppose to be the strong case for regulation. Ironically, it also provides an unseemly contrast with the case decided only five years later, striking down a very similar requirement as addressed to a newspaper.[37] Briefly then, here is the first amendment tale of two cases.

Contrary to the impression one might have from its leonine name, the Red Lion Broadcasting Company was not a particularly impressive or dominant broadcasting company.[38] Rather, it was a small one-thousand-watt radio station whose signal was received principally in a town of 5,684 persons, in Red Lion, Pennsylvania, not far from New York. Its commercial rate for one hour of "prime time" was a mere twenty-five dollars. The Red Lion station operated in competition with at least twenty AM and ten to fifteen FM radio stations readily receivable by local residents. Additionally, twelve television stations were received locally via cable in 2,080 homes in Red Lion. A nonresident (a well-known journalist residing in New York) was mentioned in a politically disparaging manner in a taped commercial program Red Lion Broadcasting Company presumed to air. In due course, the Red Lion Broadcasting Company was directed by the FCC to provide free reply time to the disparaged individual. Red Lion protested, observing that it had volunteered to let the offended person reply on its station on payment of a standard five-dollar fee, which that person concededly could afford, and otherwise claiming that the imposition of the FCC order abridged its own editorial freedom under the first amendment. The FCC and the Supreme Court disagreed. The Court held unanimously that the FCC had acted within its statutory authority and that the statute as applied did not offend the first amendment.

The contrast with the Supreme Court's subsequent decision in *Miami Herald*

Publishing Co. v. Tornillo, just five years later, could not be more striking.[39] The *Miami Herald* case tested an old and limited Florida statute applicable to newspapers. Enacted in 1913, the Florida statute required any newspaper that presumed to assail the personal character or official record of any candidate for public office to accept and publish such reply as the assailed candidate might submit in response.[40] The case arose decades later in 1972, when the *Miami Herald*, the sole metropolitan daily newspaper in the greater Miami area, ran its own editorial sharply disparaging the character of a local union leader and urging his defeat as a candidate for election to the state legislature. Refused "reply space" in the newspaper to respond to its criticism, the candidate (Pat Tornillo) sued in state court to secure compliance. Relying on the U.S. Supreme Court's decision in *Red Lion*, the Florida Supreme Court sustained the statute and held it valid as applied to these facts.[41] Without once referring to *Red Lion*, the U.S. Supreme Court unamimously reversed. In a curious opinion, the first two-thirds of which appeared to acknowledge the eminent reasonableness of the Florida statute, the Court nonetheless concluded quite emphatically: "Even if a newspaper would face no additional costs to comply with a compulsory access law and would not be forced to forego publication of news or opinion by the inclusion of a reply, the Florida Statute fails to clear the barriers of the First Amendment."[42]

The reasoning preceding this conclusion is extremely rugged and highly emphatic. It stressed overwhelmingly the free speech interests of an autonomous newspaper, and it gave no quarter at all to notions of public interest, fairness, or balance. Drawing the line very sharply, Chief Justice Burger quoted Zachariah Chafee's claim that "liberty of the press is in peril as soon as the government tries to compel what is to go into a newspaper."[43] Moving briskly to the Court's unanimous conclusion, the chief justice then declared:

> The choice of material to go into a newspaper, and the decisions made as to limitations on the size and content of the paper, and treatment of public issues and public officials—whether fair or unfair—constitute the exercise of editorial control and judgment. It has yet to be demonstrated how governmental regulation of this crucial process can be exercised consistent with First Amendment guarantees of a free press as they have evolved to this time. Accordingly, the judgment of the Supreme Court of Florida is reversed.[44]

These statements are no doubt impressive. Even so, it is not obvious, assuming that the statements are sound, how "governmental regulation of *this* crucial process" (i.e., determining content and determining the treatment of public issues and public officials) can be exercised with any greater consistency with the first amendment in respect to a private, commercial broadcaster than in respect to a private, commercial newspaper. Yet in *Red Lion* the same Court was evidently satisfied that a sufficiently safe way *had* been "demonstrated how governmental regulation of this crucial process can be exercised consistent with First

Amendment guarantees." What was that way? Apparently it involved the following elements:

1. to enact by federal statute an exclusive national licensing monopoly over an entire communications industry;
2. to criminalize any communication by any private party presuming to reach others by the government-monopolized medium, absent the possession of a license;
3. to vest sole licensing authority in a government agency to grant licenses only for such speech as would be consistent with "the public interest, convenience, and necessity";
4. to particularize that standard by requiring of every eligible applicant a subordination of its own editorial autonomy in respect to providing coverage of public issues, a fair representation of differing views respecting those issues, and a "right" of free reply to any disparaged person;
5. to enforce the compliance of all licensed parties with these standards by a power to suspend, cancel, nonrenew, or revoke the license without which it would be a federal offense for the broadcaster to continue its operation.

In comparing this arrangement with the very limited scope of the Florida reply statute, the Florida Supreme Court had thought that the statute was much more mild and therefore obviously constitutional as applied. In the U.S. Supreme Court, moreover, the *Red Lion* precedent was the principal preoccupation of the briefs submitted by both sides. In the *Miami Herald* opinion, however, *Red Lion* was not even cited.[45]

The abruptness of the Court's opinion in *Miami Herald* was additionally puzzling, moreover, because the Court itself quite readily conceded facts that would appear to make the circumstances of the *Miami Herald's* position much more appropriate for the imposition of several "public-interest" obligations than one might think to justify the imposition of such obligations on a local radio station. The Court conceded, for instance, that the *Miami Herald* was the dominant source of daily printed news (indeed, it was the sole regularly published metropolitan newspaper), whereas it was clear in *Red Lion* that that small station enjoyed nothing approaching local airwave control. It conceded, more generally, that there are overall far more single-newspaper communities in the United States than there are currently single-radio or single-television communities. It acknowledged also that "the same economic factors which have caused the disappearance of vast numbers of metropolitan newspapers have made entry into the marketplace of ideas served by the print media almost impossible."[46] The *Miami Herald* case, moreover, involved an active local candidate for public office in an immediately pending election, in essentially a one-newspaper city. Fred Cook, a distant journalist, had no equivalent stake (in rehabilitating his reputation by replying on Red Lion) in the outcome of any immediate issue of *public* concern.

In these several respects, the justification for invoking (and sustaining) the reply statute in *Miami Herald* seemed more compelling than the alleged need for overriding the editorial freedom of Red Lion. In these and several other respects (e.g., the respective remedies in each case—threatened outright license cancellation or nonrenewal versus merely a specific judicial order to print the reply), the results of the cases do seem odd.[47]

With ostensible perversity, moreover, the Supreme Court appeared to make a most peculiar use of the fact that the statutory regulation of Red Lion was *far* more pervasive that the surgically limited provision applicable to the *Miami Herald*. For at one place in its *Red Lion* opinion, the Court relied upon the relationship of the "reply" rule to all of the other FCC powers over Red Lion as a supporting reason to conclude that the reply rule itself should have but little impact upon the broadcaster's actual editorial practices. In both cases, the companies had complained that the reply rule applicable to its publication would interfere with its prerogative to assert its own strong editorial stance. In *Miami Herald*, moreover, Chief Justice Burger laid considerable stress on the pressure exerted by the reply statute to induce "self-censorship" by the newspaper as a reason to find the statute invalid. He concluded that one effect of the statute was necessarily to levy a "penalty" upon the exercise of the *Miami Herald*'s own first amendment rights.[48] Much the same argument had been made by Red Lion, where, however, it was altogether discounted. "If present licensees should suddenly prove timorous," the Court said in response to the argument (that the "reply" rule would induce broadcasters to steer clear of controversy), "the Commission is not powerless to insist that they give adequate and fair attention to public issues."[49] In brief, because the Commission could punish a broadcaster if (to avoid the reply rule) the broadcaster failed to provide "adequate" coverage of controversial issues, the reply rule could not itself be thought objectionable as an inducement for excessive caution on the broadcaster's part. This indeed may in some sense "distinguish" the *Miami Herald* case but surely not in any fashion that can ultimately be sustained. For given the overall firmness of its free press commitment in the case, it is unimaginable that the Court would have upheld the reply statute in *Miami Herald* had it been but one part of an even *larger* abridgment of freedom of the press, namely, a comprehensive statute affirmatively requiring every newspaper of general circulation to provide "fair" coverage of events. Rather, the two cases appear to proceed from fundamentally different premises.

Red Lion, *with* its government licensing system already in place, assumed that what the government permits to be broadcast it is therefore responsible for permitting, and, because it is responsible, it may surely exercise that responsibility in behalf of the public interest.[50] *Miami Herald*, unencumbered by any entangling tradition of licensing (which would plainly be unconstitutional), made no similar assumption. To the contrary, the entire emphasis of the unanimous *Miami Herald* opinion was on the protected independence of each newspaper's own policies. The point of the case lay in its conclusion respecting the *necessary* remedilessness of what others might reasonably find objectionable about a privately owned newspaper's editorial policy but which is part and parcel of its independence. The lack of right in the one (i.e., the "public" or any member of the public) to say what would go into the newspaper is precisely the meaning of the first amendment right of the other (namely, the newspaper company itself) to be the exclusive judge of that matter. It was an understanding of this very point that alone makes any sense of Jefferson's observation, lamenting "the malignity, the vulgarity, and the mendacious spirit of those who write [for newspapers]" but nonetheless concluding:

> It is however an evil for which there is no remedy, our liberty depends on the freedom of the press, and that cannot be limited without being lost.[51]

That was the whole point also of the Court's quotation from Chafee (that "liberty of the press is in peril as soon as the government tries to compel what is to go into a newspaper").[52] It is a constitutional line copied from Shakespeare's *Othello*, as it were, interpreting and defending the freedom of the press.

> I would rather be a toad,
> And breath the vapors of a dungeon,
> Than keep a place in the thing I love
> For other men's uses.[53]

The substitution of governmental commands (of what serves the public) in privately owned newspapers, for whatever reflects the publisher's *own* wishes, is thus deemed to be forbidden by the first amendment. The private publisher may be restricted by such antitrust regulations as the state (or Congress) considers appropriate. He or she may have to answer, too, in the event that what he publishes causes actionable harm that is subject to redress according to the analysis we pursued in chapter 1.[54] His practical capacity to maintain a given editorial policy may also fail for lack of advertiser revenue or because of alienated subscriptions and lost sales. But the commandeering of his publication for other people's news is altogether disallowed by the first amendment. One senses here the drawing of an essential line or at least a line the Supreme Court somehow thought to be essential. But if indeed this was the main distinction of the *Miami Herald* case, the case itself could not conceivably have come out differently had the obligation to publish such reply as any disparaged candidate cared to submit been but a small part of an even more pervasive scheme of statutory interference. The cases will not be squared on the preposterous notion that the legislative defect in *Miami Herald* was that the statute imposed too little, rather than too much, upon the publisher.

It is also clear from what we have already canvassed what else cannot provide any constitutionally significant distinctions between *Red Lion* and *Miami Herald*. It is clear, for instance, that it is *not* the de facto community influence of the particular publisher or broadcaster, the relative lack of immediate competitors of equivalent scale in the same market or medium, the felt pertinence of the subject matter to the public interest, or the relative lack of alternative means by which persons aggrieved by the publisher's (or broadcaster's) statements may attempt to register their correction or dissent. For again, in virtually all of these respects, the respective facts of the two cases are at odds with what ought to have been their respective results, if these sorts of things mattered. The winning publisher was far more dominant within its circulation area than the losing broadcaster within its broadcast area. The public interest in Pat Tornillo's possible reply was not merely to enable him to rehabilitate whatever he might deserve by way of reputation but also to prevent what might well be election ballots cast on the basis of misinformation; no equivalent public interest was at risk insofar as Fred Cook (the disparaged journalist) might not reply. Cook, moreover, could in fact have replied upon payment of a very modest, obviously affordable charge; nothing of the sort was open to Pat Tornillo. Additionally, it is not at all clear that, as a New York resident and nationally established journalist, Cook had anything much at stake in being able to "reply" to whatever small number of listeners might be tuning in to a minor local radio station months after the original, quite forgettable pretaped program in which he was mentioned. Tornillo's concern in Miami was prima facie considerably more substantial. All these things duly considered, therefore, it will not do to suggest that the imposition of public obligations on broadcasters, but not on newspaper publishers, is automatically rationalized by the greater power, control, or influence of the former as against the diversity and relatively minor influence of the latter. For tested by the facts of the two leading cases, *Red Lion* and *Miami Herald*, just the opposite was true.

Four years after the Court's unanimous opinion in *Red Lion*, moreover, many of these same points were made very forcefully in a judicial postscript written by Justice William O. Douglas, who had not participated in *Red Lion*. His views are especially interesting, as he not only served longer than any other justice but his general views respecting the proper interpretation of the first amendment are the most consistently protective of free speech of any justice in the history of the Court:

> I did not participate in [the *Red Lion* decision of the Supreme Court] and, with all respect, would not support it. . . . Both TV and radio news broadcasts frequently tip the news one direction or another and even try to turn a public figure into a character of disrepute. Yet so do the newspapers and the magazines and other segments of the press. . . . [T]he daily papers now established are unique in the sense that it would be virtually impossible for a competitor to enter the field due to the financial exigencies of this era. The result is that in practical terms the newspapers and magazines, like TV and radio, are available only to a select few. . . . But the prospect of putting Government in a position of control over publishers is to me an appalling one, even to the extent of the Fairness Doctrine. The struggle for liberty has been a struggle against Government. . . . [I]t is anathema to the First Amend-

ment to allow Government any role of censorship over newspapers, magazines, books, art, music, TV, radio, or any other aspect of the press. There is unhappiness in some circles at the impotence of Government. But if there is to be a change, let it come by constitutional amendment.[55]

Yet, despite these forceful statements by Justice Douglas, the Court has adhered to its basic *Red Lion* position (though it obviously accepts Douglas's view as to newspapers and magazines).[56] In continuing to sustain FCC superintendence of certain broadcast demands (as well as of certain broadcast restrictions), presumably at least some of the justices think that there is some constitutionally significant distinction that can be made. And, indeed, it appears that there may be such a distinction. It is not, however, that the one medium is uniformly more influential than the other, or less competitive than the other, or more expensive for new operatives to enter than the other. Rather, it is a distinction of a wholly different sort. It is that in broadcasting, unlike the rest of the publishing universe, the inability of other persons to speak at all is itself a legal disability imposed directly by the government itself.[57] It is thus in one sense the government's own obligation to redress the unfairness resulting to those locked out (by the government's own restrictive licensing policy) that rationalizes the imposition of compensatory duties upon the licensees, a circumstance that has no counterpart in the universe of newspapers and magazines.

In Atlanta, Georgia, for instance, it may be true that an underground newspaper may realistically compete only feebly with the dominant *Atlanta Constitution*, but nothing in government policy restrains it from trying. As such a paper the *Great Speckled Bird* may start out virtually as of mere handbill size and never become significant. Whatever its ultimate success or failure, however, nothing restrains it from reaching the same hands as those receiving the *Atlanta Constitution* as a matter of law. Nothing forbids it to move up, to enlist advertisers eager to appeal to whatever consumer interests in circulation of the *Great Speckled Bird* may be able to deliver. A proposed "WGSB" (i.e., "*W Great Speckled Bird*"), on the other hand, may be foreclosed from attempting to compete at all with the local radio equivalent of the *Atlanta Constitution*. Other operatives may already sit astride the only authorized AM or FM frequencies. There is no reason a priori to suppose that WGSB's version of "truth," news, entertainment, and so on could not cultivate its own radio audience, yet WGSB is forbidden by federal criminal statute even to slip the equivalent of an aural handbill into the restricted FM wave band, already largely (perhaps wholly) appropriated by others by courtesy of the federal government. The government's policy in establishing the hegemony of exclusive licensees and in criminalizing any attempt by third parties to broadcast without a license has thus precluded the first amendment from being applied to insulate incumbent radio and television licensees from the imposition of certain "public-interest" broadcast obligations. Rather, they are obliged to operate as surrogates for all others whom the government either cannot or will not also license.

The government's intervention by way of licensing AM and FM operatives (but not newspapers and magazines), on the other hand, is itself at least partly explained by a difference allegedly beyond its own power to alter and inherent in the medium. Its rule of licensing-with-strings-attached is therefore thought to be dictated strictly by the circumstances of regulatory necessity and not simply by an arbitrary desire. Were the government to begin to license newspapers or magazines in Atlanta, it could hardly defend its action as a necessary means of facilitating freedom of the press. Nothing in the ample protection of the *Atlanta Constitution*'s free press rights requires either its own licensing or the grant or denial of any license to the *Great Speckled Bird*. Indeed, even the proliferation of newspapers, magazines, or handbills by a hundred thousand different publishers in Atlanta would not require that the total number be licensed or restricted in any way, merely in order to facilitate the unencumbered circulation of each. Even with quite modern technology, however, the number of clear-signal FM channels in the Atlanta receiving area is finite. Given the (constitutionally valid) reservation of at least some channels for exigent government use (e.g., police channels), moreover, the usable spectrum of a given kind may in fact be quite modest. Thus, the finitude of the medium (i.e., the usable airwaves) imposes a physical constraint without equivalent counterpart so far as local distribution of innumerable private printed materials is concerned. Its division and allocation in order that any be able to use it intelligibly may thus be thought to compel a degree of necessary government intervention neither necessary nor appropriate to protect the intelligibility of speech in newspapers. The government's intervention, itself essential to settle clarity in radio communication, rationalizes the basic licensing arrangement. To be sure, it does not require per se that applicants be winnowed by any comparative judgment respecting their proposed program fare. Even so, it necessarily "locks out" those unable to be accommodated, even as it frees up those who are accommodated. The distinction of overcrowding, of technical scarcity, and of selecting among equally interested users, not all of whom can feasibly be accommodated, thus sets the field of *Red Lion* apart. And, indeed, in the following careful portion of its opinion, the Supreme Court noted the distinction in just this fashion:

> The lack of know-how and equipment may keep many from the air, but only a tiny fraction of those with resources and intelligence can hope to communicate by radio at the same time if intelligible communication is to be had, even if the entire radio spectrum is utilized in the present state of commercially acceptable technology.
>
> It was this fact, and the chaos which ensued from permitting anyone to use any frequency at whatever power level he wished, which made necessary the enactment of the Radio Act of 1927 and the Communications Act of 1934. . . .
>
> Where there are substantially more individuals who want to broadcast than there are frequencies to allocate, it is idle to posit an unabridgeable First Amendment right to broadcast comparable to the right of every individual to speak, write, or publish. . . .

. . . .

In view of the scarcity of broadcast frequencies, the Government's role in allocating those frequencies, and the legitimate claims of those unable without governmental assistance to gain access to those frequencies for expression of their views, we hold the regulations and ruling at issue here are both authorized by statute and constitutional.[58]

To be sure, not all of the program-content demands and limitations imposed upon licensees are necessarily well fitted to this justification, but a fair number are. For instance, the requirement of community survey is not the same thing as though the government were presuming to instruct each licensee to broadcast material the *government* itself thinks best. Rather, it is ostensibly merely to determine whether there is some degree of interest in certain kinds of program fare that others might appeal to, even on a nonprofit basis (i.e., even assuming it is of interest insufficient to attract advertiser-sponsored broadcasting), but that they are foreclosed from responding to insofar as others have absorbed the available licenses. Similarly, insofar as there are occasional local issues of sharp controversy, were there no medium constraints it does appear entirely likely that ad hoc partisans would attempt to reach local residents with their point of view by taking to the open airwaves. It scarcely seems to be an unconstitutional imposition on the exclusive licensees, given the fact that the distribution of licenses to them has soaked up the several available channels, to require that they accept a surrogate obligation to carry some portion of material reflecting those issues. As matters stand, moreover, the advocacy advantage of licensees remains much more substantial than the position of those otherwise forbidden to broadcast (because they have no licenses). The FCC does not forbid the licensee to assert extremely strong editorial positions of its own nor does the obligation of the licensee to provide some chance for the presentation of views differing from its own at all approximate a duty of "equal" time, or even fair time, for views of "all political parties no matter how small and insignificant."[59] In brief, the aggregate of these few surrogate obligations is relatively modest; indeed, the arrangement is probably at least as objectionable on the basis that it is too centrist (i.e., too reinforcing of the cultural and ideological status quo) than that it is too radical.[60] Indeed, from this perspective quite a strong case can be made that licensees might appropriately be made subject to common-carrier obligations.[61]

Usefully, too, the Court noted in *Red Lion* that "the Government could surely have decreed that *each* frequency should be shared among all or some of those who wish to use it, each being assigned a portion of the broadcast day or the broadcast week."[62] This alternative allocation technique, itself absolutely ideologically neutral and free of any program-content restrictions, presumably also would have been constitutionally unobjectionable. Like other merely parliamentary rules[63] (i.e., rules indifferently dividing an hour for argument before a city council among all those wishing to be heard or rules regulating public park use among different groups seeking exclusive use of portions of the park), it eschews profit maximization (i.e., it declines to sell off "speech-rights" to public property to the highest bidders)[64] and yet stays clear of passing any official judgment upon whose speech is "better" or "more important." Transposed to the airwaves, there is little reason to think that this hypothetical allocation technique would have raised any substantial constitutional question. The amount of time assigned to each licensee issued a time-segment license on the same wavelength shared by others would presumably be 1440 minutes (twenty-four hours) divided by the total number of applicants. Or, more exactly still, it might be a time-segment not necessarily equal in duration to each other time-segment (since certain broadcast times even on the same frequency may be plainly more valuable than others) but a time-segment that, by being longer (or shorter) than each other time-segment, would be equally as valuable as any other, or at least as nearly so as practical possibility allows.

This allocative alternative is interesting and presumably it too would be constitutionally unobjectionable, even as the Supreme Court suggested. But it may nonetheless have been highly unattractive because of what Congress could anticipate. Its use would have tended to trivialize the development of radio. The discontinuity of program service over each wavelength makes the scheme dubious. The responsibility would have remained with each time-segment licensee to provide for its own transmission facility, moreover, as nothing in the arrangement would entitle one time-segment licensee to commandeer the broadcast facility of any other licensee (any more than Pat Tornillo could commandeer the printing presses of the *Miami Herald*). Understandably chary of this alternative, Congress did not adopt it. Nor did it prefer to enact a private property system into the airwaves pursuant to which the "lock-out effect" is still produced but produced by wealth disparities among potential bidders (if a bid-auction system were used), or produced more randomly in the first instance, if a simple lottery were used. Instead, the arrangement was to award fixed, free, and exclusive licenses to private companies for minimum three-year renewable terms, contingent upon a willingness to accept certain third-party surrogate obligations.

In essence, the theory of *Red Lion* acts upon an analogy of a sort different from any we have thus far examined. The various airwave frequencies are "like" the several, laid-out, publicly owned streets of a community. The city council (i.e., Congress) clearly is without constitutional obligation to put them up for public sale. It is also under no constitutional obligation to invite competitive sealed bids such that the highest bidder in respect to each street will pay the city the market price for the fee-simple value of that particular street, purchasing by means of that bid a fee-simple owner's exclusionary command over its subsequent uses as a passageway of greater or lesser value. Nor need the city council retain ownership (in the usual full sense) and permit only city-owned vehicles or city employees alone to pass along the streets. (The analogy here is to the manner in which a number of countries restrict the airwaves altogether from any private use and confine broadcasting to government agencies or government companies alone.)

Instead, the city may strongly prefer the diverse eclecticism implicit in private development, it may appreciate the value of these streets (some highly valuable, some scarcely valuable at all), and it may also cope with both anticipated problems of congestion as well as community needs by quite an ingenious idea. Each street will be allocated to a single licensee who may generally do quite as it pleases with the "excess capacity" of the street as a delivery route or passageway. That "excess capacity" is what is left over, however, *after* the exclusive licensee discharges certain surrogate obligations it is made to observe in light of the manner in which the exclusivity of its license otherwise removes the street from public use. If any given applicant anticipates that these surrogate obligations may become so onerous that its own expense in discharging them will render the balance of the exclusive license unprofitable, that is solely for it to decide—with the assurance that no one else would be obliged to do less than it is obliged to do if it accepts.[65] If, given the marginal value of a particular street, no one may find it sufficiently attractive to apply for its exclusive use under the proposed conditions, then that may of course mean that for the time being the street will remain unlicensed. To complete the analogy, moreover, the arrangement is not one imposed upon an existing city with well-established thoroughfares, abutting buildings, and pre-existing traffic patterns of hundreds of thousands of persons and businesses who have already established immense dependencies that might be upset under the proposed arrangement.[66] Rather, this is the New Town of the airwaves, circa 1927, a proposal to deal with the discovery of new passageways in a manner attractive to private property incentives for development and yet not indifferent to other considerations.

The proper analogy in the *Miami Herald* case would be quite closely drawn in this fashion, as was already suggested back in chapter 2. If the owners of the *Miami Herald* had been awarded exclusive passage rights along even a single street in Miami, then it would have been quite a different question in that case, too, as to whether (as a condition of that exclusive license) the *Herald* could have been made to deliver other people's messages along with its own, at least on that street. As it was, in using the streets of Miami, the *Miami Herald* derived no advantage from the streets not equally available to Pat Tornillo, hawkers of handbills, or delivery agents of the *New York Times*. Nothing in the street allocation by the city of Miami having operated to the "delivery disadvantage" of any of these persons (whatever their own private "speech resources" vis-à-vis the *Miami Herald*), nothing would warrant the city of Miami imposing any special obligation on the *Miami Herald* to conduct itself in their behalf.

The *Red Lion* decision, moreover, should not be misconstrued as resting on a premise different or wider than the one we have examined. There is, for instance, nothing in the case to revive the discredited view that whatever the government controls as "property owner," it is therefore free to regulate literally as though it were itself a private fee-simple owner not subject to the first amendment at all.[67] The case rejects that view; it explicitly concedes that the reservation of the airwaves from the vicissitudes of private property claims by no means exempts the government's trusteeship licensing monopoly from the first amendment.[68]

Moreover, to the extent that any particular FCC restriction on broadcasters cannot be fitted to the specific rationale we have now examined at considerable length, it remains fully arguable that the restriction cannot be sustained unless it otherwise satisfies the usual first amendment burden imposed upon the government. One such restriction, for instance, is the restriction forbidding "profane," "indecent," or "vulgar" broadcasting.[69] There is *nothing* in the uniformity of this blanket ban that can be rationalized as an accommodation to parties lacking licenses of their own. Rather, it simply forbids such speech across the board, whether there are ample, currently unused channels for what others care to present, whether the "vulgar" broadcast is one an unlicensed party might as well have presented, or whether a candid community survey would disclose a considerable audience attraction to such material provided by an established licensee. It is instructive, correspondingly, that the particular Supreme Court decision sustaining the statute as applied made *no* effort at all to "explain" the outcome in terms of technical scarcity of frequencies, redress to unlicensed third parties, or any of the *Red Lion* rationale.[70] Rather, the decision rested narrowly and differently on the wholly conventional analysis we examined back in chapter 1. The "theory" was that the time (midafternoon), the place (homes and automobiles with very young children momentarily captured by the unexpected radio intrusion of George Carlin's "Filthy Words" record), and the manner (i.e., the repetitious use of crude sexual terms) generated a sufficiently imminent offense to the sensibilities of this partly involuntary audience that the rule as narrowly confined to the precise facts was not invalid as applied. The case, of course, may well be wrong (i.e., it may resolve the validity of the regulation as applied quite inconsistently with an appropriate regard for the first amendment or quite inconsistently with other so-called time, place, and manner cases).[71] But that is not the more important point just now. Rather, the more important point is that the regulation could gain no special insulation from the usual burden that *any* such restriction imposed by government should have to bear when appropriately challenged under the first amendment. In this respect there is no obvious reason why the prohibition of "vulgar," "profane," or "indecent" language should be sustained in an act of Congress (or FCC rule) as applied to a midafternoon FM radio broadcast but not in a state statute applicable to midafternoon, home-delivered newspapers that youngsters may equally pick up and scan without parental superintendence.[72]

Similarly, a thoroughly excellent case can be made that, where there are *not* in fact "substantially more individuals who want to broadcast than there are [in fact] frequencies" unused and available for the asking, their point of view, their program fare, or their interests in making some personal reply cannot be piggybacked upon the shoulders of an unwilling licensee.[73] Their frustration or disappointment may be altogether genuine, but it is difficult to see how it is significantly distinguishable from that of other persons who find themselves unrepresented or misrepresented in the *Miami Herald*, *Time* magazine, or the *National Inquirer*, in which the decision in the *Miami Herald* case nonetheless forbids the government to command that their own presentation be featured.

Each of these privately financed journals may obviously command a readership that the frustrated party cannot hope to reach by putting together a mere handbill or fledgling tabloid (a "Tiny Speckled Bird"), but the mere fact of their own commercial success does not permit their editorial dilution by government command. Where there are substantial numbers of unused frequencies each as readily and as clearly receivable on the same receiving sets as the frequencies existing publishers (i.e., broadcasters) use, the case for imposing surrogate responsibilities is far too ephemeral to sustain any distinction from the *Miami Herald* decision.

Surely, moreover, one should be highly skeptical of any untested assertion that the particular frequency one wants to use to piggyback own's own message through the transmission facility of its regular user is in some sense allegedly "subsidized" by the government under these circumstances. Here the notion of subsidy is quite elusive. The one fact we know, under the stipulated circumstance, is that there is no barrier of entry barring one from access to an alternative frequency that broadcasts with equal clarity into the same radio or television sets.[74] That such unused channels are not now commercially as valuable as that which the broadcaster (who says something other than what we wish to say) is using may merely reflect the fact that, in respect to the unused channels, no one has yet undertaken the time, the investment, and the effort to attract any listeners or viewers of his own. Tuning in to the call letters of an established station is in this sense not different than responding at a newsstand to one's own expectations acquired by habit. Our sheer familiarity with *Time* or *Newsweek* may mean that we merely scan the newsstand, spot the familiar identifying cover, and pick it up to read while leaving all the rest. We may scarcely even notice what else is there, including a new addition that was not there before. Our inattentiveness to these other offerings, however, provides no constitutional leverage for writers or others to call upon the government to have their messages inserted in *Time* against its will. There is nothing here to provide any genuine distinction from the *Miami Herald* decision itself. Where the newsrack space is ample, moreover, the indifferent fact that the rack happens also to be a "public" rack can surely make no difference.[75] It adds nothing to the nonexistence of government power to direct the content of *Time* magazine, either to restrict what *Time* may print or to demand ("in the public interest") what else it must also print. So, too, in the stipulated case of broadcasting that we have been supposing. At that point, the position taken by Justice Douglas seems entirely sound: "The Commission [i.e., the FCC] has an important role to play in curbing monopolistic practices, in keeping channels free from interference, in opening up new channels as technology develops. But it has no power of censorship."[76]

Despite the foregoing analysis, it has been strongly suggested elsewhere[77] that it is nonetheless constitutionally objectionable even now for the FCC to maintain *any* program-content policies limiting the complete editorial autonomy of private broadcasters. The objection holds that, even supposing spectrum constraints may still restrict some broadcast opportunities in a manner without counterpart for printed materials, the FCC position is essentially question begging.[78] Granted that the number of usable frequencies of a given sort within any particular receiving area may be limited. Is it nonetheless not obvious that any alleged broadcasting advantage resulting from that (unimpressive) fact can be fully captured in the licensing procedures of the commission such that no licensee is, in fact, any better off in this respect than was the *Miami Herald*? In brief, isn't it possible to convert airwave-frequency scarcity essentially to an ordinary problem of mere economic scarcity, pursuant to which (as illustrated by *Miami Herald*) the fact of economic scarcity per se is not a sufficient justification for requiring a private party to use his speech-property (whether a newspaper or a broadcast station) as an unwilling carrier of other people's messages?

The *Miami Herald* case reflects economic scarcity, that is, newsprint and high-speed printing presses are not free goods. But the whole point of the case was that the mere inability of others to match the *Miami Herald* with equivalent private publishing resources of their own will not permit the commandeering of the *Herald* in their behalf. To be sure, when the private property on which third-party speech easements may be established by law is not "first amendment property" as a newspaper plainly is (and as a radio transmitter equally is), the property owner's own freedom of "speech" or "press" has not been regarded as sufficiently implicated to enable him to resist the easement on that account. Thus, the Supreme Court has rejected the claim that a business corporation operating an immense, impersonal shopping plaza may successfully resist on first amendment grounds the application of a state law permitting the nondisruptive distribution of political handbills to willing customers in its most public areas.[79] The likening of these impersonal business premises to the owner's personal vocal cords, his pen, his stationery, or his newspaper has been unavailing. Indeed, a vast enough and impersonal enough expanse of private property (namely, an entire company-owned town) has been subject to speech easements of Jehovah's Witnesses whom the corporation wished to keep out, even in the absense of a pertinent state statute. The practical verisimilitude of the company-owned town to a conventional (state government) municipality has been thought sufficient by the Supreme Court to create constitutionally generated, third-party speech easements in its premises.[80]

But at least in those instances where the private property is speech-specific property, as in the *Miami Herald* case, the matter appears to have been constitutionally settled that one's editorial command cannot be diluted through some forced sharing with third parties, even if the "police power" rationale for doing so were (merely) to redress their less-than-equal economic means of competing in the ideological marketplace. As an original proposition, this proposition should apply as readily to a personal broadcasting property as to any other speech-specific property. And, should it be thought that an extremely elaborate broadcast station owned corporately might be fairly distinguishable for this purpose from, say, one's own hand-held walkie-talkie, again the matter is apparently resolved implicitly to the contrary by the *Miami Herald* case itself.

The suggestion we are now examining assumes these observations. Its proposal is to use the advantage of these several observations by converting the "technical" scarcity of (certain kinds of) broadcast frequencies into a conventional economic scarcity problem, recovering all possible profit that may otherwise redound to the advantage of any licensee from the fact of exclusive use of any given frequency in any given location, in exactly the same way that public authority so routinely and traditionally has dealt with land.[81] In brief, charge full market price for the license, exactly as full market price will at once recover the site-and-size advantage from a fixed ten-acre lot in downtown Manhattan just as well as it would recover whatever (lesser) site-and-size advantage one may get from a fixed ten-acre lot in the middle of the Mojave desert. The advantage in either case is the private advantage of fee-simple control, including, of course, the power to exclude such third-party uses as the buyer conceives to interfere with his own best interests. And, quite obviously, exactly as in the case of land, whatever its comparative site-and-size advantage, the locational advantage (including signal strength and width) of any broadcast frequency will be reflected in the amount that interested parties will be willing to bid.

The basic point is that a bid-auction method of allocating broadcast frequencies or licenses would (allegedly) have two salutary, first amendment benefits. First, it would wholly eliminate any need or justification for winnowing any list of license applicants by examining their several proposed program profiles, that is, it would withdraw the government from its (alleged) role as Big Brother, in which the FCC presumes currently to determine what kinds of programs are, or are not, in "the public interest." Second, in transforming the physical scarcity of usable frequencies in any given receiving area into the most conventional means by which economic scarcity is usually dealt with (i.e., the market pricing), it will also mean that the specific free speech uses of each frequency will be determined by their highest natural use in the marketplace rather than by government-determined preferences. In brief, the scheme copes with any problems of scarcity, it removes the government from the program-content business, and it insures that no broadcaster is subsidized by government.[82] It is not only Pareto superior to the current regime, it is also first amendment superior. It is not different from the manner in which Brentano's bookstore would come to be the successful bidder on a city-owned lot in Manhattan. Brentanos would be affected by the original competition of other bidders to thereafter offer those books and magazines most sought by the public as a necessary means of recovering the higher sum it paid in order to be the successful bidder. Having been made to pay a full, competitive price, the program fare of Brentanos will be disciplined indirectly by the market of those to whom it must appeal to make recovery of its cost effective. Thus, while it will legally possess complete "editorial control" in respect to what books and magazines it chooses to carry, free of government direction, we can also be assured that, in considerable measure, it will also necessarily be responding to the free speech interests of others. For if, indeed, it fails to do so, it will fail in business and have to make way for someone else.

The idea is quite seemingly attractive and, indeed, in some modest measure may be worth congressional consideration.[83] The current chairman of the FCC itself, moreover, has urged that it be enacted.[84] It is really not clear why *all* of the airwaves should be treated as public property, and in many respects the arrangement is more feudalistic than modern. The single model that characterizes the whole is the model of de facto government ownership, with assignments of particular parcels subject to licensing-with-strings-attached rather than \a more eclectic mix of public, quasi-public, and private complementarities. The licensing feature is more than vaguely reminiscent of pre-Milton England, and it does sit uncomfortably with the tradition of the first amendment in a constitution that derives more from Locke, Milton, and Adam Smith than from either the medievalists or, for that matter, Karl Marx. In one sense, the United States clings to the model of feudal tenure in airwave holdings according to which there is no alienability without the principal lord's (i.e., the government's) consent and no escape from the ritual rendering of modern socage, that is, "public-interest" duties. The basic essence of the Radio Act of 1927, of which the current Federal Communications Act is but an expanded version, was captured in the remark of a sponsoring congressman. "If enacted into law," he suggested, "the broadcasting privilege will not be a right of selfishness. It will rest upon an assurance of public interest to be served."[85] It is true that the arrangement battens down the hatch of selfishness to some extent, but to the same extent it thus also interferes with "selfness," which is more synonymous with personality and which need not be derided as merely or as necessarily selfishness per se. The rubric of "the public interest" has usually been the basis for suppressing individuality in societies that are averse to risk and possessed by a good degree of self-canceling jealousies. It, and licensing-with-strings-attached, is not the more robust and more diverse society of which Milton wrote in the *Areopagitica*, which Mill celebrated in his essay *On Liberty*, or which the overall tradition of our first amendment seems otherwise to embrace. The presence of a government licensing agency whose membership rotates among political appointees, with powers of grant, renewal, nonrenewal, suspension, and cancellation of everything that moves through the electromagnetic spectrum, is very disturbing in its first amendment implications.

Even so, it would almost surely be a serious mistake literally to "privatize" the airways completely. In a society where the effective speech-rights of all are already by no means equal (to the extent that they obviously depend significantly upon one's "speech-property" holdings), it is not obvious that *the* freedom of speech would be appropriately enhanced by exclusive reliance upon a private property system that would literally drive out all those unable to compete effectively with dollars. Noticing how the exclusivity of that arrangement necessarily makes the exercise of free speech even more dependent than it already is upon the circumstance of private wealth must surely give us pause.

The problem of the deregulation-by-privatization proposal is that it conflates "demand" for certain kinds of speech (as well as for certain kinds of rights to speak) with something that sounds as though it is the same thing but which is not at all the same thing. That is, it conflates "demand" with "*effective* demand," it sorts out the interests both of "sellers" of speech and of "buyers" of speech not merely by willingness to pay dollars but by ability to pay dollars. But nothing we know of the first amendment suggests that it commands the allocation of effective speech-rights in the United States solely according to this economic class-conscious single model. Indeed, in earlier parts of this chapter, we have already dealt with this idée fixe.[86] We did so, for instance, in examining the hypothetical suggestion that the public streets be auctioned off to reduce congestion by clearing away those who would be unable to pay their "proper cost" of being there, once such proper costs were internalized in the efficient rationing system of a competitive array of profit-maximizing private owners.

If the streets were auctioned off in competitive bidding, each successful bidder would thereafter have to serve the community better than anyone else by offering the best mix of transport services to meet "effective" demand, namely, the transport needs of those able, as well as willing, to pay the real economic cost of carrying them. So, too, for those interested in stopping to talk to others, to give a speech, or to pass around handbills. The impersonal rigor of the system simply eliminates those unable to pay the real costs (e.g., the opportunity costs) of their proposed use of this scarce resource. But nothing we know about the first amendment commands the use of so insensitive a device, even were there no practical objections that otherwise stood in its way. Nor does the first amendment command that public parks be put up for auction, following which the successful bidder may then (like the *Miami Herald*?) determine solely to its own satisfaction, subject only to market discipline, who may assemble there.

In brief, the Constitution does not ordain that the less affluent must scratch about to bid either to speak (through their own "speech-property") or to hear only what their personal budget constraint will enable them to buy in a nation consisting exclusively of privately owned, fee-simple "speech estates." To the contrary, it authorizes them to march off to a different market in which each "bid" (i.e., vote) has the same outcome efficacy as every other, despite the poverty of the voter. By casting that vote for certain persons, the less affluent may readily secure (indeed, they do secure) the partial socialization of many speech resources, including parks, streets, civic auditoriums, and to some extent the airwaves too. Essentially, the airwaves were partly socialized in 1927, though they are also now very substantially driven by the usual discipline of the market, which does indeed furnish incentives to broadcasters to meet "effective" demand. While the proliferation of new technology may well sufficiently collapse the original scarcity preoccupations such that it may make little sense to regulate broadcasters as they are now regulated in many respects (and *Red Lion*, in light of *Miami Herald* plus these developments, may no longer itself be sound),[87] the problem of reserving *some* airwave use from the wealth-disparity consequence of an unmitigated private property system will remain with us indefinitely.

The Möbius strip of the first amendment thus imagines a great deal of public property held by government, yet subject to the first amendment, which will forbid its ideological corruption or purely ideological rationing by that government.[88] It also imagines a very great deal of private property as well, nonetheless subject to ideologically neutral free speech easements not seriously inconsistent with its most ordinary commercial uses.[89] And, as in the *Miami Herald* case, it does indeed provide shelter for a rugged and diverse array of private property places that the government may not commandeer or flatten out, places in which no owner need keep some corner for any idea he detests, whatever others may think. Still, it is quite true that even on the bicentennial of our Constitution we have not yet reconciled the interpretive difficulties of the first amendment in respect to scarcity, property, and government policy.[90] The antecedents are mostly those of John Locke, but the presence of the reproachful Rousseau and of an angry Marx can be felt as well.

Notes

Introduction

1. 5 U.S. (1 Cranch) 137 (1803).

2. Medicus, *Federal Republic of Germany*, in 1 INTERNATIONAL ENCYCLOPEDIA OF COMPARATIVE LAW F1, F3; Irani, *India*, *id.* at 110; Noda, *Japan*, *id.* at J8.

3. P. NORTON, THE CONSTITUTION IN FLUX 244–61 (1982); Lloyd, *Do We Need a Bill of Rights?*, 39 MOD. L. REV. 121, 124 (1976). *See generally* Griffith, *The Political Constitution*, 42 MOD. L. REV. 1 (1979).

4. The current law in England is still as it was in 1700 in this respect: "An Act of Parliament can do no wrong, though it may do several things that look pretty odd." City of London v. Wood, 88 Eng. Rep. 1592, 1602 (1700). "In Britain, the phrase 'judicial review' is merely a flattering way of describing statutory interpretation—the judicial approach to which it is confined by strict rules, though there are signs in recent cases of a more liberal approach developing." Scarman, *Fundamental Rights, The British Scene*, 78 COLUM. L. REV. 1575, 1585 (1978). *See also* Karst, *Judicial Review and the Channel Tunnel*, 52 S. CAL. L. REV. 447 (1980).
For a review of legal developments in New Zealand respecting freedom of the press, see ESSAYS ON HUMAN RIGHTS (K. Keith 9th ed. 1968); Burrows, *The Law and the Press*, 4 OTAGO L. REV. 119 (1978). For a review in Australia, see E. CAMPBELL & H. WHITMORE, FREEDOM IN AUSTRALIA (1973). *See also* Hunt & McCarthy, *Why No First Amendment? The Role of the Press in Relationship to Justice*, in AM./AUSTL./N.Z. L. 133, 147 (1980).
The background to the newly entrenched Canadian Bill of Rights is presented in Tarnopolsky, *The Historical and Constitutional Context of the Proposed Canadian Charter of Rights and Freedom*, 44, LAW & CONTEMP. PROBS. 169 (1981), and an assessment of the most recent changes is presented in *Reshaping Confederation: The 1982 Reform of the Canadian Constitution*, 45 LAW & CONTEMP. PROBS. 1 (1983).

5. See P. NORTON, *supra* note 3, at 148–51, and the several writings by John Griffiths on this subject.

6. The reference is, of course, to Lochner v. New York, 198 U.S. 45 (1905). The large number of related decisions are summarized in B. WRIGHT, THE GROWTH OF AMERICAN CONSTITUTIONAL LAW 173–75 (1942) and in *The Constitution of the United States* (G.P.O. 1972). For a recent and elaborate defense of that era, see B. SIEGAN, ECONOMIC LIBERTIES AND THE CONSTITUTION (1980).

7. THE FEDERALIST NO. 84, at 514–15 (A. Hamilton) (C. Rossiter ed. 1961). For a modern view that Hamilton may have been correct in his skepticism, see Kurland, *The Irrelevance of the Constitution: The First Amendment's Freedom of Speech and Freedom of the Press Clauses*, 29 DRAKE L. REV. 1, 5–6 (1979–80). And for more general statements respecting the ultimate undependability of judicial review to secure the Bill of Rights, see, e.g., R. JACKSON, THE SUPREME COURT IN THE AMERICAN SYSTEM OF GOVERMNMENT 80 (1955) ("I know of no modern instance in which any judiciary has saved a whole people from the great currents of intolerance, passion, usurpation, and tyranny which have threatened liberty and free institutions."); THE SPIRIT OF LIBERTY, PAPERS AND ADDRESSES OF LEARNED HAND 1289 (I. Dillard ed. 1953) ("I often wonder whether we do not rest our hopes too much upon constitutions, upon laws and upon courts.").

8. Letter from Thomas Jefferson to James Madison, from Paris (Mar. 15 1789), *reprinted in part in* THE LIFE AND SELECTED WRITINGS OF THOMAS JEFFERSON 462, 462–63 (A. Koch & W. Peden eds. 1944).

9. Letter from James Madison to Thomas Jefferson (Oct. 17, 1788), *reprinted in* 5 THE WRITINGS OF JAMES MADISON 269, 271 (G. Hunt ed. 1904).

10. Address by James Madison before the United States House of Representatives (June 8, 1789), reprinted in *id.* at 370, 380.

11. *Id.* at 370, 385.

12. *Id.* at 370, 389.

13. *E.g.*, THE FEDERALIST NO. 78, at 485–86 (A. Hamilton) (H. Lodge ed. 1888):

The interpretation of the laws is the proper and peculiar province of the courts. A constitution is in fact, and must be regarded by the judges, as a fundamental law. It therefore belongs to them to ascertain its meaning, as well as the meaning of any particular act proceeding from the legislative body. If there should happen to be an irreconcilable variance between the two, that which has the superior obligation and validity ought, of course, to be preferred; or, in other words, the Constitution ought to be preferred to the statute, the intention of the people to the intention of their agents.

See also materials and references in R. BERGER, CONGRESS VERSUS THE SUPREME COURT (1969) (while not useful as a source respecting the scope of the clause it purported to deal with, i.e., the clause in article III respecting "such exceptions" as Congress may make to the Supreme Court's appellate jurisdiction, this is nonetheless a very full collection of materials respecting the widespread understanding that substantive constitutional review, incidental to adjudication, would be a feature of the judicial power); A. BICKEL, THE LEAST DANGEROUS BRANCH 14 (1962); Currie, *The Constitution in the Supreme Court: The Powers of the Federal Courts, 1801–1835*, 49 U. CHI. L. REV. 646, 655–57 (1982); Van Alstyne, *A Critical Guide to Marbury v. Madison*, 1969 DUKE L.J. 1, 38–45.

14. Proposed by Congress as the twenty-seventh amendment on March 22, 1972; and the extended ratification deadline having expired on June 30, 1982 (three states [of the requisite 38] short of ratification), the amendment would have provided:

Section 1. Equality of rights under the law shall not be denied or abridged by the United States or by any State on account of sex.
Section 2. The Congress shall have power to enforce by appropriate legislation, the provision of this article.
Section 3. This amendment shall take effect two years after the date of ratification.

15. In Marbury v. Madison, 5 U.S. (1 Cranch) 137 (1803), it was obvious that several plausible interpretations of those clauses in article III describing congressional power in the allocation and regulation of the judicial power were available to sustain the act of Congress. *see* Van Alstyne, *supra* note 13, at 30–32.

16. *See* McCulloch v. Maryland, 17 U.S. (4 Wheat.) 316 (1819).

17. *See, e.g.*, Fletcher v. Peck, 10 U.S. (6 Cranch) 87 (1810) ("contract" impairment clause of Article I, § 10 interpreted to include legislative grant of land that a state was held to have no power to "impair" by rescinding on grounds of fraud and corruption); Dartmouth College v. Woodward, 17 U.S. (4 Wheat.) 518 (1819) (similarly activist interpretation of contracts clause to invalidate state acts). For additional examples and an excellent review, see generally Currie, *supra* note 13.

The seed of the rationale for more aggressive review of state vis-à-vis federal laws generally (both procedural and substantive activism), keyed to a special theory of rationing the occasions and substance of constitutional review according to the representative adequacy of the legislative source, appears in McCulloch v. Maryland, 17 U.S. (4 Wheat.) 316 (1819). It was given a systematic push in an unduly famous essay by James B. Thayer, *The Origin and Scope of the American Doctrine of Constitutional Law*, 7 HARV. L. REV. 129 (1893), once identified by Justice Felix Frankfurter as perhaps the single most important piece of writing on American constitutional law. *See also* A. BICKEL, *supra* note 13, at 35–40. The essential thesis similarly figures centrally in Wechsler, *The*

Political Safeguards of Federalism: The Role of the States in the Composition and Selection of the National Government, 54 COLUM. L. REV. 543 (1954). An extreme version (literally removing judicial review of any exertion of national power brought into question on the ground that it exceeded any enumerated or implied power) is proposed in J. CHOPER, JUDICIAL REVIEW AND THE NATIONAL POLITICAL PROCESS 175 (1980) ("The federal judiciary should not decide constitutional questions respecting the ultimate power of the national government vis-à-vis the states.").

18. Dred Scott and McCulloch are at 60 U.S. 393 (1857) and 17 U.S. 316 (4 Wheat.) (1819), respectively.

19. *E.g.*, Mr. Justice Black's textual literalism was defended instrumentally as most conducive to strong protection of civil rights. *See* Black, *Mr. Justice Black, The Supreme Court and the Bill of Rights*, Harper's, Feb. 1961, at 63; Reich, *Mr. Justice Black and the Living Constitution*, 76 HARV. L. REV. 673 (1963). His jurisprudence, however, often resulted in quite the opposite application. *See, e.g.*, Street v. New York, 394 U.S. 576 (1969); Tinker v. Des Moines School Dist., 393 U.S. 503 (1969); Adderly v. Florida, 385 U.S. 39 (1966); Griswold v. Connecticut, 381 U.S. 479 (1965).

20. *See* Currie, *supra* note 13, at 647:

This was a time of vigorous affirmation of national authority and of vigorous enforcement of constitutional limitations on the states; a time of extensive opinions in the grand style we have come to associate with Marshall; a time, moreover, of remarkable stability and official unanimity. . . . The rarity of recorded dissent during this period was so great as to be almost incredible by modern standards.

21. *See supra* note 17.

22. *See, e.g.*, J. CHOPER, *supra* note 17, at 263 ("The federal judiciary should not decide constitutional questions concerning the respective powers of Congress and the President vis-à-vis one another.").

23. To a considerable extent, the proposition is embedded in Thayer's rule, which obliges the Court to sustain unconstitutional acts of Congress not merely when challenged on grounds of insufficient enacting authority but also when challenged on grounds that they interfere with affirmatively protected rights. Thayer, *supra* note 17, at 151. Relatedly, insofar as John Ely endorses a tougher substantive standard of equal protection review contingent upon the (judicially perceived) extent to which certain group interests are not given equal dignity or respect within a legislative process, necessarily the idea is equivalently that no similar conformity to the equal protection clause should be required insofar as judges think other group interests are given sufficient respect in legislative processes. J. ELY, DEMOCRACY AND DISTRUST: A THEORY OF JUDICIAL REVIEW 146–65 (1980). The general reference for this sort of thinking is footnote four in Justice Stone's opinion in United States v. Carolene Prods. Co., 304 U.S. 144, 152–53 n.4 (1938). On its face, Stone's footnote was merely a justification for *procedural* judicial activism. It suggested that judges ought to be selectively willing to take such cases, and willing to take a harder look at them ("more searching judicial inquiry") than other kinds of cases. It did not decide that such cases, upon examination, should necessarily also result in holding the law invalid unless they satisfied a more exacting *substantive* standard of constitutional demand. The footnote was, however, developed into an independent, sociological rationale for differentiated substantive standards as well. Most of its favored categories are hopelessly far removed from the separate historical basis that would reserve a unique standard for race-based laws alone. The conventional standard of equal protection review is one that virtually no law can fail. *See* Gunther, *In Search of Evolving Doctrine on a Changing Court: A Model for a New Equal Protection*, 86 HARV. L. REV. 1 (1972). For a few of the many lucubrations on *Carolene Products'* footnote, see J. ELY, *supra*, at 75–77; Lusky, *Footnote Redux: A Carolene Products Reminiscence*, 82 COLUM. L. REV. 1087 (1982).

24. *See, e.g.*, J. ELY, *supra* note 23, at 222. *See also* Ely, *The Constitutionality of Reverse Racial Discrimination*, 41 U. CHI. L. REV. 723 (1974); Ely, *Democracy and Judicial Review*, 17 STAN. LAW. REV. 3 (1982).

25. Critically reviewed in Grano, *Judicial Review and a Written Constitution in a Democratic Society*, 28 WAYNE L. REV. 1 (1981), and in Monaghan, *Our Perfect Constitution*, 56 N.Y.U. L. REV. 359 (1981). For leading examples, see A. MILLER, TOWARD INCREASED JUDICIAL ACTIVISM (1982); P. BOBBITT, CONSTITUTIONAL FATE 94–97, 137, 144–45, 159–67 (1982) (arguing for the appropriateness of "ethical" argument that, to the extent that it is distinguishable from a liberal interpretation of particular clauses [e.g., the ninth amendment, the privileges and immunities clause of the fourteenth amendment], proceeds essentially by posing broad normative statements, eliciting audience concurrence that surely legislation inconsistent with such statements simply must be unconstitutional, and concluding, therefore, according to the ethos of the American polity, such legislation is indeed unconstitutional); Parker, *The Past of Constitutional Theory And Its Future*, 42 OHIO ST. L.J. 223 (1981) (condemning the political pluralism characteristic of process-oriented theory and advocating exposure of underlying asssumptions made by the theory to strive toward more democratic approach); Perry, *Noninterpretive Review in Human Rights Cases: A Functional Justification*, 56 N.Y.U. L. REV. 278 (1981) (reprinted in M. PERRY, THE CONSTITUTION, THE COURTS, AND HUMAN RIGHTS 91, 97–102, 123 (1982)) (arguing for a "religious" function for the Supreme Court, i.e., an obligation to discover contemporary vital values as the ligaments that bind an enlightened society, to enact them as appropriately protected rights); Richards, *Human Rights as the Unwritten Constitution: The Problem of Change and Stability in Constitutional Intepretation*, 4 U. DAYTON L. REV. 295 (1979) (claiming a shift to human rights in constitutional development); Saphire, *Professor Richards' Unwritten Constitution of Human Rights: Some Preliminary Observations*, 4 U. DAYTON L. REV. 305 (1979) (critizing validity of Richards' theory as failing to develop the role of history in human rights pardigm); Saphire, *The Search for Legitimacy in Constitutional Theory: What Price Purity?*, 42 OHIO ST. L.J. 335 (1981) (exploring theories focusing on the process of decision making and arguing that such theories sacrifice constitutional moral function in serving society by subordinating concern for substantively "just" decisions). For related ideas, see C. BLACK, DECISION ACCORDING TO LAW (1981); Fiss, *The Supreme Court, 1978 Term— Foreword: The Forms of Justice*, 93 HARV. L. REV. 1 (1979); Grey, *Do We Have an Unwritten Constitution?*, 27 STAN. L. REV. 703 (1975); Grey, *Origins of the Unwritten Constitution: Fundamental Law In American Revolutionary Thought*, 30 STAN. L. REV. 843 (1978); Murphy, *An Ordering of Constitutional Values*, 53 S. CAL. L. REV. 703 (1980).

26. *See supra* sources cited note 25. *See also* Michelman, *In Pursuit of Constitutional Welfare Rights: One View of Rawls' Theory of Justice*, 121 U. PA. L. REV. 962 (1973); Michelman, *The Supreme Court, 1968 Term—Foreword: On Protecting the Poor Through the Fourteenth Amendment*, 83 HARV. L. REV. 7 (1969); Michelman, *Welfare Rights in a Constitutional Democracy*, 1979 WASH. U.L.Q. 659; Stone, *Equal Protection and the Search for Justice*, 22 ARIZ. L. REV. 1 (1980); Tribe, *Unraveling National League of Cities: The New Federalism and Affirmative Rights to Essential Government Services*, 90 HARV. L. REV. 1065 (1977).

27. The term *noninterpretivism* may not go back beyond its appearance in Grey I, *supra* note 25, at 703. The reason may be obvious. It signals a frank resolve to detach judicial review from the Constitution itself by stipulating it purports not to be interpreting the Constitution. It may say too much about the current condition of constitutional scholarship that "noninterpretivism" is willingly adopted as a mode of describing one's own work in constitutional law. If there were not writers who evidently welcome its fit, *e.g.*, Perry, *supra* note 25, at 278, one might have supposed that its use was limited and purely pejorative, a mere epithet cast cruelly against a judge or another writer—a harsh opinion of their work (*e.g.*, that judge so-and-so rendered another "noninterpretation" of the first amendment in his latest opinion). Compare the following comment by James White on these tendencies:

> To say, as some do, that "we" ought to regard ourselves as "free" from the constraints of meaning and authority, free to make "our" Constitution what "we" want it to be, is in fact to propose the destruction of an existing community, established by our laws and Constitution, extending from "we" who are alive to those who have given us the materials of our cultural world, and to substitute for it another, the identity of which is most uncertain indeed. In place of the constituted "we" that is the achievement of our past to have given us, we are offered an unconstituted "we," or a "we" constituted on the pages of law journals. One can properly ask of such a person, and mean it literally, "Who are you to speak as you do? Who is the 'we' of whom you speak?" To answer that the new "we" is defined not by the Constitution we have, but by the

Constitution we wish we had, is no answer at all; for who is the "we" doing the wishing? In the new world, who shall be king?

White, *Law as Language: Reading Law and Reading Literature*, 60 TEX. L. REV. 415, 442–43 (1982) (footnote omitted).

Volunteers are evidently not in short supply. Having persuaded himself that "noninterpretivism" is inevitable in any case (*see* Tushnet, *Following the Rules Laid Down: A Critique of Interpretivism and Neutral Principles*, 96 HARV. L. REV. 183 (1982)), Mark Tushnet presumes to respond to the unasked question:

> When I reach this point in the argument . . . I am invariably asked, "Well . . . How would *you* decide the X case?"
>
> . . . .
>
> My answer, in brief, is to make an explicitly political judgment; which result is, in the circumstances, likely to advance the cause of socialism? Having decided that, I would write an opinion in some currently favored version of Grand Theory.

Tushnet, *The Dilemmas of Liberal Constitutionalism*, 42 OHIO STATE. L. J. 424 (1981).

28. Nor is there the slightest reason to think that any of these formulations would be acceptable as a proposed, express provision for inclusion explicitly in article III.

29. *E.g.*, Frontiero v. Richardson, 411 U.S. 677 (1973) (Brennan, J., for a plurality). *See also* Craig v. Boren, 429 U.S. 190 (1976). *Compare* Van Alstyne, *The Proposed Twenty-Seventh Amendment: A Brief, Supportive Comment*, 1979 WASH. U. L. Q. 189 *with* Note, *Sex Discrimination and Equal Protection: Do We Need a Constitutional Amendment?*, 84 HARV. L. REV. 1499 (1971). Others, unimpressed with the straining required to adapt the fourteenth amendment to render superfluous any new amendment, nonetheless urge essentially the same outcome via some other existing provision (*e.g.*, the ninth amendment). *Compare* C. BLACK, *supra* note 25, at 35 *with* Van Alstyne, *Slouching Toward Bethlehem with the Ninth Amendment*, 91 YALE L. J. 207 (1981).

30. "Congress shall make no law . . . abridging the freedom of speech or of the press . . . ." U.S. Const. amend. I.

31. "Neither slavery nor involuntary servitude . . . shall exist within the United States . . . ." *Id.* amend. XIII, § 1.

32. "[N]or shall any state . . . deny to any person within its jurisdiction the equal protection of the laws." *Id.* amend. XIV, § 1.

33. "The right . . . to vote shall not be denied or abridged . . ., on account of race, color, or previous condition of servitude." *Id.* amend. XV, § 1.

34. "The right . . . to vote shall not be denied . . . on account of sex." *Id.* amend. XIX, § 1.

35. "The right . . . to vote . . . shall not be denied . . . by reason of failure to pay any poll tax or other tax." *Id.* amend. XXIV, § 1.

36. "The right of citizens of the United States, who are eighteen years of age or older, to vote shall not be denied . . . on account of age." *Id.* amend. XXVI, § 1.

37. *See* Thayer, *supra* note 17, at 151. I characterized as "unduly famous" this original and most influential article, in note 17. Perhaps I should say why.

With respect to the adjudication of cases involving challenges to the constitutionality of state statutes, Thayer held that it was the duty of the judiciary "to allow to [the] constitution nothing less than its just and true interpretation." *Id.* at 155. In fully equivalent cases involving acts of Congress, however, it was not Thayer's view that the Court was to allow the Constitution nothing less than "its just and true interpretation"; rather, it was to allow *much* less than a just and true interpretation. The Court was urged to do so, moreover, whether the issue of constitutionality turned on an alleged failure of enumerated or implied constitutional power vested in Congress to presume to do as it had done, or whether the issue turned on the inconsistency of the act with some positive prohibition in the Bill or Rights. Thus, Thayer acknowledged that his proposed rule will operate against "private rights" as well, though it has a "tendency to drive out questions of justice and right . . . ." *Id.* In brief, acts of Congress were to be upheld and enforced by the Supreme Court unless founded on a preposterous, rather than an erroneous, misinterpretation of the Constitution. Moreover, even if the legislative record were to make it quite clear that Congress had in fact never even considered the constitutionality of its proposed action, Thayer took the view that the Court should nonetheless pretend that it had, pretend also that Congress treated the issue (of constitutional interpretation) conscientiously, and pretend that Congress would not have enacted the bill but for a good faith belief in its consistency with the Constitution. Indeed, even if the congressional record made it quite clear that Congress enacted the bill despite its own expressed doubts and in express expectation that the issue would be more appropriately resolved in court, still the Supreme Court was to treat the bill as (falsely) reflecting a conscientious debate in Congress and a conscientious conclusion that the bill was not inconsistent with the Constitution. See *id.* at 146 (dealing with the problem and airily concluding that "we must assume that the legislature have done their duty . . . .").

Taken at face value, Thayer's "analysis" should produce Supreme Court rulings along any of the following lines. None of them seems the least bit attractive:

1. The act as applied in this case does not in our view rest within any enumerated or implied power of Congress; moreover, despite the able argument by counsel representing the government whose views we have heard respectfully, we are persuaded that as applied, this act also abridges the petitioner's freedom of speech contrary to the first amendment. However, as our view is not controlling, as Congress is irrebuttably presumed to have concluded otherwise, and as its view though incorrect is merely incorrect and no worse, we now sustain the act as applied; [or]

2. We hold that the act of Congress as applied is not unconstitutional either for lack of power to enact it or for conflict with some affirmative prohibition in the Constitution (although, of course, this in fact is not our view); [or]

3. We hold that the argument respecting the unconstitutionality of the act of Congress is correct and has not been refuted, but since reasonable persons might conclude otherwise we therefore hold the act to be constitutional.

I think none of this would have been the least bit attractive but for the character of practical results that the thesis was expected to yield; namely, that acts of Congress that a conservative Court would hold invalid might, under Thayer's rule, be sustained. Of course, that kind of outcome more favorable to Congress might well be desirable and defensible by rules of constitutional interpretation eminently persuasive in their own right, yet (unlike Thayer's rule) not in the least derogating from the independence of judicial constitutional review. It requires no fictitious imputation of constitutional interpretation within Congress (and no nonsense suppositions about either the representativeness or scruples of Congress) for the judiciary itself to apply a rule of generous construction in respect to the enumerated powers of Congress. The rule of generous construction, like Thayer's rule of "clear error," may of course result in upholding more acts of Congress than otherwise might be sustained. While not free from criticism on its own account (federalism critics will tend to fault it), it is not contingent upon doubtful assumptions respecting the capacity of the president or the Congress fairly to assess the scope of their respective powers for the purpose of binding courts as well. Neither does it make any assumptions (irrebuttable or otherwise) that the president or Congress actually made such an inquiry before acting, or acted only after conscientious anguishing. Certainly it does not invite a tendency to ration the independence of judicial review inversely to the degree of consideration that those departments may have given the matter. In brief, there is no renunciation of independent judicial review and no subordination of the Court's own view of the "just and true" interpretation of the Constitution according to the politically driven and self-serving rhetoric of the political departments.

38. An example is readily furnished by Justice Brennan's opinion in Regents of the Univ. of Cal. v. Bakke, 438 U.S. 265, 361 (1978) (Brennan, J., concurring and dissenting), in which the analysis based on representativeness jurisprudence is either clearly unsophisticated or seriously disingenuous. Compare the opinion in the same case by Justice Powell. *Id.* at 265. *See also* Van Alstyne, *Rites of Passage: Race, the Supreme Court, and the Constitution*, 46 U. CHI. L. REV. 775, 800–02 (1979).

39. For a discussion and interesting case review applying this point of view, see C. BLACK,

Structure and Relationship in Constitutional Law 76–95 (1969). According to this view, the degree of "presumption of constitutional validity" will move from zero in the case of an individual police officer's on-the-spot decision to take certain action (which is subsequently challenged), through "1" when the officer acted pursuant to a (mere) local ordinance adopted by a city council, through "3" when anchored in a clearly framed state law, through "8" when in the form of a clear act of Congress.

40. Note, then, that what would be "held" unconstitutional when reflected merely in the practice of a given police officer may (and sometimes must) logically be "held" constitutional if reflected in a state statute. Of course, that inconsistency could be avoided by treating the first decision on the merits as a binding precedent (though by hypothesis the "first decision" itself would have been different had that "first decision" involved a state statute [or federal statute] rather than an individual police officer's act), but this way of coping with inconsistency then makes the content of the prevailing constitutional rule very much the accident of which kind of "case" happened to be adjudicated first. How very strange. One may attempt other permutations, but most will be found to exhibit similar difficulties. The point illustrated here is distinct from the different point discussed in note 43 *infra*, in the example taken from Katzenbach v. Morgan, 384 U.S. 641 (1966).

41. *But see* Katzenbach v. Morgan, 384 U.S. 641 (1966), yielding to Congress the determination of what kinds of state legislative distinctions are forbidden by the equal protection clause, though the provisions of the act in question affected a very limited portion of the nation and in fact received virtually *no* attention in Congress. A refinement to this approach would qualify it, however, by reinstating the nearly insurmountable presumption of substantive constitutional consistency insofar as the Court is of the view that, despite the regional or otherwise restricted field of impact of the proposed act, the economic and/or sociological position of those to whom it may apply is such that their political influence with the legislature is bound to be substantial. *See, e.g.*, Southern Pac. Co. v. Arizona, 325 U.S. 711, 767 n.2 (1945); South Carolina Highway Dep't v. Barnwell Bros., 303 U.S. 177, 185 n.2 (1938).

42. Legislation unfavorable to women is treated generally in this respect, partly on the conjecture that women are (sometimes) not adequate to represent their own interests because of self-victimization of "stereotype," *e.g.*, that they would have effectively acted to forestall certain legislation but for the damaging effects of our culture, which precludes them from taking their own constitutional rights seriously within the legislative process, and obliging the Court to do so in their behalf. *See, e.g.*, Frontiero v. Richardson, 411 U.S. 677, 686 n.17 (1973). *Compare* discussion in J. Ely, *supra* note 23, at 166–69 *with* Note, *supra* note 29, at 1505 n.48. Legislation favorable to women may likewise be treated the same way, insofar as the same school of political sociology can persuade some justices that such legislation, unfavorable to men, is only *seemingly* unfavorable to men (but actually favorable to them [in the Court's view] insofar as it is favorable to women in respect to some reinforcement of "woman's role"). *See, e.g.*, Mississippi Univ. of Women v. Hogan, 1092 S. Ct. 3331, 3339 (and compare the dissent at 3347); Orr v. Orr, 440 U.S. 268, 283 (1979); Craig v. Boren, 429 U.S. 190, 220 n.2 (1976).

43. This use of representativeness jurisprudence in the rationing of substantive judicial activism should also be distinguished from the relevance of legislative facts in constitutional litigation. *See, e.g.*, Karst, *Legislative Facts in Constitutional Litigation*, 1960 Sup. Ct. Rev. 75. The distinction is illustrated by comparing Katzenbach v. Morgan, 384 U.S. 641 (1966), with South Carolina v. Katzenbach, 383 U.S. 301 (1966). In the first case, *Morgan*, an act of Congress forbade the use of voter-literacy tests because in its view the use of such tests was per se sufficiently unfair as to deny equal protection to such persons as could not pass them. In the second case, *South Carolina*, an act of Congress suspended the use of voter-literacy tests in certain jurisdictions as an efficient means of enforcing the fifteenth amendment's prohibition against otherwise-difficult-to-detect racial misapplications of such tests by local registrars.

In *South Carolina*, no novel or different construction of the fifteenth amendment was relied upon by Congress than the judiciary, acting independently, regarded as entirely sound and conventional. The question, then, was the sufficiency of the factual predicate relied upon by Congress, the sufficiency of the "legislative facts": i.e., was there sufficient evidence of difficult-to-detect registrar misapplications of certain literacy tests to support Congress's conclusion that, given these conditions, the remedy it proposed (suspending the tests in jurisdictions in which less than half of the eligible-age population registered and voted in 1964) was legislation "appropriate" to enforce the fifteenth amendment's prohibition of such racial misapplications? The Court agreed that the evidence was sufficient.

In *Morgan*, Congress presumed to legislate its view respecting the constitutional consistency of literacy tests and the obligation of each state to deny to no person the equal protection of its laws. The Court had previously held that there was no inconsistency between minimal English literacy-test requirements and the equal protection restriction on the several states. A majority of the Court nonetheless concluded that insofar as it could "perceive a basis" for the contrary (legal) conclusion reached by Congress, it would yield to the reasonableness of that view. *But see* Oregon v. Mitchell, 400 U.S. 112 (1970).

The implications of the *Morgan* case can, of course, be confined. *See, e.g.*, Choper, *Congressional Power to Expand Judicial Definitions of the Substantive Terms of the Civil War Amendments*, 67 MINN. L. REV. 299 (1982); Cohen, *Congressional Power to Interpret Due Process and Equal Protection?*, 27 STAN. L. REV. 603 (1975). Nonetheless, *Morgan* does provide a strong opening wedge for additional "representativeness" determinations as, say, that the Court should similarly yield if it could "perceive a basis" for a (legal) conclusion reached by Congress that two-month-old fetuses are as deserving of protection as seven-month-old fetuses such that it shall be a federal crime for physicians whose medical practice may affect such commerce as it is within the congressional power to regulate, or physicians either directly or indirectly receiving federal funds, to perform an abortion resulting in death or damage to a fetus more mature than sixty (thirty? ten?) days old. *Compare* Roe v. Wade, 410 U.S. 113 (1973).

44. These uses of "representativeness" jurisprudence in adjusting the substantive standards of various clauses, incidentally, should be distinguished from their uses in respect to *procedural* (as distinct from *substantive*) judicial restraint and judicial activism. The four thousand plus caseload of the Supreme Court (the majority of which cases are on its certiorari rather than its appeal docket) obviously requires some rationing system in determining which cases to hear. The tendency of judges to employ their own notions of political sociology in deciding which cases to hear (e.g., because certain types of laws seem "fishy") may not be very sophisticated and may, of course, engender its own frustrations. But it produces no important body of substantive constitutional law with the ramified inconsistencies and the sheer vagrancy of keying the "meaning" of clauses to perceived "representativeness."

45. *See* U.S. Const. art. I, § 2, cl. 3 (direct taxes shall be apportioned . . . by adding to the whole number of free Persons . . . .") (encourages slavery because congressional representation directly correlates to the number of slaves brought into the state); *id.* art. IV. § 2, cl. 3 ("fugitive slave" clause recognizing and enforcing slaveowners' rights). *See also id.* art. I. § 19, cl. 1; *id.* art. V. *See generally* THE CONSTITUTION, A PRO SLAVERY COMPACT (W. Phillips ed. 1845).

46. *See supra* note 12 and accompanying text.

47. United States v. Butler, 297 U.S. 6, 62 (1936).

48. *See, e.g.*, A. BICKEL, *supra* note 13, at 90.

49. The phrase is Marshall's, from McCulloch v. Maryland, 17 U.S. (4 Wheat.) 316, 406–07 (1819), in which the immediate point is that while the government "can exercise only the powers granted to it," because "it is a *constitution* we are expounding," the "fair and just interpretation" of those powers ought not to be grudging. The same useful proposition is asserted quite forcefully in a memorable Holmes opinion a century later, as well. *See* Missouri v. Holland, 252 U.S. 416 (1920). The rule of generous construction of express national powers is analytically quite different from a suggestion that an interpretation that the Court would conclude was erroneous (though "merely" erroneous and not preposterously so) should nonetheless be applied for adjudicative purposes by the judiciary if the erroneous interpretation is preferred by Congress. *Compare supra* note 37.

50. *See* J. ELY, *supra* note 23, at 183 ("At that point you'd hardly be acting like a judge . . . .").

51. "[P]recisely because it is *a constitution* we are expounding, we ought not to take liberties with it." National Mut. Ins. Co. v. Tidewater Transfer Co., 337 U.S. 582, 647 (1949) (Frankfurter, J., dissenting) (citation omitted).

52. A. BICKEL, *supra* note 13, at 90.

53. *See supra* materials collected notes 25–26.

54. *See* J. ELY, *supra* note 23, at 191.

55. *E.g.*, *id.* at 87 ("The remainder of this chapter [actually, of the whole book] will comprise three arguments in favor of a participation-oriented, representation-reinforcing approach to judicial review.")

56. Colleagues have suggested that it would be useful to refer here to at least one example of an issue examined by fairly ordinary standards of constitutional interpretation, to provide contrast with nonstandard theories of judicial review. An excellent example is provided in chapter 2, *infra* pages 53–54, in the recapitulation of the several bases according to which "freedom of the press" might be held to yield a somewhat different and stronger set of first amendment rights for journalists than the equivalent set of first amendment rights provided solely by the free speech clause. Note that the discussion there, as elsewhere, is conducted wholly as a concern with interpreting the first amendment and not as a reprise incidental to article III (the article of the Constitution that describes the judicial power). Note also that the treatment of the issue makes no use at all of how representative the legislative body may have been that enacted the law drawn into question as applied to a newspaper, or whether the interpretation in dispute would or would not advance the interests of historically neglected minorities. Similarly, there is no suggestion that were the interpretation in dispute otherwise convincing, the Court ought nonetheless reject it as applied to some act of Congress on the Marshall-Thayer assumption that Congress shall be irrebuttably presumed to have considered the consistency of every proposed act with the Constitution and to have adopted only such acts as in its considered view are constitutional, and that the Court should reexamine such congressionally implied interpretations only for the remote possibility of "clear error." In respect to the latter consideration, compare also Justice Jackson's dictum in West Virginia State Bd. of Education v. Barnette, 319 U.S. 624, 638 (1943):

> The very purpose of a Bill of rights was to withdraw certain subjects from the vicissitudes of political controversy, to place them beyond the reach of majorities and officials and to establish them as legal principles to be applied by the courts. One's right to life, liberty, and property, to free speech, a free press, freedom of worship and assembly, and other fundamental rights may not be submitted to vote; they depend on the outcome of no elections.

The approach of the main chapters on interpreting the first amendment may also be seen in contrast with R. LADENSON, A PHILOSOPHY OF FREE EXPRESSION (1983). There, the author suggests an adjustment according to which the first amendment ought to be interpreted according to Rawlsian notions of "valid principles of social justice . . . that rational people would unanimously advocate under equal conditions" (p. 12) in order that judicial review in cases involving the Bill of Rights can be reconciled with democracy. Further, in that author's view, since "protection of fundamental rights" is postulated by the author as the "basic purposes [sic]" to be served by interpreting the first amendment (p. 26), it is made to follow that whatever view of the best moral philosophy commands one's sense of reflective equilibrium as to what ought ideally to be protected, the first amendment shall be interpreted accordingly.

57. The suggestion that the ninth amendment's adjudicative futility ought not be assumed in the absence of serious investigation is meant earnestly. Despite the criticism that has been made of Moore v. City of East Cleveland, 431 U.S. 494 (1977) (*see, e.g.*, Grano, *supra* note 25, at 8–11), it may very well be an instance of a law that, as applied, was seriously subject to objection on ninth amendment grounds. The case involved a zoning ordinance applied to forbid a grandmother from sharing her own home with her own two grandsons. The ordinance was applied despite the utter lack of any evidence of crowding, interference with others, impact on property values, or any other distinction from any other family living together (as otherwise provided by the same ordinance) or, indeed, anything whatever that should plausibly be disturbing. The integrity of ordinary families, the historical centrality of close, consanguinal ties, the sense of duty and care of "one's own," the almost certain sense of profound impropriety that (I think) research would show would have greeted

the mere suggestion of jailing an unoffending grandmother for sharing her home with her own grandchildren, and the extremely well-developed paths of pre-existing decisional law absorbing the presumed "right" to some positive sense of family, may well sum to a rare instance of a compelling ninth amendment case. The ninth amendment need not be seen as an empty sack simply from fear that, unless one insists upon making it so, it must at once become every judicial moralist's cornucopia. The burden would appropriately be upon Mrs. Moore to establish the foundations of her claim. In her case, however, it is likely that history would support her very well indeed. But see Caplan, *The History and Meaning of the Ninth Amendment*, 69 VA. L. REV. 223 (1983).

58. *See, e.g.*, Bonfield, *The Guarantee Clause of Article IV, Section 4: A Study in Constitutional Desuetude*, 46 MINN. L. REV. 513 (1962).

59. Marbury v. Madison, 5 U.S. (1 Cranch) 137 (1803), merely confirmed the separate obligation of the judiciary to determine the consistency of acts of Congress with provisions in the Constitution as an incident of adjudicating "cases" properly before the courts. Despite a few pretentious dicta in other cases (*see, e.g.*, Cooper v. Aaron, 358 U.S. 1, 17–19 (1958)), there is no basis in Marbury or in any other source for the suggestion that the sole "correct" interpretation of the Constitution is that which is sufficiently convincing for courts to accept. *See* G. GUNTHER, CONSTITUTIONAL LAW—CASES AND MATERIALS 25–30 (10th ed. 1980); Brest, *The Conscientious Legislator's Guide to Constitutional Interpretation*, 27 STAN L. REV. 585, 589 (1975) ("Decisions *not* striking down laws do not always mean that the laws are constitutional . . . for a court's failure to invalidate may only reflect its institutional limitations.") (emphasis in original).

60. The point is suggested in Justice Harlan's dictum that "[t]he suggestion that courts lack standards by which to decide such cases . . . is relevant not only to the question of 'justiciability,' but also, and perhaps more fundamentally, to the determination whether any cognizable constitutional claim has been asserted . . . ." Baker v. Carr, 369 U.S. 186, 337 (1962) (Harlan, J., dissenting).

61. The point of the reference to "some combination of clauses" is of course to acknowledge that there is an architecture in the Constitution. The crowding clauses obviously bear upon one another, their particular grouping in particular articles likewise may have an illuminating significance, and indeed it may be useful to consider the "structure" of the Constitution as well as the relationship of its features in the course of quite standard and conscientious judicial review. *See* C. BLACK, *supra* note 39.

62. For a better understanding of this claim, see Aptheker v. Secretary of State, 378 U.S. 500 (1964).

63. "[T]he specific prohibitions of the first ten amendments and the same prohibitions when adopted by the Fourteenth Amendment leave no opportunity for presumption of constitutionality where statutes on their face violate the prohibition." Letter from Justice Stone to Chief Justice Hughes, Apr. 19, 1938, *quoted in* Lusky, *supra* note 23, at 1098. See also Brandenburg v. Ohio, 395 U.S. 444 (1969).

64. And to the extent that it may not, the means of legitimate fundamental change are still at hand. It is by amendment that a constitution records a nation's fundamental changes as an act of will, actively and positively, an observation that cannot be made of such transfigurations merely perpetrated by unimpeached and "not overruled" judges on the skeleton of an inadequate document. By way of concrete example, it seems clear enough that the amendments of 1791, and those also of 1866–70, made our Constitution better by far than what it was without those alterations. So, too, in this respect is it better by far than were those alterations not in the Constitution itself, but merely discoverable in the Shepardized inventions of judges. So, as well, with equal matters of fundamental concern today. It is one of the ironies of judicial self-justification that it operates to inhibit the nation's authentic means of making improvements in the Constitution by (a) "proving" that amendments are not needed and by (b) "proving" also that (given the special theories of some judges) none of any significance can safely even be considered.

1. A Graphic Review of the Free Speech Clause

1. Act of July 21, 1798, ch. 74, § II, 1 Stat. 596, *critically reviewed in* L. LEVY, LEGACY OF SUPPRESSION (1960) *and* J. SMITH, FREEDOM'S FETTERS—THE ALIEN AND SEDITION LAWS AND AMERICAN CIVIL LIBERTIES (1956).

2. Metromedia, Inc. v. City of San Diego, 453 U.S. 490, 501 (1981).

3. *See, e.g.,* Wolston v. Reader's Digest Ass'n, 443 U.S. 157 (1979); Hutchinson v. Proxmire, 443 U.S. 111 (1979); Time, Inc. v. Firestone, 424 U.S. 448 (1976); Gertz v. Robert Welch, Inc., 418 U.S. 323 (1974); New York Times Co. v. Sullivan, 376 U.S. 255 (1964).

4. *See, e.g.,* Eaton, *The American Law of Defamation Through Gertz v. Robert Welch, Inc. and Beyond: An Analytical Primer,* 61 VA. L. REV. 1349, 1450–51 (1975).

5. Jacobellis v. Ohio, 388 U.S. 184, 197 (1964).

6. Three versions that will not be reviewed here are the "bad tendency," "advocacy of illegal conduct," and "no prior restraint" versions. The first tended to characterize the Supreme Court majority position throughout the 1920's. *See, e.g.,* Whitney v. California, 274 U.S. 357 (1927); Gitlow v. New York, 268 U.S. 652 (1925); Abrams v. United States, 250 U.S. 616 (1919). The second was put forward by Learned Hand in Masses Pub. Co. v. Patten, 244 F. 535 (S.D.N.Y. 1917), and is well described in Gunther, *Learned Hand and the Origins of Modern First Amendment Doctrine: Some Fragments of History,* 27 STAN. L. REV. 719 (1975). The third was the sole concern of the common law as summarized in 4 W. BLACKSTONE, COMMENTARIES ON THE COMMON LAW 150–54 (1st Am. ed. 1772), *discussed in* Z. CHAFEE, FREE SPEECH IN THE UNITED STATES 9–12 (1942). For an excellent recent review of contending doctrines early in this century, see Rabban, *The First Amendment in Its Forgotten Years,* 90 YALE L.J. 514 (1981).

7. *See* United States v. O'Brien, 391 U.S. 367 (1968) (burning of draft card, in the context of an antiwar rally, given marginal first amendment protection). Compare Tinker v. Des Moines School District, 393 U.S. 503 (1969) (armbands treated as "closely akin to 'pure speech' . . . entitled to comprehensive protection under the First Amendment."). See also F. SCHAUER, FREE SPEECH: A PHILOSOPHICAL INQUIRY 95–101 (1982); Ely, *Flag Desecration: A Case Study in the Roles of Categorization and Balancing in First Amendment Analysis,* 88 HARV. L. REV. 1482 (1975). Generally, conduct not literally "speech" is treated for first amendment purposes as speech if: (1) characteristically communicative in fact (*e.g.,* wearing an armband); or (2) subjected to regulation only when communicative (*i.e.,* the legislature regulated it as speech); or (3) the particular conduct was in the particular instance communicative and, though the law on its face forbade that conduct whether or not it was communicative, there is clear and convincing evidence that the law was adopted for the purpose (as well as applied with the effect) of suppressing the message sought to be conveyed.

8. A surprising number of commentators have concluded that, for this reason alone, the first amendment cannot be taken literally because it would leave unrestrained, incorrigible opportunities for the executive and judicial departments of the United States to suppress free speech in ways that must have been meant to be forbidden under the first amendment. It is not clear, however, whether such easy criticism is well founded. The extent of the problem depends partly upon one's view of how much of the executive power and how much of the judicial power do not depend upon acts of Congress.

Most of what the president can do may in fact be derived from enabling legislation by Congress rather than by force of his power as provided in article II. The same is true of our federal courts under article III. When particular uses of the executive and judicial power proceed pursuant to authorizations and enabling legislation by Congress, they are subject to the first amendment, which makes no exception for acts of Congress merely because they may also be in aid of the executive or judicial powers, as distinct from acts of Congress in aid of its own enumerated powers. The consequence may be that the actual ambit of executive and judicial power unaffected by a literal first amendment (because not consequential to any act of Congress) would be very small, confined at the outset, and not as important to restrict as that of Congress. I have dealt with this problem obliquely in a different article, however, and there is little reason to deal with it here. *See* Van Alstyne, *The Role of Congress in Determining Incidental Powers of the President and the Federal Courts*, 40 LAW & CONTEMP. PROB. 102 (1976).

9. The inquiry may not be ended if it is the kind of speech that the copyright clause enables Congress to control (by confiding an exclusive property right in others), pursuant to its power under art. I, § 8, cl. 8, "to promote the Progress of Science and useful Arts, by securing for limited Times to Authors and Inventors the exclusive Right to their respective Writings and Discoveries." For an opening discussion, see Nimmer, *Does Copyright Abridge the First Amendment Guarantee of Free Speech and Press?*, 17 U.C.L.A. L. REV. 1180 (1970).

10. Note, for instance, how the first amendment differs from the second amendment in this respect. The first amendment does not link the protection it provides with any particular objective and may accordingly be deemed to operate without regard to anyone's view of how well the speech it protects may or may not serve such an objective. The second amendment expressly links the protection it provides with a stated objective ("A well regulated Militia, being necessary to the security of a free state") and might therefore be deemed to operate only insofar as the right it protects ("the right of the people to keep and bear arms") can be shown to be connected with that objective, *i.e.*, the maintenance of a well-regulated militia.

The different modes of the first and second amendments are not unique in this regard. The enumeration of powers vested in Congress, in art. I, § 8, reflects a similar pattern of difference. For instance, whatever the reasons contributing to the grant, the vesting of power in Congress to "regulate commerce among the several states" is textually not bounded by any statement of purpose or objective in respect to the exercise of that power. On the other hand, the vesting of power in Congress to secure "to Authors and Inventors the exclusive Right to their respective Writings and Discoveries" has two textual qualifications. The first may be implied by the introductory phrase accompanying the grant of power, that this power is vested in Congress "to promote the Progress of Science and useful Arts." The second is express in that the power is one to grant an "exclusive Right" for "limited Times," and not in perpetuity. Thus, while the Supreme Court might defer to Congress on both matters, it might also, consistent with the text, check Congress with respect to either matter. The Court might, for example, hold unconstitutional a vesting of exclusive patent or copyright that in the Court's view has no rational connection with promoting the progress of science or any useful art, or it might hold unconstitutional a vesting of exclusive patent or copyright that in the Court's view is unnecessarily long or excessive to fair protection. On the other hand, the Court would regard the commerce power as plenary, as indeed it has in an overwhelming number of cases. *See, e.g.*, Prudential Ins. Co. v. Benjamin, 328 U.S. 408 (1946) (congressionally approved discriminatory state tax statute sustained); Champion v. Ames, 188 U.S. 321 (1903) (act of Congress destroying, rather than enhancing, interstate commerce sustained); Gibbons v. Ogden, 22 U.S. (9 Wheat.) 1 (1824).

11. "The Congress, whenever two thirds of both Houses shall deem it necessary, shall propose Amendments to this Constitution, or, on the Application of the Legislatures of two thirds of the several States, shall call a Convention for proposing Amendments, which, in either Case, shall be valid to all Intents and Purposes, as part of this Constitution, when ratified by the Legislatures of three fourths of the several States, or by Conventions in three fourths thereof, as the one or the other Mode of Ratification may be proposed by the Congress . . . ."

12. Schenck v. United States, 249 U.S. 47, 52 (1919) ("The most stringent protection of free speech would not protect a man in falsely shouting fire in a theatre and causing a panic.").

13. In several cases, Justice Black wrote strongly and approvingly of a first amendment with no exceptions. *See, e.g.*, his opinions in New York Times Co. v. Sullivan, 376 U.S. 254, 293 (1964) (Black, J., concurring); Konigsberg v. State Bar, 366 U.S. 36, 56 (1961) (Black, J., dissenting); Barenblatt v. United States, 360 U.S. 109, 135 (1959) (Black, J., dissenting). Even so, his own discernment of "speech plus" led him to vote to sustain many laws believed to be unconstitutional under the first amendment even by more conservative colleagues not sharing his "absolute" commitment to the first amendment. *See, e.g.*, Cohen v. California, 403 U.S. 15 (1971); Street v. New York, 394 U.S. 576, 609 (1969) (Black, J., dissenting); Tinker v. Des Moines School Dist., 393

U.S. 503, 515 (1966) (Black, J., dissenting); Cox v. Louisiana, 379 U.S. 559 (1965); Giboney v. Empire Storage & Ice Co., 336 U.S. 490 (1949). *See also* Kalven, *Upon Rereading Mr. Justice Black on the First Amendment*, 14 U.C.L.A. L. Rev. 428 (1967). Efforts at such distinctions have created difficulties for other "strong" first amendment writers as well. *See, e.g.*, T. Emerson, The System of Freedom of Expression 80–89 (1970).

14. The point has not escaped theatrical parody. *See* T. Stoppard, Rosencrantz & Guilden-stern Are Dead, Act II, at 60 (1967).

15. *But see* F. Schauer, *supra* note 7, at 89 ("Perjury and extortion have nothing to do with what free speech is all about."). Perhaps, or perhaps not, but in either case this quite misses the point. The point is that a compelling (literal) first amendment is threatened in the first place insofar as one must not merely show that he or she is being prosecuted and prosecuted for what was said but show additionally that what was said is "what free speech is all about," *i.e.*, speech-of-a-kind (*the* kind?)-not-excluded-from-the-first-amendment. Who has what burden in these matters is the point.

The point additionally is that words such as *perjury* and *extortion* are easy to dismiss as (some-how) not "speech" within the first amendment (although in fact pure speech) but are less easy to dismiss once one concedes that in the first instance such speech is clearly within the first amendment and the burden is on the government to explain why it should be taken out. "Perjury" may consist of submitting a willful and false affidavit. But if the (false) affidavit is itself one the government may not (consistent with the first amendment itself) require, is it still clear that that perjury can be punished? (*See* Justice Black's dissent in Dennis v. United States, 384 U.S. 855, 875 (1966).) "Extortion" involves threats of coercion to gain one's object. Whether it is "what free speech is all about" is frequently extremely debatable. See discussion and examples in note 47 *infra*. Calling a thing "perjury" or "extortion," as calling that which is utterly speech "not-speech," is precisely the point. Professor Schauer and many others work from the notion that one must settle the purposes to be served by the first amendment and, having done so, then match those purposes against varic-ties of speech to determine which of the latter are "speech" within the first amendment. May it not be far better to take the amendment as it is, and let those who imagine purposes for the first amend-ment carry their own burden to show why, accordingly, that which is concededly speech is none-theless not to be protected under the circumstances?

16. This view is evidently shared by seemingly "strong" first amendment proponents such as Zechariah Chafee. *See* Z. Chafee, *supra* note 6, at 14, 145, 149–50 ("We can all agree that the free speech clauses do not wipe out the common law as to obscenity, profanity, and defamation of individuals. . . . [O]bscenity, profanity, and gross libels upon individuals . . . fall outside the pro-tection of the free speech clauses as I have defined them . . . [as do criminal solicitation or even talking scurrilously about the flag].")*. See also* Justice Holmes's opinion in Frohwerk v. United States, 249 U.S. 204, 206 (1919) ("We venture to believe that neither Hamilton nor Madison, nor any other competent person then or later, ever supposed that to make criminal the counseling of a murder . . . would be an unconstitutional interference with speech."). Other (and much more dis-piriting) early Holmes opinions are comprehensively reviewed in Rabban, *supra* note 6, at 533–40.

17. For example, Professor Chafee concluded that the central minimum intention of the drafters and ratifiers of the first amendment was "to wipe out the common law of sedition, and make further prosecutions for criticism of the government, without any incitement to law-breaking, forever im-possible in the United States of America." Z. Chafee, *supra* note 6, at 21. The Supreme Court has accepted this conclusion. New York Times Co. v. Sullivan, 375 U.S. 254, 276 (1964) ("Although the Sedition Act was never tested in this Court, the attack upon its validity has carried the day in the court of history. . . . [There has been] a broad consensus that the Act, because of the restraint it imposed upon criticism of government and public officials, was inconsistent with the First Amendment.").

However, the matter did not always appear so clear. There is, for instance, a growth in the changing impressions of Justice Holmes on the same question. He wrote in 1907:

> [T]he main purpose of such constitutional provisions is "to prevent all such *previous restraints* upon publications as had been practiced by other governments," and they do not prevent the subsequent punishment of such as may be deemed contrary to the public welfare.

Patterson v. Colorado, 205 U.S. 454 (1907).
Then, by 1919, he wrote:

> It well may be that the prohibition of laws abridging the freedom of speech is not confined to previous restraints, although to prevent them may have been the main purpose, as intimated in *Patterson v. Colorado* . . . .

Schenck v. United States, 249 U.S. 47, 51–52 (1919).
Finally and much more emphatically, he stated in the same year: "I wholly disagree with the argument of the Government that the First Amendment left the common law as to seditious libel in force. History seems to me against the notion." Abrams v. United States, 250 U.S. 616, 630 (1919) (Holmes, J., dissenting opinion).
Yet in 1960, Professor Levy reluctantly concluded:

> If . . . a choice must be made between two propositions, first, that the clause [*i.e.*, the freedom of speech and press clause] substantially embodied the Blackstonian definition and left the law of seditious libel in force, or second, that it repudiated Blackstone and superseded the common law, the known evidence points strongly in support of the former proposition. Contrary to Justice Holmes, history favors the notion.

L. LEVY, *supra* note 1, at 248. And yet, for an impressive article that Holmes came to his conclusions conscientiously and not merely as a matter of pragmatic considerations, see Bogen, *The Free Speech Metamorphosis of Mr. Justice Holmes*, 11 HOFSTRA L. REV. 97 (1982). For a recent article essentially agreeing with Holmes and Chafee, see Mayton, *Seditious Libel and the Lost Guarantee of a Freedom of Expression*, 84 COLUM. L. REV. 91 (1984).

18. Roth v. United States, 354 U.S. 476, 483, 485 (1957) ("In light of this history, it is apparent that the unconditional phrasing of the First Amendment was not intended to protect every utterance. . . . We hold that obscenity is not within the area of constitutionally protected speech or press."). The principle was subsequently reaffirmed. Miller v. California, 413 U.S. 15, 23 (1973) ("This much has been categorically settled by the Court, that obscene material is unprotected by the First Amendment."). The most recent effort to defend this distinction is Schauer, *Speech and "Speech"—Obscenity and "Obscenity": An Exercise in the Interpreting of Constitutional Language*, 67 GEO. L.J. 899, 905–06 (1979). *See also* T. EMERSON, *supra* note 13, at 401–12. A more general defense of "definitional balancing" (*i.e.*, judicially defining which kinds of speech are, and which are not, within the protection of the first amendment) is presented in Nimmer, *The Right to Speak from Times to Time: First Amendment Theory Applied to Libel and Misapplied to Privacy*, 56 CALIF. L. REV. 935 (1968).

19. The grounds are "rather shaky" principally because the historical evidence respecting the early common law and the early statutes that punish obscene public expression is taken almost exclusively from state practice, which of course the first amendment does not even purport to affect. The federalism component of free speech protection tends to be overlooked in many treatments of the first amendment. The extent to which state regulation of speech could be imitated by Congress (in all cases in which Congress would otherwise have legislative power pursuant to its enumerated powers in article I) is itself a crucial question. It is certainly not at all clear that the first amendment meant to do no more than to restrict Congress in respect to its enumerated powers to refrain from acts abridging speech that even none of the states reserved the power to regulate as they might wish, pursuant to the tenth amendment. Some of the conflicting views on this question are canvassed in the materials, *supra* notes 17 and 18. We return to the subject later in this chapter, in discussing the final federalism graphic (figure 11).

20. The subject is comprehensively reviewed in Greenawalt, *Speech and Crime*, 1980 AM. B. FOUNDATION RESEARCH J. 645.

21. Chaplinsky v. New Hampshire, 315 U.S. 568, 571–72 (1942) ("There are certain well-defined and narrowly limited classes of speech, the prevention and punishment of which have never been thought to raise *any* constitutional problem. These include the lewd and obscene, the profane, the libelous, and the insulting or 'fighting' words.") (emphasis added), *overruled in part*, New York Times Co. v. Sullivan, 376 U.S. 255, 268 (1964) ("[L]ibel can claim no talismanic immunity from constitutional limitations. It must be measured by standards that satisfy the First Amendment."). *See also* Gooding v. Wilson, 405 U.S. 518, 520 (1972) (reversing conviction of person scuffling with a police officer who had told him, "White son of a bitch, I'll kill you"; "you son of a bitch,

I'll choke you to death"); Terminiello v. Chicago, 337 U.S. 1, 4 (1949) (modifying *Chaplinsky* to apply only when the willfully provocative language "rises far above public inconvenience, annoyance, or unrest," without regard to whether it "stirs people to anger"). For an impressive recent case, see Collin v. Smith, 447 F. Supp. 676 (N.D. Ill.), *aff'd*, 578 F.2d 1197 (7th Cir. 1978) (proposed Nazi march planned for neighborhood inhabited by many Jews personally victims of German concentration camps). *See also* Skokie v. National Socialist Party, 69 Ill. 2d 605, 373 N.E.2d 21 (1978).

22. Valentine v. Chrestensen, 316 U.S. 52 (1942), *overruled in part*, Virginia State Bd. of Pharmacy v. Virginia Citizens Consumer Council, 425 U.S. 748, 760–62 (1976) ("Here, . . . [the] question whether there is a First Amendment exception for 'commercial speech' is squarely before us . . . . Our question, then, is whether this communication is wholly outside the protection of the First Amendment . . . . Our answer is that it is not.").

23. *See, e.g.*, Laird v. Tatum, 408 U.S. 1 (1972) (allegations of present speech-inhibiting consequences of Army intelligence surveillance of dissident civilian groups held insufficient to secure ripeness or standing under article III); Boyle v. Landry, 401 U.S. 77 (1971) (allegations of chilling effect from enacted antispeech criminal statutes insufficient); United Pub. Workers v. Mitchell, 330 U.S. 75 (1947) (denial of declaratory judgment sought by federal civil servants alleging they were intimidated from pursuing particular political activities by a federal statute prohibiting "any active part in political management or in political campaigns."). An exceptionally able review of this subject is provided in Albert, *Justiciability and Theories of Judicial Review: A Remote Relationship*, 50 S. CAL. L. REV. 1139 (1977). Contrary to most of the case law, an excellent argument can be made that because of the very language of the first amendment, it establishes its own special doctrine of litigative ripeness. Persons able to show that a law made by Congress is applicable to their speech, and able to show also that the formal enrollment of the bill necessarily chills their continuing freedom to engage in that speech (and thus "abridges" it), should have standing to have the enrolled bill tested at once in the courts. They would be appropriately confined to a testing of the statute according to the factual setting of their own complaint (*i.e.*, the court would have no obligation to render a sweeping, purely advisory opinion), but they would not be dismissed for failure to satisfy more conventional standards of ripeness.

24. In this respect, the Supreme Court does take the first amendment literally. It examines the law as made and holds it invalid if, as made, the law abridges speech, even though as applied the law does not contravene the first amendment because the speech involved is not protected. *See, e.g.*, Gooding v. Wilson, 405 U.S. 518, 520 (1972) ("It matters not that the words appellee used might have been constitutionally prohibited under a narrowly and precisely drawn statute."). *See also* Coates v. Cincinnati, 402 U.S. 611 (1971) (conviction reversed due to facial overbreadth of ordinance); Shuttlesworth v. Birmingham, 394 U.S. 147 (1969) (conviction reversed because ordinance as drafted was unconstitutionally broad, although as subsequently construed by state supreme court it would presumably be valid as applied to the very facts of the case). The use of these doctrines thus tends to offset the inability of parties to secure a more timely adjudication of an act when first made, although at the corresponding cost of enabling some guilty (*i.e.*, otherwise punishable) parties to go free.

In one respect, the doctrines of "void-on-its-face" for first amendment overbreadth or vagueness are identical to the exclusionary rule disallowing evidence gained by means inconsistent with fourth amendment protection against unreasonable searches and seizures. *See* Mapp v. Ohio, 367 U.S. 643 (1961). In the one case, the criminal goes free because the constable blundered. In the other, the criminal goes free because the legislature blundered. Still, there are grounds for distinguishing the bases of the two rules. Nothing in the text of the fourth amendment itself precludes the use of evidence, however wrongfully secured. But, since the text of the first amendment forbids Congress to make a law abridging protected speech, when the only law applicable abridges speech, it is logical for a court to hold that it cannot be invoked. For an able review of rationales addressed to these problems, see BeVier, *The First Amendment and Political Speech: An Inquiry into the Substance and Limits of Principle*, 30 STAN. L. REV. 299 (1978).

25. For an additional example of judicial discretion that defeats the protection of the first amendment, see Kime v. United States, 103 S.Ct. 266 (1982) and especially the dissent by Justice Brennan at 267–69. (The decision is one declining to review a criminal conviction for "knowingly

casting contempt" upon a replica of the flag in the course of a peaceful political protest in a public place.) In addition to the Brennan dissent, see Ely, *supra*, note 7, at 1482.

26. 341 U.S. 494, 510 (1951).

27. Whitney v. California, 274 U.S. 357, 377–78 (1927) (concurring opinion).

28. *Compare* Edwards v. South Carolina, 372 U.S. 229 (1963) (breach of peace convictions reversed in circumstances of large-scale and somewhat boisterous racial demonstration on state house grounds), *with* Adderly v. Florida, 385 U.S. 39 (1966) (criminal trespass convictions affirmed in circumstances of smaller, less boisterous racial demonstration on jail grounds); *compare* Brown v. Louisiana, 383 U.S. 131 (1966) (breach of peace conviction reversed for silent racial protest stand-in in public library anteroom), *with* Grayned v. City of Rockford, 408 U.S. 104, 116 (1972) (breach of peace conviction sustained for noisy demonstration within one hundred feet of high school during school day) ("The nature of a place, 'the pattern of its normal activities, dictates the kinds of regulations of time, place, and manner that are reasonable.'"). The most recent decision in this heavily case-congested subject is Heffron v. International Soc'y for Krishna Consciousness, Inc., 101 S. Ct. 2559 (1981).

29. These are cases in which no speech is forbidden by law but where, for instance, being obliged to say something may under the circumstances indirectly inhibit one's ability or willingness to speak candidly. *See, e.g.,* Miami Herald Pub. Co. v. Tornillo, 418 U.S. 241 (1974) (duty to publish a reply by any candidate for office disparaged by the newspaper, held invalid); Lamont v. Postmaster Gen., 381 U.S. 301 (1965) (compelled indication of wanting to receive certain mail, as a condition of having such mail delivered, held invalid); Talley v. California, 362 U.S. 60 (1960) (prohibition of anonymous handbills, held invalid). Frequently, although there is no prohibition upon what may be said, it is the "indirect effect" of a "reasonable time, place, and manner" restriction that effects the speech or press abridgment. *See, e.g.,* Houchins v. KQED, 438 U.S. 1 (1978) (restriction on press access to jail of questionable condition, upheld).

30. *See* cases at note 28 *supra.*

31. Terminiello v. Chicago, 337 U.S. 1 (1949) (breach of peace conviction of speaker reversed where demagogic auditorium harangue attracted angry crowd outside).

32. Feiner v. New York, 340 U.S. 315 (1951) (disorderly conduct conviction for refusing police officer's request to cease street corner harangue attracting hostile crowd at busy intersection, affirmed); Kovacs v. Cooper, 336 U.S. 77 (1949) (misdemeanor conviction for "loud and raucous sounding truck" in business district, upheld; dicta suggesting court would be favorable to similar restriction in residential areas).

33. *See* cases and discussion at note 29 *supra. See also* Baird v. State Bar, 401 U.S. 1 (1971) (ineligibility for bar from refusal to disclose membership in certain organization reversed as unduly discouraging citizens "from exercising rights protected by the Constitution"); Gibson v. Florida Legislative Investigative Comm., 372 U.S. 539 (1963) (six-month jail term and $1,200 fine for contempt in refusing to identify names of NAACP members to state legislative committee, reversed).

34. *See, e.g.,* Branzburg v. Hayes, 408 U.S. 665 (1972) (rejection of blanket refusal by journalist to appear before grand jury investigating possible crimes reported by the journalist in newspaper with information allegedly derived from confidential sources).

35. Dennis v. United States, 341 US. 494, 510 (1951).

36. 18 U.S.C. § 2385 (1976).

37. The point is vigorously emphasized in the Douglas dissent in *Dennis*, 341 U.S. at 582, 584 ("So far as the present record is concerned, what petitioners did was to organize people to teach and themselves teach the Marxist-Leninist doctrine contained chiefly in four books. . . . Not a

single seditious act is charged in the indictment. To make a lawful speech unlawful because two men conceive it is to raise the law of conspiracy to appalling proportions.").

38. The point was well made by Justice Douglas in *Terminiello*, 337 U.S. at 4: "[A] function of free speech under our system of government is to invite dispute. It may indeed best serve its high purpose when it induces a condition of unrest, creates dissatisfaction with conditions as they are, or even stirs people to anger." That provocative, offensive, or gratuitous language, attention getting by its willful offensiveness, may for that reason be highly protected as well, is eloquently defended in Justice Harlan's majority opinion in Cohen v. California, 403 U.S. 15 (1971). No doubt the classic exposition of this view in the case law is in Justice Holmes's dissent in Abrams v. United States, 250 U.S. 616, 624 (1919). Exquisite reiterations appear in his dissenting opinion in Gitlow v. New York, 368 U.S. 652, 672 (1925), and the Brandeis concurring opinion in Whitney v. California, 274 U.S. 357, 375 (1927).

39. 341 U.S. at 579, 581. *See* note 37 *supra*. The shortcomings of *Dennis* in this regard are further explored in J. ELY, DEMOCRACY AND DISTRUST 107 8 (1980); M. SHAPIRO, FREEDOM OF SPEECH: THE SUPREME COURT AND JUDICIAL REVIEW 63–65 (1965); Strong, *Fifty Years of "Clear and Present Danger": From Schenck to Brandenburg—and Beyond*, 1969 SUP. CT. REV. 41, 52–53. The *Dennis* formulation is nonetheless defended. *See, e.g.* Bork, *Neutral Principles and Some First Amendment Problems*, 47 IND. L.J. 1, 32–35 (1971).

40. *See* note 1 *supra* and the critical reviews of the Espionage Act and Smith Act in Z. CHAFEE, *supra* note 6, at 36–140 (in more than two thousand prosecutions, "[a]lmost all the convictions were for expressions of opinions about the merits and conduct of the war," *id.* at 51); A. KELLY & W. HARBISON, THE AMERICAN CONSTITUTION: ITS ORIGIN AND DEVELOPMENT 664–70 (1955); T. EMERSON, D. HABER, & N. DORSEN, POLITICAL AND CIVIL RIGHTS IN THE UNITED STATES 104–55 (3d ed. 1967).

41. John Stuart Mill's powerful essay, *On Liberty*, contains an extraordinarily resolute anticipation of the clear-and-present-danger test in the concrete example of "tyrannicide," a topic that in contemporary terms might embrace advocating the desirability of presidential assassination. Note the anticipation of later defenses as to why advocacy of illegal (and clearly dangerous) action is deemed defensible:

> If the arguments of the present chapter are of any validity, there ought to exist the fullest liberty of professing and discussing, as a matter of ethical conviction, any doctrine, however immoral it may be considered. It would, therefore, be irrelevant and out of place to examine here, whether the doctrine of Tyrannicide deserves that title. I shall content myself with saying that the subject has been at all times one of the open questions of morals; that the act of a private citizen in striking down a criminal, who, by raising himself above the law, has placed himself beyond the reach of legal punishment or control, has been accounted by whole nations, and by some of the best and wisest of men, not a crime, but an act of exalted virtue; and that, right or wrong, it is not of the nature of assassination, but of civil war. As such, *I hold that the instigation of it, in a specific case, may be a proper subject of punishment, but only if an overt act has followed, and at least a probable connection can be established between the act and the instigation.*

J. S. Mill, *On Liberty*, in UTILITARIANISM, LIBERTY, & REPRESENTATIVE GOVERNMENT 78 n.1 (1910) (emphasis added).

42. 249 U.S. 47, 52 (1919) (emphasis added).

43. 395 U.S. 444, 447 (1969). The equivalent to the requirement that the danger must be "clear and present" is that the lawless action must be "imminent . . . and . . . likely." The *Brandenburg* formulation is additionally rigorous in its scienter requirement, *i.e.*, that the advocacy must be "directed to" produce the lawless action (the "evil"). The formulation thus protects the speaker to the extent that it forbids making the speaker an insurer of his audience; it holds him criminally responsible only insofar as he meant to produce the imminent lawless action likely in fact to be produced by his utterances. In this respect, then, it borrows the advantage of Learned Hand's original formulation in Masses Pub. Co. v. Patten, 244 F. 535 (S.D.N.Y. 1917), and combines it with

the advantage of the Holmes formulation. *See* Gunther, *supra* note 6, at 754–55. The intent requirement mitigates a problem in the clear-and-present-danger test well illustrated in the following example by Justice Rutledge:

> It is axiomatic that a democratic state may not deny its citizens the right to criticize existing laws and to urge that they be changed. And yet, in order to succeed in an effort to legalize polygamy it is obviously necessary to convince a substantial number of people that such conduct is desirable. But conviction that the practice is desirable has a natural tendency to induce the practice itself. Thus, depending on where the circular reasoning is started, the advocacy of polygamy may either be unlawful as inducing a violation of law, or be constitutionally protected as essential to the proper functioning of the democratic process.

Musser v. Utah, 333 U.S. 95, 101–2 (1948) (dissenting opinion).

In the original clear-and-present-danger formulation, intent was an alternative standard. Thus, in his *Abrams* dissent, Justice Holmes had declared: "It is only the present danger of immediate evil *or* an intent to bring it about that warrants Congress in setting a limit to the expression of opinion where private rights are not concerned." Abrams v. United States, 250 U.S. 616, 628 (1919) (emphasis added). Currently, even when merely "private rights" such as reputation are concerned, *some* degree of scienter (at least negligence) must be established to provide recovery of money damages. The foundation case on this point is unquestionably New York Times Co. v. Sullivan, 376 U.S. 254 (1964). *See* Gertz v. Robert Welch, Inc., 418 U.S. 323 (1974). The first amendment need for some kind of scienter requirement to avoid the self-censoring consequences of a strict liability standard is self-evident.

For an excellent general review of the *Brandenburg* standard, see Comment, *Brandenburg v. Ohio: A Speech Test for All Seasons*, 43 U. Chi. L. Rev. 151 (1975).

44. In Tinker v. Des Moines School Dist., 393 U.S. 503 (1969), the Supreme Court upheld the right of public school students to wear black (protest) armbands on campus, despite the claim that the other children would regard the armbands as provocative and that the armbands might cause some degree of mental anguish to students whose fathers had died fighting in Vietnam. The Illinois Supreme Court adhered quite faithfully to the case in refusing to sustain a municipal ban on armbands involved in the Nazi march, Skokie v. National Socialist Party, 69 Ill. 2d 605, 373 N.E.2d 21 (1978), and was severely criticized for not sustaining the restriction on a "fighting words" and "avoidance of mental suffering" rationale. *See, e.g.*, Horowitz & Bramson, *Skokie, The ACLU and the Endurance of Democratic Theory*, 43 Law & Contemp. Probs. 328 (1979); Rabinowitz, *Nazis in Skokie: Fighting Words or Heckler's Veto?*, 28 De Paul L. Rev. 259 (1979). For a related discussion, see Comment, *The Fighting Words Doctrine—Is There a Clear and Present Danger to the Standard?*, 84 Dick. L. Rev. 75 (1979).

45. Whitney v. California, 274 U.S. 357, 377 (1927).

46. Thus, Justice Brandeis used the example of advocacy of a moral right or duty "to cross unenclosed, unposted, waste land" as an example of an instance when such advocacy could not be punished—even when directed to the urging of such trespass, "even if there was imminent danger that advocacy would lead to a trespass," and even assuming that the trespassers, acting on the advocacy, could themselves be punished. *Id.* at 377–79 ("[T]he evil apprehended [must be] relatively serious . . . . There must be the probability of serious injury to the states . . . . [T]he evil apprehended [must be] so substantial as to justify the stringent restriction interposed by the legislature."). This rule was applied in Grayned v. City of Rockford, 408 U.S. 104, 115 (1972) ("The right to use a public place for expressive activity may be restricted only for weighty reasons."); Cohen v. California, 403 U.S. 15 (1971) (reversing breach of peace conviction for exhibiting jacket with "Fuck the Draft" in a courthouse corridor before women and children, holding that the privacy interests of the unwilling and offended persons from distasteful vulgarities in such a place were insufficiently "substantial"); Terminiello v. Chicago, 337 U.S. 1, 4 (1949) ("[F]reedom of speech, though not absolute, . . . is nevertheless protected against censorship or punishment, unless shown likely to produce a clear and present danger of a serious substantive evil that rises far above public inconvenience [or] annoyance . . . ."); Bridges v. California, 314 U.S. 252, 263 (1941) ("[T]he substantive evil must be extremely serious and the degree of imminence extremely high before utterances can be punished."); Schneider v. State, 308 U.S. 147, 162 (1939) (public interest in clean streets insufficient to justify antihandbilling ordinance). *See also* Time, Inc. v. Hill, 385 U.S. 374 (1976) (family who had declined to sell rights in their story involving intrusion by escaping

felons into their home, who plainly wanted no attention, and who were placed in false (but not unflattering) light by a Life Magazine story, recovered money damages under New York privacy statutes but the judgment was reversed in the Supreme Court). See the excellent discussion of these issues in Kalven, *Privacy in Tort Law—Were Warren and Brandeis Wrong?*, 31 LAW & CONTEMP. PROBS. 326 (1966); Kalven, *The Concept of the Public Forum*, 1965 SUP. CT. REV. 1.

There is, incidentally, a tendency to say that a statute directly abridging speech must serve a "compelling state interest" rather than that it must be necessary to avoid a "serious evil." *See, e.g.*, L. TRIBE, AMERICAN CONSTITUTIONAL LAW 602 (1978). In certain respects, this different figure of speech seems to be just as good, retaining as it does the notion that something more than interests suitable to sustain the police power in general must clearly be forthcoming in first amendment cases. Because of the facile use of this phrase ("compelling state interest") in connection with other clauses in the Constitution (*e.g.*, the equal protection clause of the fourteenth amendment), however, we may come to regret the tendency to use it in connection with the free speech clause. Other clauses are not as emphatic as the first amendment, a difference that sets this clause apart. If (as seems desirable) one wants to retain a special stringency for the first amendment, it may be vital to avoid linguistic usages that tend to blur or merge its treatment with cases, doctrines, and standards drawn from less robust sections in the Constitution.

47. An excellent example is raised by the facts of Missouri v. National Org. for Women, Inc., 620 F.2d 1301 (1980), *cert. denied*, 101 U.S. 122 (1981). The NOW campaign for convention boycotts of states that had not ratified the equal rights amendment was found to be protected by the first amendment right to petition the government and was not an illegal restraint of trade or intentional infliction of economic harm. Since the NOW boycott was causing revenue losses by Missouri motel and restaurant owners as part of its efforts to influence the votes of state legislators, the issue was whether the government can forbid such economic "persuasion." It is factually correct to characterize such efforts as a "conspiracy" to induce a "secondary boycott" that has as its objective the coercion of third parties (business enterprises) to express support for legislative changes they do not in fact desire. It is also factually correct to characterize such efforts as the peaceful communication of truthful information enabling each citizen to decide according to his own conscience whether, in these circumstances, he or she wishes to take the information into account and, indeed, in what way to take it into account. *See also* NAACP. v. Claiborne Hardware Co., 102 S. Ct. 3409 (1982), and compare International Longshoreman's Ass'n, AFL-CIO v. Allied International, 102 S. Ct. 1656 (1982).

The Supreme Court has suggested that even high-powered private propaganda, aimed at the body politic to persuade the public to influence Congress to adopt laws destructive to competition and of selfish economic advantage to the group mounting that campaign, is fully protected by the first amendment. Eastern R.R. Presidents Conf. v. Noerr Motor Freight, Inc., 365 U.S. 127 (1961). *See also* First National Bank of Boston v. Bellotti, 435 U.S. 765 (1978). The Court has also made clear, however, that government itself may not exert duress on private parties to compel insincere expression of political support. Wooley v. Maynard, 430 U.S. 705 (1977); West Virginia State Bd. of Education v. Barnette, 319 U.S. 624 (1943). *See also* Branti v. Finkel, 100 S. Ct. 1287 (1980); Elrod v. Burns, 427 U.S. 347 (1970). But none of these cases is especially instructive.

A bit closer to the point, the Court has sustained state laws that would restrict the dissemination of even truthful information when done for the purpose of stimulating an economic boycott to induce a business practice that would itself violate a valid law (Giboney v. Empire Storage & Ice Co., 336 U.S. 490 (1949)), but that issue is plainly not involved in this problem since an insincere expression of enthusiasm for the equal rights amendment by Missouri businessmen would violate no law. In dicta, the Court has also suggested that circulating information to induce a boycott to force a change in the targeted business's own business practice may not be constitutionally prohibitable, despite the boycott's coercive effect. *See* Organization for Better Austin v. Keefe, 402 U.S. 415, 419 (1971) ("The claim that the expressions were intended to exercise a coercive impact on respondent does not remove them from the reach of the First Amendment."); NAACP. v. Claiborne Hardware Co., *supra*. But this, too, is inconclusive.

Indeed, the critical question has been avoided by judicial hesitancy to find any existing law addressed squarely to the crucial issue. A fair test would suppose a statute framed in the following way:

It shall be unlawful for any person or combination of persons to coerce or attempt to coerce any other person in respect to his vote in any election or the manner in which he chooses to exercise his freedom to speak or not to speak on any political issue or candidate, including within this prohibition the truthful communication to third-party persons of information imparted for the purpose and with the effect of inducing a boycott of the person whose vote or expression of political belief is meant thereby to be coerced, except insofar as that person holds public office or is a candidate for public office.

Doubtless, speech may be used to coerce legislators to vote for propositions, despite their views respecting the merits, under the duress of being boycotted at the polls. Whether it is consistent with the first amendment that private citizens may also be coerced into insincere expressions of political support by speech-induced economic pressure, however, has not yet been determined.

In Osborn v. Pennsylvania-Delaware Serv. Station Dealers Ass'n, 449 F. Supp. 553 (D. Del. 1980), a motion to dismiss a private (consumer) antitrust action was denied in an opinion disapproving the court of appeals' reasoning in the NOW case and holding that boycotts instituted to induce consumers to exert political pressure on government are neither exempt from the Sherman Act nor protected by the first amendment. *Id.* at 558 n.8. For a discussion (and reference to cases) related to this fascinating problem, see Hersbergen, *Picketing by Aggrieved Consumers—A Case Law Analysis*, 59 IOWA L. REV. 1097 (1974); Note, *NOW or Never: Is There Antitrust Liability for Noncommercial Boycotts?*, 80 COLUM. L. REV. 1317 (1980); Note, *Concerted Refusals to Deal by Non-Business Groups: A Critique of Missouri v. NOW*, 49 GEO. WASH. L. REV. 143 (1980); Note, *Political Boycott Activity and the First Amendment*, 91 HARV. L. REV. 659 (1978); Note, *First Amendment Analysis of Peaceful Picketing*, 28 ME. L. REV. 203 (1976); Note, *Protest Boycotts under the Sherman Act*, 128 U. PA. L. REV. 1131 (1980).

48. *See* notes 18–22 and accompanying text *supra*.

49. *See* quotations and references at notes 16 and 43 *supra*.

50. A timely example is provided by the Supreme Court's recent commercial case, Metromedia, Inc. v. City of San Diego, 101 S. Ct. 2882 (1981). The plurality opinion bifurcates commercial speech, declaring that some is not protected at all by the first amendment and that the protected speech is subject to restriction if (but only if) three conditions are met:

> We [have] adopted a four-part test for determining the validity of government restrictions on commercial speech as distinguished from more fully protected speech. (1) The First Amendment protects commercial speech only if that speech concerns lawful activity and is not misleading. A restriction on otherwise protected commercial speech is valid only if it (2) seeks to implement a substantial governmental interest, (3) directly advances that interest, and (4) reaches no farther than necessary to accomplish the given objective.

Id. at 2892.

51. *See* notes 6, 16, 20 *supra*. *See also* E. HUDON, FREEDOM OF SPEECH AND PRESS IN AMERICA (1963); F. SIEBERT, FREEDOM OF THE PRESS IN ENGLAND 1476–1776 (1952); sources cited in Rabban, *supra* note 6, at 560 nn.236–41; Bogen, *The Origins of Freedom of Speech and Press*, 42 MD. L. REV. 429 (1983).

52. *See* note 17 *supra* for an example of the vigor and confidence with which mutually exclusive views have been put forth respecting the ratification of the first amendment as a repudiation, or as an absorption, of the common law of seditious libel.

53. *See* notes 16 and 18 *supra*.

54. This sort of dichotomy within the speech clause has also been defended on purely prudential grounds. Thus, Professor Tribe suggests:

> In retrospect, the two-level theory may well have served a vital purpose in protecting first amendment doctrine from general erosion by walling out entirely those categories of expression that the Court was unready to protect but could not hold punishable as clear and present dangers without diluting the meaning of that phrase.

L. TRIBE, *supra* note 46, at 671.

55. The following observation is, alas, not a parody of the case law of the last twenty years but

a concise summary of it: "[T]he Court ha[s] moved from a view in which the obscene was unprotected because utterly worthless (Roth), to an approach in which the obscene was unprotected if utterly worthless (Memoirs), to a conclusion in which obscenity was unprotected even if not "utterly" without worth (Miller)." *Id.* at 661.

56. Probably the leading example is the differentiated first amendment standards that must be met as prerequisite for recovering damages for libel, *e.g.*, whether the plaintiff is a political official (or at least a "public figure") or a private figure uninvolved in government. *See* Time, Inc. v. Firestone, 424 U.S. 448 (1976); Gertz v. Robert Welch, Inc., 418 U.S. 323 (1974); New York Times Co. v. Sullivan, 376 U.S. 254 (1964). For general discussions ranking speech protection according to its bearing upon government and social change, see A. MEIKLEJOHN, FREE SPEECH AND ITS RELATIONS TO SELF-GOVERNMENT (1948); Blasi, *The Checking Value in First Amendment Theory*, 1977 AM. B. FOUNDATION RESEARCH J. 521; Kalven, *The New York Times Case: A Note on "The Central Meaning of the First Amendment*," 1964 SUP. CT. REV. 191.

57. As previously noted (note 49 *supra*), the Court currently takes the view that some commercial speech is wholly unprotected while that which is protected nonetheless is subject to restriction on grounds less demanding than if noncommercial ideological communication were involved. Metromedia, Inc. v. City of San Diego, 101 S. Ct. 2882, 2890 nn.11 and 12 (1981). For a recent helpful review and analysis on the subject, see Farber, *Commercial Speech and First Amendment Theory*, 74 Nw. U.L. REV. 372 (1979).

58. *See* Cohen v. California, 403 U.S. 15 (1971).

59. U.S. Const. amend. XIV, § 1 (1868).

60. Gitlow v. New York, 268 U.S. 652, 666 (1925) (dictum). Stromberg v. California, 283 U.S. 359 (1931), and Fiske v. Kansas, 274 U.S. 380 (1927), reversed state convictions on free speech related grounds. Finally, in 1931 the Supreme Court for the first time held a state statute invalid under the fourteenth amendment as violative of first amendment free speech standards. Near v. Minnesota, 283 U.S. 697 (1931), *reviewed in* F. FRIENDLY, MINNESOTA RAG (1981). Not until 1965 was an act of Congress actually held invalid under the free speech clause of the first amendment. Lamont v. Postmaster Gen., 381 U.S. 301 (1965).

61. Whitney v. California, 274 U.S. 357, 373 (1927) (Brandeis, J., dissenting) ("Despite arguments to the contrary which had seemed to me persuasive, it is settled that the due process clause of the Fourteenth Amendment applies to matters of substantive law as well as to matters of procedure.").

62. Roth v. United States, 354 U.S. 476, 503 (1957) (dissenting opinion).

63. The most recent examination of this endlessly discussed question, with suitable references to the principal previous writings and cases, is Curtis. *The Fourteenth Amendment and the Bill of Rights*, 14 CONN. L. REV. 237 (1982); Curtis, *The Bill of Rights as a Limitation on State Authority: A Reply to Professor Berger*, 16 WAKE FOREST L. REV. 45 (1980). As others have also noted, Mr. Curtis quite sensibly suggests that the privileges and immunities clause of the fourteenth amendment, as compared with the due process clause, is semantically less awkward and historically better linked as the principal clause in the association of substantive rights with protection from abridgments by state government.

64. As suggested by Chief Justice Stone in United States v. Carolene Prods. Co., 304 U.S. 144, 152 n.4 (1938):

> There may be a narrower scope for operation of the presumption of constitutionality when legislation appears on its face to be within a specific prohibition of the Constitution, such as those of the first ten amendments, which are deemed equally specific when held to be embraced within the Fourteenth.

Or, as separately defined in the implications of an additional paragraph in the same footnote:

It is not necessary to consider now whether legislation which restricts those political processes [such as freedom of speech and particularly of political criticism?], which can ordinarily be expected to bring about repeal of undesirable legislation, is to be subjected to more exacting judicial scrutiny under the general prohibitions of the Fourteenth Amendment than are most other types of legislation.

65. As suggested by Justice Holmes in Gitlow v. New York, 268 U.S. 652, 672 (1925):

The general principle of free speech, it seems to me, must be included in the Fourteenth Amendment, in view of the scope that has been given to the word "liberty" as there used, although perhaps it may be accepted with a somewhat larger latitude of interpretation than is allowed to Congress by the sweeping language that governs or ought to govern the laws of the United States.

66. Professor Tribe's observation, quoted at note 54 *supra*, respecting the prudential advantage of the Court's "two-level" address to freedom of speech might apply at least as well in this context.

67. Consider Justice Harlan's observation in Roth v. United States, 354 U.S. 476, 506 (1957) (dissenting opinion):

The danger is perhaps not great if the people of one State, through their legislature, decide that [a given book] goes so far beyond the acceptable standards of candor that it will be deemed offensive and non-sellable, for the State next door is still free to make its own choice. At least we do not have one uniform standard. But the dangers to free thought and expression are truly great if the Federal government imposes a blanket ban over the Nation on such a book . . . . [T]hat the people of one State cannot read some [books] seems to me, if not wise or desirable, at least acceptable. But that no person in the United States should be allowed to do so seems to be intolerable, and violative of both the letter and spirit of the First Amendment.

68. *Id.* at 506–7. This proposal encompasses two separate issues. First, it addresses the attenuation of the federal interest (*i.e.*, the commerce power or postal power may provide little foundation for legislating in respect to a variety of subjects of no national significance). Second, it assumes the states have the prerogative to experiment with a more robust regime of free speech when, indeed, the speech subject matter that an act of Congress seeks to regulate is not of such demonstratable importance to submit it to a flat, uniform national policy.

This is but the logical corollary of the proposition that the extent to which states may restrict speech should be at its weakest where states presume to address matters in no way peculiar to local or state concerns but rather address concerns common to the nation at large, *e.g.*, speech deemed threatening to national security. *See* Gilbert v. Minnesota, 254 U.S. 325, 334 (1920) (dissenting opinion); Z. CHAFEE, *supra*, note 6, at 285–98. *See also* Pennsylvania v. Nelson, 350 U.S. 497 (1956) (state law presuming to protect United States from possible sedition deemed preempted); Hines v. Davidowitz, 312 U.S. 52 (1941) (state law imposing additional restrictions on aliens deemed preempted).

69. 426 U.S. 833 (1976). *Usery* was the first case in four decades holding unconstitutional an act of Congress under the interstate commerce power. The tenth amendment was found to limit the authority of the federal government to regulate wage rates of state and local government employees.

70. *See* the quotation from Justice Harlan at note 67 *supra*. Dissenting in *Roth*, Harlan nonetheless concurred in the companion case of Alberts v. California, 354 U.S. 476 (1957), upholding a state anti-obscenity statute and relying on the federalism distinction that states have greater latitude in respect to this subject than does the national government.

71. *See* discussion and case at note 68 *supra* for the suggestion that the states' police powers are weakest in the face of free speech claims when the states presume to act on behalf of interests not particular to the state or local community but on subjects of national concern or of international implication.

72. United States v. Butler, 297 U.S. 1, 62 (1936).

73. Whether under the common law of seditious libel, the Race Relations Act, the Official Secrets Act, varieties of contempt powers, anti-obscenity (or "decency") acts, privacy laws, disorderly conduct, breach of peace, commercial regulations, permit controls, parliamentary supremacy principles, or the simple absence of a "first amendment" as the basis for resisting equivalent "laws," it is at least highly doubtful whether equivalently protective decisions can be found among the English decisions for any but a very few of the following cases: Bates v. State Bar, 433 U.S. 350 (1977); Linmark Assocs. v. Township of Willingboro, 431 U.S. 85 (1977); Wooley v. Maynard, 430 U.S. 705 (1977); Nebraska Press Ass'n v. Stuart, 427 U.S. 539 (1976); Virginia State Bd. of Pharmacy v. Virginia Citizens Consumer Council, 425 U.S. 748 (1976); Erznoznik v. City of Jacksonville, 22 U.S. 205 (1975); Cox Broadcasting Corp. v. Cohn, 420 U.S. 469 (1975); Miami Herald Publishing Co. v. Tornillo, 418 U.S. 241 (1974); Lewis v. City of New Orleans, 415 U.S. 130 (1974); Hess v. Indiana, 414 U.S. 105 (1973); Grayned v. City of Rockford, 408 U.S. 104 (1972); Gooding v. Wilson, 405 U.S. 518 (1972); New York Times Co. v. United States, 403 U.S. 713 (1971); Rosenbloom v. Metromedia, Inc., 403 U.S. 29 (1971); Cohen v. California, 403 U.S. 15 (1971); Organization for Better Austin v. Keefe, 402 U.S. 415 (1971); Brandenburg v. Ohio, 395 U.S. 444 (1969); Tinker v. Des Moines School Dist., 393 U.S. 503 (1969); United States v. Robel, 389 U.S. 258 (1967); Redrup v. New York, 386 U.S. 767 (1967); Time, Inc. v. Hill, 385 U.S. 274 (1967); Brown v. Louisiana, 383 U.S. 131 (1966); Rosenblatt v. Baer, 383 U.S. 75 (1966); Cox v. Louisiana, 379 U.S. 559 (1965); Garrison v. Louisiana, 379 U.S. 64 (1964); New York Times Co. v. Sullivan, 376 U.S. 254 (1964); Kunz v. New York, 340 U.S. 290 (1951); Terminiello v. Chicago, 337 U.S. 1 (1949); Craig v. Harney, 331 U.S. 367 (1947); Pennakamp v. Florida, 328 U.S. 331 (1946); Thomas v. Collins, 323 U.S. 516 (1945); Hartzel v. United States, 322 U.S. 680 (1944); Bridges v. California, 314 U.S. 252 (1941); Schneider v. State, 308 U.S. 147 (1939); Lovell v. City of Griffin, 303 U.S. 444 (1938); Grosjean v. American Press Co., 297 U.S. 233 (1936). The vast majority of cases providing effective vindication of first amendment rights against state and local measures do not generate any review in the Supreme Court. For an impressive recent example, see Collin v. Smith, 447 F. Supp. 676 (N.D. Ill.), aff'd, 578 F.2d 1197 (7th Cir. 1978). See also Skokie v. National Socialist Party, 69 Ill. 2d 605, 373 N.E.2d 21, 14 Ill. Dec. 890 (1978).

74. See H. STREET, FREEDOM, THE INDIVIDUAL AND THE LAW (1982), and compare the first amendment cases at note 73 supra.

75. See note 1 supra.

2. The Controverted Uses of the Press Clause

1. Schenck v. United States, 249 U.S. 47 (1919).

2. New York Times Co. v. Sullivan, 376 U.S. 254 (1964).

3. Schneider v. State, 308 U.S. 147 (1939); Lovell v. City of Griffin, 303 U.S. 444 (1938).

4. Branzburg v. Hayes, 408 U.S. 665 (1972).

5. See cases and discussion at note 7 chapter 1 supra.

6. For other discussions on these questions, see, e.g., Abrams, The Press Is Different: Reflections on Justice Stewart and the Autonomous Press, 7 HOFSTRA L. REV. 563 (1979); Bezanson, The New Free Press Guarantee, 63 VA. L. REV. 731 (1977); Blanchard, The Institutional Press and Its First Amendment Privileges, 1978 SUP. CT. REV. 225; Ingber, Defamation: A Conflict Between Reason and Decency, 65 VA. L. REV. 785 (1979); Jaxa-Debicki, Problems in Defining the Institutional Status of the Press, RICH. L. REV. 177 (1976); Lange, The Speech and Press Clauses, 23 U.C.L.A. L. REV. 77 (1975); Lewis, A Preferred Position for Journalism?, 7 HOFSTRA L. REV. 595 (1979); Nimmer, Introduction—Is Freedom of the Press a Redundancy: What Does It Add to Freedom of

Speech?, 26 HASTINGS L.J. 639 (1975); Oakes, *Proof of Actual Malice in Defamation Actions: An Unsolved Dilemma*, 7 HOFSTRA L. REV. 655 (1979); Sack, *Reflections on the Wrong Question: Special Constitutional Privilege for the Institutional Press*, 7 HOFSTRA L. REV. 629 (1979); Stonecipher, *Safeguarding Speech and Press Guarantees: Preferred Position Postulate Reexamined*, in THE FIRST AMENDMENT RECONSIDERED 89 (1982) (B. CHAMBERLAIN & C. BROWN eds.); Comment, *Examining the Institutional Interpretation of the Press Clause*, 58 TEX. L. REV. 171 (1979).

7. 4 W. BLACKSTONE, COMMENTARIES ON THE LAWS OF ENGLAND 151 (Oxford 1769). *See also* Lord Mansfield's charge to the jury in Miller's Case, 20 Howell's State Trials, 860, 895 (1770): "As for freedom of the press, I will tell you what it is; the liberty of the press is, that a man may print what he pleases without license; as long as it remains so the liberty of the press is not restrained."

8. *See, e.g.*, Nebraska Press Ass'n v. Stuart, 427 U.S. 539 (1976), and New York Times Co. v. United States, 403 U.S. 713 (1971), and compare Times Film Corp. v. Chicago, 375 U.S. 43 (1961) (sustaining a municipal film licensing board).

9. The principal cases are reviewed, and the media-nonmedia distinction critically examined in Note, *Mediaocracy and Mistrust: Extending New York Times Defamation Protection to Nonmedia Defendants*, 95 HARV. L. REV. 1876 (1982).

10. Address by Justice Stewart before the Yale Law School Sesquicentennial Convocation, New Haven, Conn. (Nov. 2, 1974), *reprinted in part* as *Or of the Press*, 26 HASTINGS L.J. 631 (1975).

11. Branzburg v. Hayes, 408 U.S. 665, 721 (1972) (Douglas, J., dissenting).

12. The subject is discussed and supportive cases are provided in Van Alstyne, *The Specific Theory of Academic Freedom and the General Issue of Civil Liberty*, in THE CONCEPT OF ACADEMIC FREEDOM 59 (E. Pincoffs ed. 1972), *reprinted in* THE CONSTITUTIONAL STATUS OF ACADEMIC FREEDOM (W. Metzger ed. 1977). *See also* R. HOFSTADER & W. METZGER, THE DEVELOPMENT OF ACADEMIC FREEDOM IN THE UNITED STATES (1955); LOVEJOY, 1 ENCYCLOPEDIA OF THE SOCIAL SCIENCES 384–88 (1937); Morrow, *Academic Freedom*, ENCYCLOPEDIA OF SOCIAL SCIENCES (1968).

13. Regents of the Univ. of Calif. v. Bakke, 438 U.S. 265 (1978) (emphasis added).

14. Branzburg v. Hayes, 408 U.S. 665, 721 (1972) (Douglas, J., dissenting).

15. Saxbe v. Washington Post Co., 417 U.S. 843, 863 (1974) (Powell, J., dissenting).

16. *See* Blasi, *The Checking Value in First Amendment Theory*, 1977 AM. B. FOUNDATION RESEARCH J. 521; Mills v. Alabama, 384 U.S. 214, 219 (1966) ("Thus the press serves and was designed to serve as a powerful antidote to any abuses of power by governmental officials and as a constitutionally chosen means for keeping officials elected by the people responsible to all the people whom they were selected to serve."); Madison, in 4 ANNALS OF CONG. 934 (1794) ("If we advert to the nature of Republican Government, we shall find that the censorial power is in the people over the Government, and not in the Government over the people.").

17. 1 ANNALS OF CONG. 451 (1789) (emphasis added). The particularly strong emphasis upon the press is similar to that in the Virginia Resolution of Independence, adopted June 12, 1776. ("The freedom of the press is one of the greatest bulwarks of liberty, and can never be restrained by any despotic government.") See also the impressive review of this subject in Anderson, *The Origins of the Press Clause*, 30 U.C.L.A. L. REV. 456 (1983).

18. *See* Stewart, *"Or of the Press,"* 26 HASTING L.J. 631, 634 (1975); L. LEVY, LEGACY OF SUPPRESSION: FREEDOM OF SPEECH AND PRESS IN EARLY AMERICAN HISTORY (1960); L. LEVY, FREEDOM OF THE PRESS FROM ZENGER TO JEFFERSON (1966); F. SIEBERT, FREEDOM OF THE PRESS

IN ENGLAND, 1476–1776 (1952); *discussion and citations in* Lange, *The Speech and Press Clauses*, 23 U.C.L.A. L. REV. 77, 88–97 (1975).

19. *See e.g.*, his letter to John Norvell, written in 1807, *reprinted in part in* THE LIFE AND SELECTED WRITINGS OF THOMAS JEFFERSON 581 (A. Koch & W. Peden eds. 1944):

Nothing can now be believed which is seen in a newspaper. Truth itself becomes suspicious by being put into that polluted vehicle. . . . I will add, that the man who never looks into a newspaper is better informed than he who reads them; inasmuch as he who knows nothing is nearer to truth than he whose mind is filled with falsewords and errors.

See generally L. LEVY, JEFFERSON AND CIVIL LIBERTIES (1953).

20. *Recorded in* W. CHENERY, FREEDOM OF THE PRESS 29 (1955).

21. Note 1 *supra*.

22. Gitlow v. New York, 268 U.S. 652 (1925).

23. Note 2 *supra*.

24. 448 U.S. 555 (1980). For a case (prematurely) suggesting quite a different view, see Gannett Co. v. DePasquale, 443 U.S. 368 (1979). For subsequent cases enlarging upon the *Richmond Newspapers* holding, see Globe Newspaper Co. v. Superior Court, 102 S. Ct. 2613 (1982); Press-Enterprise Co. v. Superior Court, 52 U.S.L.W. 4113 (1984). For an elaborate exploration of the implications, see Note, *Press Access to Government-Controlled Information and the Alternative Means Test*, 59 TEXAS L. REV. 1289 (1981).

25. *See, e.g.*, Gannett Co. v. DePasquale, note 24 *supra* (access sought to pretrial hearing); Houchins v. KQED, Inc., 438 U.S. 1 (1978); Pell v. Procunier, 417 U.S. 817 (1974); Saxbe v. Washington Post Co., 417 U.S. 843 (1974) (access to prisons and to prisoners). The efforts are supported by James Madison's observation that "[a] popular Government, without popular information, or the means of acquiring it, is but a prologue to a Farce or a Tragedy; or, perhaps both." 9 WRITINGS OF JAMES MADISON 103 (G. Hunt ed. 1910).

26. 307 U.S. 496 (1939).

27. *See* Kalven, *The Concept of the Public Forum*, 1965 SUP. CT. REV. 1; Stone, *Fora Americana: Speech in Public Places*, 1974 SUP. CT. REV. 233. The decision in *Hague* discarded the earlier prevailing view of Holmes, in Davis v. Massachusetts, 162 Mass 510, *aff'd*, 167 U.S. 43 (1897) ("For the legislature absolutely or conditionally to forbid public speaking in a highway or public park is no more an infringement on the rights of a member of the public than for the owner of a private house to forbid it in the house."). For a general review tracing the change in Holmes' thinking and the gradual change in first amendment interpretation, see Van Alstyne, *The Demise of the Right-Privilege Distinction in Constitutional Law*, 81 HARV. L. REV. 1439 (1968); Bogen, *The Free Speech Metamorphosis of Mr. Justice Holmes*, 11 HOFSTRA L. REV. 97 (1982).

28. *Compare* Lamont v. Postmaster General, 381 U.S. 301 (1965) (addressee of mail has first amendment standing successfully to contest conditions attached to withholding of mail sent from abroad). The case is of special interest; not only is it the first to establish a reciprocal (addressee's) first amendment right, it is actually the first decision ever to hold invalid an act of Congress on first amendment grounds.

29. 448 U.S. 555, 582 (1980).

30. *See* the rephrasing (and discussion) of that general first amendment standard at p. 48, chapter 1.

31. 448 U.S. 572–73 (1980).

32. *Id.* at 581, n. 18.

33. *Id.* at 586, n. 2.

34. Houchins v. KQED, Inc., 438 U.S. 1 (1978).

35. *See, e.g.*, Branzburg v. Hayes, 408 U.S. 665 (1972) (grand jury subpoena of journalist sustained against claim of privilege); Zurcher v. Stanford Daily, 436 U.S. 547 (1978) (search warrant for mere evidence in newspaper files sustained against claim of privilege); Herbert v. Lando, 441 U.S. 153 (1979) (endless deposition of journalist sustained against claim of privilege).

36. Dissenting in *Zurcher* (*supra*), Justice Potter Stewart tentatively moved to the position he had suggested in his Yale Law School address (436 U.S. at 576):

> Perhaps as a matter of abstract policy a newspaper office should receive no more protection from unannounced police searches than, say, the office of a doctor or the office of a bank. But we are here to uphold a Constitution. And our Constitution does not explicitly protect the practice of medicine or the business of banking from all abridgments by government. It does explicitly protect freedom of the press.

On the other hand, rejection of the notion that the press is unique within the first amendment does not mean that therefore the first amendment is of no importance when compelled disclosure may well have an inhibiting effect on third-party, highly protected free speech interests (*e.g.*, political interests). Toward the conclusion of chapter 1, we noted that the more central to political participation the subject of one's speech may be, the more protected from otherwise valid regulations it is as well. Within first amendment cases of compelled disclosure, that consideration has tended to be well respected. *See, e.g.*, Gibson v. Florida Legislative Investigation Comm., 372 U.S. 539 (1963) (refusal to disclose members of NAACP sustained); Shelton v. Tucker, 364 U.S. 479 (1960) (refusal to list memberships sustained); Slochower v. Board of Higher Educ., 350 U.S. 551 (1946) (refusal to disclose substance of university lectures sustained); Brown v. Socialist Workers '74 Campaign Committee, 103 S. Ct. 416 (1982) (refusal to list contributors to minor and unpopular political party sustained). The question is thus not simply from whom the disclosure is sought (whether a newspaper, a bank, an attorney, or a political party) but rather of whom and with respect to what subject, and why.

37. That is, this is the "general rule" for defamation of private (as distinct from public) figures, although arguably persons not members of "the press" may not be protected even to this extent. *See, e.g.*, cases cited at note 32 of Abrams, *The Press is Different: Reflections on Justice Stewart and the Autonomous Press*, 7 HOFSTRA L. REV.. 563 (1979). See Gertz v. Robert Welch, Inc., 418 U.S. 323 (1974); Wolston v. Reader's Digest Ass'n, 443 U.S. 157 (1979). *See also* the discussion in Ingber, *supra* note 6, at 785.

The general case for calibrating the degree of protection according to the subject matter of the speech is well defended in BeVier, *The First Amendment and Political Speech: An Inquiry Into the Substance and Limits of Principle*, 30 STAN. L. REV. 299 (1978). Having originally accepted the notion that "the press" should absorb special (*i.e.*, institutional) protection, Judge James Oakes subsequently concluded (for reasons not unlike those canvassed *infra*, in this chapter) that the approach was fundamentally unsound. Oakes, *Proof of Actual Malice in Defamation Actions: An Unsolved Dilemma*, 7 HOFSTRA L. REV.. 655, 720 (1979):

> [M]y concurring opinion in *Herbert* [the case involving prolonged civil discovery in a libel action] partly relied upon a differentiation between the free press and free speech clauses, a position that Justice Stewart first expressly advanced. That differentiation, however, is both unprovable from the perspective of the Framers' intent and conceptually debatable; its most serious failing is that it can be construed to afford greater protection to the "institutional" press than to the individual speaker or publisher and contains no justification for such a special privilege.

38. *See, e.g.*, Torcaso v. Watkins, 367 U.S. 448 (1961); United States v. Seeger, 380 U.S. 163 (1965); Welsh v. United States, 398 U.S. 333 (1979); United States v. Ballard, 322 U.S. 78 (1944);

Note, *Toward a Constitutional Definition of Religion*, 91 HARV. L. REV. 1056 (1978). For a recent effort to narrow the controlling definition substantially, see Choper, *Defining "Religion" in the First Amendment*, 1982 U. ILL. L. REV. 579 (1982); Note, *The Sacred and the Profane: A First Amendment Definition of Religion*, 61 TEX. L. REV. 139 (1982).

39. Miami Herald Publishing Co. v. Tornillo, 418 U.S. 241 (1974), discussed at length in chapter 3 *infra*. For recent writing reflecting the persistence of efforts to commandeer newspapers in the public interest, see, e.g., Yackle *Confessions of a Horizontalist: A Dialogue on the First Amendment*, 27 KAN. L. REV. 541 (1979); Note, *Access to the Press: A Teleological Analysis of a Constitutional Double Standard*, 50 GEO. WASH. L. REV. 530 (1982).

40. *See* 1 E. ARBER, A TRANSCRIPT OF THE REGISTERS OF THE COMPANY OF STATIONERS OF LONDON xxviii (1975); C. BLAGDEN, THE STATIONERS COMPANY: A HISTORY (1960). Henry VIII had issued an index of prohibited books in 1529; licensing set in the following year. F. SIEBERT, *supra* note 18, at 2.

41. *Id. See also* F. SIEBERT, T. PETERSON & W. SCHRAMM, FOUR THEORIES OF THE PRESS 2 (1956) ("Since the beginnings of mass communication, in the Renaissance, there have been only two or four basic theories of the press—two or four, that is, according to how one counts them. . . . [T]he oldest is the Authoritarian."); E. HUDON, FREEDOM OF SPEECH AND PRESS IN AMERICA 9–11 (1963). The reference to general warrants and writs of assistance makes it useful to remember that the first amendment is not the only portion of the American Constitution influenced by historic speech-and-press concerns. See, e.g., the fourth amendment (forbidding general warrants); article III sec. 3 (defining "treason" to eliminate constructive treason); article I sec. 6 (specially protecting speech and debate in either house of Congress). Insofar as the first amendment itself was but a restriction on Congress (leaving to the states whatever regimes of control each preferred), the legacy of press prosecutions was depressing. *See* L. LEVY, LEGACY OF SUPPRESSION: FREEDOM OF SPEECH AND PRESS IN EARLY AMERICAN HISTORY (1960); L. LEVY, FREEDOM OF THE PRESS FROM ZENGER TO JEFFERSON (1966).

42. *See* materials cited in nn. 40 and 41 *supra*.

43. *See* H. STREET, FREEDOM, THE INDIVIDUAL AND THE LAW (5th ed. 1982).

44. W. BLACKSTONE, *supra* note 7, at 151–52:
The liberty of the press is indeed essential to the nature of a free state: but this consists in laying no *previous* restraints upon publications, and not in freedom from censure for criminal matter when published. Every freeman has an undoubted right to lay what sentiments he pleases before the public: to forbid this, is to destroy the freedom of the press: but if he publishes what is improper, mischievous, or illegal, he must take the consequences of his own temerity.

45. J. LOFTON, THE PRESS AS GUARDIAN OF THE FIRST AMENDMENT 279 (1980).

46. Lewis, *A Preferred Position for Journalism?*, 7 HOFSTRA L. REV. 595, 626 (1979) (footnotes omitted).

47. *See* discussion and notes in chapter 3 *infra*.

48. CBS v. Democratic Nat'l Comm., 412 U.S. 94 (1973) (Douglas, J., concurring).

49. T. JEFFERSON, DEMOCRACY 150–51 (S. Padover ed. 1939).

50. *See* authors cited at note 6 *supra*. *See also* J. BARRON, PUBLIC RIGHTS AND THE PRIVATE PRESS (1981); J. BARRON, FREEDOM OF THE PRESS FOR WHOM? THE RIGHT OF ACCESS TO MASS MEDIA (1973); T. EMERSON, THE SYSTEM OF FREEDOM OF EXPRESSION 670–71 (1970); Barron, *Access to the Press—A New First Amendment Right*, 80 HARV. L. REV. 1641 (1967).

51. Nadel, *A Unified Theory of the First Amendment: Divorcing the Medium from the Message*, 11 FORDHAM URBAN L.J. 163 (1983).

3. Scarcity, Property, and Government Policy

1. *See* chapter 2, pp. 61, 64–65 *supra*.

2. The development of the FCC's various speech-content regulations is very well (and elaborately) presented in Simmons, *Fairness Doctrine: The Early History*, 29 FED. COM. B. J. 207 (1976); Hegelin, *The First Amendment Stake in New Technology: The Broadcast-Cable Controversy*, 44 U. CIN. L. REV. 427 (1975). A critical, updated review is provided by Fowler and Brenner, *A Marketplace Approach to Broadcast Regulation*, 60 TEXAS L. REV. 207–33 (1982). The last comprehensive summary of the fairness doctrine rules is in *In re the Handling of Public Issues under the Fairness Doctrine and the Public Interest Standards of the Communications Act*, 30 RAD. REG. 2d (P & F) 1261 (July 12, 1974). A description of applicant responsibilities to ascertain community problems is provided in Ascertainment of Community Problems by Broadcast Applicants, 57 F.C.C.2d 418 (1975), *modified*, 61 F.C.C.2d 1 (1976). A description of the fourteen program categories broadcasters are obliged to consider (to meet the "public-interest" standard) is in 44 F.C.C. 2303 *et seq.* (1960).

3. Red Lion Broadcasting Co. v. FCC, 395 U.S. 367 (1969); Miami Herald Publishing Co. v. Tornillo, 418 U.S. 241 (1974).

4. W. Parker, unpublished paper at Duke Law School.

5. 47 U.S.C. §§ 151–609 (1970) (originally enacted as Federal Communications Act of June 19, 1934, ch. 652, 48 Stat. 1064).

6. Radio Act, ch. 169, 44 Stat. 1162 (pt. II) (1927) (repealed 1934). *See also* Radio Act of 1912, ch. 287, 37 Stat. 302 (1912), *repealed by* Communications Act of 1934, ch. 652 § 602(a), 48 Stat. 1064, 1192.

7. *See* discussion and references at note 40, chapter 2 *supra*.

8. 48 Stat. 1091, 47 U.S.C. § 326:

Nothing in this Act shall be understood or construed to give the Commission the power of censorship over the radio communications or signals transmitted by a radio station, and no regulation or condition shall be promulgated or fixed by the Commission which shall interfere with the right of free speech by means of radio communication.

9. FCC v. Pacifica Foundation, 438 U.S. 726, 735 (1978). ("The prohibition against censorship unequivocally denies the Commission any power to edit proposed broadcasts in advance [but does not] deny the Commission the power to review the content of completed broadcasts in the performance of its regulatory duties.") The case sustained an FCC declaratory order against the midafternoon radio broadcast of a satiric commercial record (George Carlin's "Filthy Words" monologue), with the FCC's order being placed in the licensee's file for such subsequent use as the FCC would be empowered to make of such infractions, including license revocation, nonrenewal, or imposition of a monetary forfeiture. The decision by the Supreme Court is critically reviewed in Krattenmaker & Powe, *Televised Violence: First Amendment Principles and Social Science Theory*, 64 VA. L. REV. 1123 (1978). The case is troubling as it does not involve "obscene" speech, and the context is clearly one of social comment. The decision as reasoned in Justice Stevens's opinion is very limited, going solely to time, place, and manner. *See also* Young v. American Mini Theatres, Inc., 427 U.S. 50 (1976) (sustaining restrictive zoning of "adult" book stores). *Compare* Cohen v. California, 403 U.S. 15 (1971) (holding unconstitutional a disturbing-the-peace ordinance as applied to a person sporting a vulgar political slogan on the back of his jacket, in the corridor of a county courthouse).

10. 47 U.S.C. §§ 303, 307 (1976).

11. The Interstate Commerce Commission was created in the nineteenth century by the Interstate

Commerce Act, ch. 104, 24 Stat. 379 (1887), but the licensing provisions (current version at 49 U.S.C. § 1(18)–(19) (1970) were not added until 1920. (Subsection (19) was subsequently repealed, Pub. L. No. 94–210, § 801(b), 90 Stat. 127 (1976).

12. *See* references at note 2 *supra*; E. BARNOUW, A HISTORY OF BROADCASTING IN THE UNITED STATES: A TOWER IN BABEL (1966).

13. 47 U.S.C. § 315 (1976). More recently (in 1972), Congress added still another self-favoring provision, namely, a new subsection requiring networks and licensees to furnish "reasonable access" for legally qualified candidates for federal elective office. *See* 47 U.S.C. § 312 (a)(7)(1976), sustained as applied in CBS, Inc. v. FCC, 453 U.S. 367 (1981).

14. NBC v. United States, 319 U.S. 190 (1943). See also Associated Press v. United States, 326 U.S. 1 (1944).

15. Reviewed and sustained in FCC v. National Citizens Committee for Broadcasting, 436 U.S. 775 (1978).

16. "Because these criteria [*i.e.*, program-content criteria] most directly predict what service to expect from an applicant, the Commission cannot avoid considering such criteria under the judgmental directive of the 'public interest.'" Fowler and Brenner, *A Marketplace Approach to Broadcast Regulation*, 60 TEXAS L. REV. 207, 218 (1982).

17. Thus, in NBC v. United States, 319 U.S. 190, 215–16 (1943), Justice Frankfurter noted that "the Act does not restrict the Commission merely to supervision of the traffic. It puts upon the Commission the burden of determining the composition of that traffic."

18. FCC v. Midwest Video (II), 99 S. Ct. 1435 (1979), applying 47 U.S.C. § 153(h) (1976) ("a person engaged in radio broadcasting shall not, insofar as such a person is so engaged, be deemed a common carrier.").

19. *See* Red Lion Broadcasting Co. v. FCC, 395 U.S. 367 (1969), construing the wording of certain amendments to § 315, in 1959 (Act of Sept. 14, 1959, § 1, 73, Stat. 557), as "positive legislation" ratifying nearly all aspects of the "fairness" doctrine as it had been developed administratively over the decades, from "the public interest, convenience, and necessity" language of the original act.

20. *See, e.g.*, references at notes 2 and 12 *supra*. *See also* E. FOSTER, UNDERSTANDING BROADCASTING (1982); M. FRANKLIN, MASS MEDIA LAW—CASES AND MATERIALS 736–922 (2d ed. 1982).

21. *See* Brandywine Main Line Radio, Inc. v. FCC, 473 F.2d 16, 68–80 (D.C. Cir. 1972) (Bazelon, J., dissenting, *aff'g* 27 F.C.C.2d 565 (1972), *cert. denied*, 412 U.S. 922 (1973)).

22. *See, e.g.*, Lange, *The Role for the Access Doctrine in the Regulation of Mass Media: A Critical Review and Assessment*, 52 N.C.L. REV. 1 (1973).

23. Fairness Doctrine and Public Interest Standards, Fairness Report Regarding Handling of Public Issues, 39 Fed. Reg. 26, 372 (1974).

24. *Id. See also* 30 RAD. REG. 2d (P & F) 1277–78 (July 12, 1974); *In re the Handling of Public Issues under the Fairness Doctrine and the Public Interest Standards of the Communications Act*, 30 RAD. REG. (P & F) 1261 (July 12, 1974).

25. All as applied and sustained in Red Lion Broadcasting Co. v. FCC, note 19 *supra*, and as more fully described in the text, *infra* note 36.

26. *See* note 8 *supra*.

27. *See* notes 9, 16, 17, and 21 *supra.*

28. FCC v. Pacifica Foundation, 438 U.S. 736 (1978); Yale Broadcasting Co. v. FCC, 478 F.2d 594 (D.C. Cir.), *cert. denied*, 414 U.S. 914 (1973); Sonderling Broadcasting Corp. v. WGLD-FM, 27 RAD. REG. 2d (P & F) 285 (1973). *Compare* the critical review in Note, *Filthy Words, the FCC and the First Amendment: Regulating Broadcast Obscenity*, 61 VA. L. REV. 579 (1975); Krattenmaker & Powe, *supra* note 9.

29. *See Hearings on Freedom of Expression Before the Senate Comm. on Commerce, Science and Transportation*, 97th Cong., 2d Sess. 3, 115, 123 (1982).

30. Reviewed in M. FRANKLIN, *supra* note 20, at 882–87.

31. *See, e.g.*, National Ass'n of Indep. Television Producers & Distributors v. FCC, 516 F.2d 526 (2d Cir. 1975):

> The result has been . . . that it is largely the cheaper productions, daytime fare, that have been put into cleared prime time slots. What was not anticipated by the Commission was the monotony of the product . . . . The fact is, as the Commission concedes, that the degree of diversity in programming for access time has been disappointing. In the entertainment area, the emphasis has largely been on game shows and animal shows . . . .

32. *See* Writers Guild of America v. FCC, 423 F. Supp. 1064 (C.D. Cal. 1976), vacated and remanded, 609 F.2d 355 (9th Cir. 1979), *cert. denied*, 449 U.S. 824 (1980). For an excellent critical discussion, see Bazelon, *FCC Regulation of the Telecommunications Press*, 1975 DUKE L.J. 213.

33. An elegant example is furnished by FCC v. WNCN Listeners Guild, 482 U.S. 582 (1981). The FCC declined to disallow a format change (from "classical" to "rock" music) incidental to a proposed license transfer; the D.C. Circuit reversed and required that a hearing be held to determine whether the "public interest" would be better served by locking in the original format; on remand the FCC promulgated a policy rejecting the court of appeals approach; the court of appeals over-turned the policy, and the Supreme Court (finally) sustained the commission. For additional ex-amples (of various groups encouraged to intervene in license renewals or transfers, contingent upon their dissatisfaction with what the broadcaster has presented), see M. FRANKLIN, note 20 *supra*, at 782–817.

34. 453 U.S. 367 (1981).

35. Cited at note 13 *supra*.

36. Red Lion Broadcasting Co. v. FCC, 395 U.S. 367 (1969).

37. Miami Herald Publishing Co. v. Tornillo, 418 U.S. 241 (1974).

38. Few of these facts about the *Red Lion* case are taken from the judicial reports of the case. Most, instead, are taken from the excellent description in F. FRIENDLY, THE GOOD GUYS, THE BAD GUYS, AND THE FIRST AMENDMENT (1975), and especially from pp. 5–7.

39. 418 U.S. 241 (1974).

40. FLA. STAT. ANN. § 104.38 (Harrison 1975) (repealed 1975).

41. 287 So. 2d 78 (Fla. 1973).

42. 418 U.S. 258 (1974).

43. 2 Z. CHAFEE, GOVERNMENT AND MASS COMMUNICATIONS 633 (1974), *quoted in* Miami Herald Pub. Co. v. Tornillo, 418 U.S. 254, 258 (1974).

44. 418 U.S. 258 (1974).

45. Noted and ably discussed in B. SCHMIDT, FREEDOM OF THE PRESS VS. PUBLIC ACCESS (1976).

46. 418 U.S. at 251; and see also discussion *id.* at 248–54.

47. Correspondingly, there is an immense diversity of professional writing respecting the relative "rightness" of *Red Lion* and *Tornillo. See e.g.*, J. BARRON, PUBLIC RIGHTS AND THE PRIVATE PRESS (1981); J. BARRON, FREEDOM OF THE PRESS FOR WHOM? (1973); 2 Z. CHAFEE, GOVERNMENT AND MASS COMMUNICATIONS (1947); T. EMERSON, THE SYSTEM OF FREEDOM OF EXPRESSION 670–71 (1970); F. FRIENDLY, THE GOOD GUYS, THE BAD GUYS AND THE FIRST AMENDMENT (1975); W. HOCKING, FREEDOM OF THE PRESS, A FRAMEWORK OF PRINCIPLE (1947); B. OWEN, ECONOMICS AND FREEDOM OF EXPRESSION (1975); B. SCHMIDT, FREEDOM OF THE PRESS VS. PUBLIC ACCESS 1976); Barrow, *The Fairness Doctrine: A Double Standard for Electronic and Print Media*, 26 HASTINGS L.J. 659 (1975); Barrow, *The Equal Opportunities and Fairness Doctrines in Broadcasting: Pillars in the Forum of Democracy*, 37 U. CIN. L. REV. 447 (1968); Bazelon, *FCC Regulation of the Telecommunications Press*, 1975 DUKE L.J. 213; Blake, *Red Lion Broadcasting Co. v. FCC: Fairness and the Emperor's New Clothes*, 23 FED. COM. B.J. 75 (1969); Bollinger, *Freedom of the Press and Public Access: Toward a Theory of Partial Regulation of the Mass Media*, 75 MICH. L. REV. 1 (1976); Coase, *Evaluation of Public Policy Relating to Radio and Television Broadcasting: Social and Economic Issues*, 41 LAND ECON. 161 (1965); Coase, *The Federal Communications Commission*, 2 J.L. & ECON. 1 (1959); Emerson, *Legal Foundations of the Right to Know*, 1976 WASH. U.L.Q. 1; Fowler and Brenner, *A Marketplace Approach to Broadcast Regulation*, 60 TEXAS L. REV. 207 (1982); Freund, *The Great Disorder of Speech*, 44 AM. SCHOLAR 541 (1975); Jaffe, *The Editorial Responsibility of the Broadcaster: Reflections on Fairness and Access*, 85 HARV. L. REV. 768 (1972); Jaffe, *The Fairness Doctrine, Equal Time, Reply to Personal Attacks, and the Local Service Obligation: Implications of Technological Change*, 37 U. CIN. L. REV. 550 (1968); Kalven, *Broadcasting, Public Policy and the First Amendment*, 10 J.L. & ECON. 15 (1967); Karst, *Equality as a Central Principle in the First Amendment*, 43 U. CHI. L. REV. 20 (1975); Loevinger, *Free Speech, Fairness, and Fiduciary Duty in Broacasting*, 34 LAW & CONTEMP. PROB. 278 (1968); Powe, "*Or of the [Broadcast] Press*," 55 TEXAS L. REV. 39 (1976); Robinson, *The FCC and the First Amendment: Observations on 40 Years of Radio and Television Regulation*, 52 MINN. L. REV. 67 (1967); Robinson, *The Federal Communications Commission: An Essay on Regulatory Watchdogs*, 64 VA. L. REV. 169 (1978).

48. 418 U.S. at 256.

49. 395 U.S. at 393.

50. It has been argued, indeed, that the government's regulatory relationship with licensees (pursuant to which it grants an exclusive use-right in public property [an airwave] and stands ready to vindicate that use-right against unlicensed parties) is sufficiently in the nature of a joint ventureship that the FCC is subject to a first amendment obligation to provide access rights in behalf of third parties. For a discussion, see Note, *Constitutional Ramifications of a Repeal of the Fairness Doctrine*, 64 GEO. L.J. 1293 (1976). *Compare* Burton v. Wilmington Parking Authority, 365 U.S. 715 (1961) *with* CBS v. Democratic Nat'l Comm., 412 U.S. 94 (1973).

51. T. JEFFERSON, DEMOCRACY 150–51 (S. Padover ed. 1939), *quoted* in CBS v. Democratic Nat'l Comm., 412 U.S. 94, 153 (1973) (Douglas J., concurring).

52. See note 43 *supra.*

53. Act III, Scene 3. *Compare* Measure for Measure, Act I, Scene 1 ("What's mine is yours, and what is yours is mine.") See also the discussion in note 90 *infra.*

54. It is quite arguable, moreover, that compelled publication of a retraction (or even of a reply), would be entirely appropriate as a remedy incidental to a successful libel action brought against the publisher. In their brief concurring opinion in *Miami Herald*, Justices Rehnquist and Brennan explicitly reserved such a possibility, 418 U.S. at 258.

55. CBS v. Democratic Nat'l Comm., 412 U.S. 94, 148–61 (1973) (Douglas, J., concurring).

56. See, e.g., CBS, Inc. v. FCC, 453 U.S. 367 (1981).

57. See the extended quotation from *Red Lion* at note 58 *infra*, and see also the discussion and references at note 47 *supra*. The "legal disability" referred to, of course, is the fact that by federal statute it is a federal crime to broadcast without a license.

Since it *is* a crime to broadcast even over wavelengths not already licensed to others or reserved exclusively for exigent government use (*e.g.*, police frequencies), this may be the appropriate place to take notice of an interesting first amendment possibility that may not have been adequately considered. The airways are a "natural speech" medium, *i.e.*, their most obvious and traditional use is for communicative purposes. Their use as a means of communication between willing speakers and willing listeners is at least as impressive as the "speech uses" of public streets and public parks where the speech uses of such places often come at the marginal expense of other sorts of uses, *e.g.*, as efficient thoroughfares (in the case of streets) or as quiet places of recreation (in the case of parks). It is very well established first amendment doctrine that the bare fact of government ownership or trusteeship does not exempt such places as streets and parks from use by persons simply wishing to speak there. Rather, such constraints as may be imposed may be justified only as necessary to prevent substantial interference with some other, incompatible activity lawfully taking place there. (See the cases and discussion at note 26 *supra*, in chapter 2.) It is thus a fair question to ask whether an unlicensed party's ad hoc use of an *unused* wavelength can (constitutionally) be deemed a crime or an enjoinable wrong, the Federal Communications Act to the contrary notwithstanding. Applying the general analysis provided in chapter 1, what can be the sufficient basis for abridging a "pirate" broadcaster's speech in these circumstances?

58. 395 U.S. 388, 400–401 (1969) (emphasis added).

59. 30 RAD. REG. 2d (P & F) at 1282 (July 12, 1974).

60. For an impressive critique, see Lange, *the Role of the Access Doctrine in the Regulation of the Mass Media: A Critical Review and Assessment*, 52 N.C.L. REV. 1 (1973).

61. See the very interesting discussion in Geller & Lampert, *Cable, Content Regulation and the First Amendment*, 32 CATH. U.L. REV. 603 (1983).

62. 395 U.S. at 390–91 (emphasis added).

63. For an excellent argument that only such "parliamentary" rules may be both appropriate and constitutionally safe in the government's superintendence of the airwaves as a public forum, see Kalven, *Broadcasting, Public Policy and the First Amendment*, 10 J.L. & ECON. 15 (1967); Kalven, *The Concept of the Public Forum: Cox v. Louisiana*, 1965 SUP. CT. REV. 1.

64. This alternative rationing mechanism, with several variations, is discussed in more detail in the text at note 77 *infra*. It has been strongly advocated by the current chairman of the FCC (1983), Mark Fowler. *See* Fowler & Brenner, *A Marketplace Approach to Broadcast Regulation*, 60 TEXAS L. REV. 207, 242 (1982). ("The Commission would hold an auction to select new users and frequency rights would go to the highest bidders, who under a market theory should put the frequencies to their best use.") The basic analysis was provided by Ronald Coase. See Coase, *Evaluation of Public Policy Relating to Radio and Television Broadcasting: Social and Economic Issues*, 41 LAND ECON. 161 (1965); Coase, *The Federal Communications Commission*, 2 J.L. & ECON. 1 (1959). Additional principal support is offered by B. OWEN, ECONOMICS AND FREEDOM OF EXPRESSION: MEDIA STRUCTURE AND THE FIRST AMENDMENT (1975); De Vany, Eckert, Meyers, O'Hara & Scott, *A Property System for Market Allocation of the Electromagnetic Spectrum: A Legal-Economic-Engineering Study*, 21 STAN L. REV. 1499 (1969). For an argument that such an allocation is required by the first amendment, see Note, *Reconciling Red Lion and Tornillo: A Consistent Theory of Media Regulation*, 28 STAN. L. REV. 563 (1976). (*But see* Van Alstyne, *Perspectives on Red Lion*, 29 S.C.L. REV. 539 (1978) and discussion in text at note 83 *infra*.) For an excellent argument as to why a bid-auction system might in fact be less inegalitarian than first impressions may suggest (principally because of the high private cost already involved in FCC practices and

because of factors and practices common to the industry), see the reflections of a recent FCC Commissioner, Robinson, *The Federal Communications Commission: An Essay on Regulatory Watchdogs*, 64 VA. L. REV. 169 (1978).

65. Some readers, conversant with constitutional doctrines, may at this point wonder whether the analogy overlooks a difficulty that needs further attention, namely, that the arrangement being discussed may offend the doctrine of "unconstitutional conditions." The doctrine originates in a dictum by Justice Sutherland, in Frost & Frost Trucking Co. v. Railroad Comm'n, 271 U.S. 583, 593 (1926), in which he observed:

> It would be a palpable incongruity to strike down an act of . . . legislation which, by words of express divestment, seeks to strip the citizen of rights guaranteed by the federal Constitution, but to uphold an act by which the same result is accomplished under the guise of a surrender of a right in exchange for a valuable privilege which the state threatens otherwise to withhold.

As applied here, the thought might be that if the government cannot compel one to carry other people's messages against one's own wishes by threatening imprisonment (because such an imposition would violate one's own freedom of speech), neither may it accomplish the same end indirectly, by attaching such an obligation in exchange for the "valuable privilege which the state threatens otherwise to withhold," namely, the "valuable privilege" of (exclusive) street use. Moreover, the fact that any other person applying for the same privilege would be subject to the same agreement, it may be argued, can make no difference; if the condition of securing the privilege is one that otherwise violates the first amendment, the willingness of someone else to submit to it cannot alter its impropriety. To the contrary. *See, e.g.*, Branti v. Finkel, 445 U.S. 507 (1980); Elrod v. Burns, 427 U.S. 347 (1976); Sherbert v. Verner, 374 U.S. 398 (1963); Speiser v. Randall, 357 U.S. 513 (1968). And see discussions in Hale, *Unconstitutional Conditions and Constitutional Rights*, 35 COLUM. L. REV. 321 (1935); O'Neil, *Unconstitutional Conditions: Welfare Benefits with Strings Attached*, 54 CALIF. L. REV. 443 (1966); discussion and additonal citations in Note, *Constitutional Problems in the Execution of Foreign Penal Sentences: The Mexican-American Prisoner Transfer Treaty*, 90 HARV. L. REV. 1500, 1525 (1977).

But the trick, of course, is to be very careful in determining whether the arrangement now being objected to is in fact the "same" thing (in disguise) as that with which it is being compared, *i.e.*, whether the context of the arrangement is without a differentiating significance of its own. The doctrine of unconstitutional conditions does not answer that question. Rather, it merely raises that question—it imposes upon government the burden to demonstrate a constitutionally significant difference sufficient to account for a condition (namely, the duty to carry other people's messages) distinguishably relevant to this context. Here, of course, the "distinguishably relevant" fact is the exclusivity of use-rights granted the successful applicant, and the justification of mitigating the excluded use-rights of others in the same street. Imposition of a common carrier's duty may be no more remarkable here, though the "freight" being carried includes other people's messages, than in respect to a regulated, privately owned, publicly secured monopoly. For an additional discussion, see Van Alstyne, *The Constitutional Rights of Public Employees: A Comment on the Inappropriate Uses of an Old Analogy*, 16 U.C.L.A. L. REV. 751 (1969). And compare with the cases cited above, United States Civil Serv. Comm'n v. National Ass'n of Letter Carriers, 413 U.S. 548 (1973); Pickering v. Board of Educ., 391 U.S. 563 (1968); Garrity v. New Jersey, 385 U.S. 493 (1967).

66. *Cf.* B. ACKERMAN, PRIVATE PROPERTY AND THE CONSTITUTION (1977) and see also the discussion and references at note 85 *infra*, as well as Michelman, *Property as a Constitutional Right*, 38 WASH. & LEE L. REV. 1097 (1981).

67. *See* discussion and references at note 27, chapter 2.

68. 395 U.S. at 386 ("broadcasting is clearly a medium affected by a First Amendment interest").

69. *See* 47 U.S.C. § 303(m)(1)(D) (1970); Yale Broadcasting Co. v. FCC, 478 F.2d 594 (D.C. Cir.), *cert. denied*, 414 U.S. 914 (1973); Sonderling Broadcasting Corp. WGLD-FM, 27 RAD. REG. 2d (P & F) 285 (1973). For a superior critical review, see Note, *Filthy Words, the FCC and the First Amendment: Regulating Broadcast Obscenity*, 61 VA. L. REV. 579 (1975).

70. FCC v. Pacifica Foundation, 438 U.S. 726 (1978).

71. As argued in Krattenmaker & Powe, *Television Violence: First Amendment Principles and Social Science Theory*, 64 VA. L. REV. 1123 (1978); Feinberg, *Obscene Words and the Law*, 2 LAW AND PHILOSOPHY 139 (1983); and see Note cited note 69 *supra*; Erznoznik v. Jacksonville, 422 U.S. 205 (1975) (ordinance prohibiting drive-in movies from showing nudity in films visible from public street held invalid); Cohen v. California, 403 U.S. 15 (1971) (disorderly conduct ordinance as applied to "fuck the draft" slogan on jacket worn in public courthouse corridor held invalid). *But see* Young v. American Mini Theatres, 427 U.S. 50 (1976) (commercial zoning restriction on "adult" theaters upheld).

72. *Cf.* Rowan v. Post Office Department, 397 U.S. 728 (1970) (federal statute forbidding sending of mail to addressee who has filed notice indicating it is not to receive such mail, sustained). *Compare* Butler v. Michigan, 352 U.S. 380 (1957) (holding invalid a law forbidding theaters to show films thought unfit for children).

73. The point is potentially significant. Current technological developments may substantially meet this qualification. *See, e.g.*, M. FRANKLIN, MASS MEDIA LAW 630.44 (1982); Watts, *A Major Issue of the 1980's: New Communications Tools*, in B. CHAMBERLIN & C. BROWN, THE FIRST AMENDMENT RECONSIDERED 181 (1982); *Hearings on Freedom of Expression and the Electronic Media before the Senate Committee on Commerce, Science, and Transportation*, 97th Cong. 2d Sess. (1982). Additionally, insofar as ordinary home receivers accept a range of signals (*e.g.*, AM as well as FM, UHF as well as VHF), it is a very nice question whether saturation of available frequencies of one "type" justifies imposition of third-party obligations even when alternative channels (albeit of a nominally different type) remain unclaimed. The practical inability to proceed to use such a channel is doubtless most typically a function of personal budget constraint, rather than lack of equivalent, available channels to reach those interested in listening or seeing.

These nuances aside, it is also strongly arguable that most of the program-content powers vested in the FCC should be withdrawn in view of: (a) the *actual* administration of the FCC (*i.e.*, its tendency both to underenforce and overenforce the several program-content rules); (b) the practical (financial and administrative) barriers that affect the current arrangement; (c) the deep political hazards that lie close to the surface of the FCC's basic licensing powers (*i.e.*, its fundamental anti–first amendment kinship with the Stationers' monopoly and the temptation the arrangement provides for government abuse); and (d) the immense variety of other sources of news and views freely available (*e.g.*, special-interest printed material has in fact proliferated, not diminished, in the United States). Quite a strong case can be made that despite the prevailing theory, the prevailing fact is that the current regime diminishes, rather than promotes, either freedom or diversity. *See, e.g.*, Robinson, *The Federal Communications Commission: An Essay on Regulatory Watchdogs*, 64 VA. L. REV. 169 (1978); Lange, *The Role of the Access Doctrine in the Regulation of the Mass Media: A Critical Review and Assessment*, 52 N.C.L. REV. 1 (1973). See also the dissent by Bazelon in Brandywine-Main Line Radio, Inc. v. FCC, 473 F.2d 16 (D.C. Cir. 1972), *cert. denied*, 412 U.S. 922 (1973).

74. To the extent that the FCC may refuse to license new channels in order to protect existing licensees (*compare* FCC v. Sanders Bros. Radio Station, 309 U.S. 470 (1940) *with* Carroll Broadcasting Co. v. FCC, 258 F.2d 440 (D.C. Cir. 1958)), the metaphor of the publicly owned magazine rack (discussed *infra* in this same paragraph of the text), capable of accepting additional magazines, should be highly instructive. Imagine a policy of forbidding new magazines to be placed on the rack, despite the availability of ample space, on the rationale that the "public interest" is already adequately served by the current users. The better first amendment argument is to strike directly at that restriction. It is not to permit the government (a) to lock out other competitors and then (b) to utilize the fact of such a restriction as a justification to continue to regulate the content of magazines it does allow to be placed on the rack, on the bootstrap rationale that insofar as it insulates those magazines from competition it provides them with a subsidy for which it may exact a concession respecting some control over each magazine's content.

The very suggestion that "public property" (which the airwaves are alleged to be) can be denied to some because "the public interest" is deemed to be already adequately served by the communications of others (whose capacity to serve that "public interest" would be placed at risk by the competing communications of newcomers) turns the first amendment upside down. The reasoning implicit in such an argument is no better than if Florida, in a modified *Miami Herald* case, had (a) directed the *Miami Herald* what to print "in the public interest"; (b) criminalized the operation of any rival newspaper sufficiently likely to cut into *Herald* revenues to compromise its economic ability to continue to carry the government-directed "public-interest" features; and (c) used its suppression of such other papers as the ultimate fortifying rationale for justifying its interference with the *Herald.*

75. If any distinction remained to be made, it would be a distinction both very different in kind and sharply more limited in effect than the general, content-sensitive regime of the FCC as we now know it. For instance, it may be objected that a large number of media-related enterprises (*e.g.*, AT&T and certain cable companies) do not fit the metaphor likening the airways to a publicly owned newsrack or broadcast companies to newspapers at all well. Rather, they are primarily commercial entities in the business of carrying messages for hire, and accordingly, in respect to that aspect of their business, quite a strong case may still be made that they may be subjected to the nondiscrimination obligations of common carriers. The analogy here is appropriately to Western Union as a private company, as well as to the U.S. Post Office. *See* Geller & Lampert, *Cable, Content Regulation and the First Amendment*, 32 CATH. U.L. REV. 603 (1983). Note, however, that application of this observation is not merely different in its theory. It is also different in its implications. For an additional recent analysis, see I. POOL, TECHNOLOGIES OF FREEDOM (1983).

The analogy, moreover, is surely one that would have to be pursued with considerable modesty, consistent with the interpretations of the first amendment we have reviewed. For instance, although it is doubtless true that newspapers must sell advertising space to survive and that they do so as a regular part of their business, it cannot readily be supposed that therefore they, too, might be compelled by law to accept advertisements inconsistent with the editorial policy of the publisher, consistent with the implications of the *Miami Herald* case. The new effort to impose common-carrier duties on newspaper advertising space would rest on the suggestion of cutting legal pieces out of allegedly separable parts of a newspaper, *i.e.*, of separating common-carrier advertising duties from full editorial autonomy limited strictly to news stories and/or editorials. But obviously the editorial color of a newspaper or journal (*e.g.*, the National Review, Ms. Magazine) cannot realistically be identified solely with the publisher's full editorial discretion over only a part of the journal. The idiosyncrasy of most of the press is at least partly reflected in its editorial policies respecting advertising. Even for the majority of newspapers that do in fact pursue a private advertising policy like that of a common carrier, moreover, it is still because the publisher (doubtless influenced by competitive factors) desires to present the publication in that way—and not because, contrary to editorial choice, a "common-carrier" law forces them to publish a product different from what they wish to present. *Compare* Nadel, *A Unified Theory of the First Amendment: Divorcing the Medium from the Message*, 11 FORDHAM URBAN L.J. 163 (1983).

76. CBS v. Democratic Nat'l Comm., 412 U.S. 94, 162 (1973) (Douglas, J., concurring).

77. See references at note 64 *supra.*

78. The insight was originally offered by Ronald Coase, *The Federal Communications Commission*, 2 J.L. & ECON. 1 (1959), and the following summary in the text is reflected in the subsequent writings of others cited in note 64 *supra.*

79. Pruneyard Shopping Center v. Robins, 447 U.S. 74 (1980).

80. Marsh v. Alabama, 326 U.S. 501 (1946). *See also* Amalgamated Food Employees Union v. Logan Valley Plaza, Inc., 391 U.S. 308 (1968), *limited by* Lloyd Corp. v. Tanner, 407 U.S. 551 (1972), and *overruled by* Hudgens v. NLRB, 424 U.S. 507 (1976).

81. See text and references at note 64 *supra.*

82. And despite what is reflected in the text immediately hereafter, to a considerable extent the argument we are now examining does in fact effectively respond to most of the Supreme Court's opinion in *Red Lion*, which is far more obfuscating than convincing. For instance, at several places the Court puts a part of the rationale on the need to avoid "the cacophony of competing voices, none of which could be clearly and predictably heard" (p. 376), and it likens radio broadcasts to the use of a sound truck that might, if left unregulated, "snuff out the free speech of others" (p. 387). But that, of course, does no more than demonstrate the need for some sort of property rules

and legal analogies to the common law of nuisances, according to which injunctive judicial relief can be sought as when one homeowner plays his stereo so loud as to interfere with his neighbors; assuredly it requires no license to operate a stereo and certainly no obligation to play anything on one's stereo other than what one decides to play. Elsewhere, the Court emphasizes the limited divisibility of the usable spectrum (thus attempting to distinguish it from "mere" economic scarcity), but here, too, the land analogy (fixed sites, some favored by downtown locations, some subject to zoning on size, etc., but *not* including surrogate program-content duties [may a motion picture theater be compelled to show a "diversity" of films?]) makes the point either too weak or too strong. That more will apply for licenses than there are frequencies to allocate is similarly indistinguishable from "free" land access of variable site-and-size advantage; the cost internalization of any such advantages, pursuant to a property-rights regime, eliminates both the subsidy and the length of the line of erstwhile license seekers. In any event, it is quite plain that *choice*, not necessity, underlies the arrangement of the airwaves.

83. It is surely noteworthy, for instance, that the FCC has itself already conceded the inappropriateness of continuing compulsory program-diversity formats within each radio licensee's broadcast fare, given the very large number of AM and FM stations readily receivable in virtually every part of the country and given also the diversity of alternative media sources readily available within every community. For more on this and related deregulation developments affecting radio, see De-regulation of Radio, 84 F.C.C.2d 968, 49 RAD. REG.2d 1, *reconsideration denied*, 87 F.C.C.2d 797, 50 R.R.2d 93 (1981). Except as a "right of reply" might sometimes be available against newspaper defamation (see note 54 *supra*), the basic case to sustain it as applied to a broadcaster now does appear to be exceedingly weak. In respect to new developments in direct broadcast satellites (DBS), moreover, the tentative position of the FCC is essentially that of market forces and minimum regulation. *See* Report and Order, 51 RAD. REG.2d (P & F) 1341 (1982); Comment, *Cable Television vs. Direct Broadcast Satellites: Market Competition Replaces the FCC as the Guarantor of the Public Interest*, 34 SYRA. L. REV. 851 (1983). For evidence of recent deregulation developments even for regular television (as well as radio) licensees, see references and discussion in Black Citizens for a Fair Media v. FCC, 719 F.2d. 407 (D.C. Cir. 1983).

84. Cited and quoted at note 64 *supra*.

85. Quoted in *Red Lion* at 395 U.S. 376, n.5.

86. See text at note 64 *supra*.

87. See discussion and suggestions in text at notes 69.76, 84 *supra*.

88. *See, e.g.* Hague v. CIO, 307 U.S. 496 (1939) (public park); Southeastern Promotions Ltd. v. Conrad, 420 U.S. 546 (1975) (civic auditorium); Elrod v. Burns, 427 U.S. 347 (1976) (public jobs).

89. Marsh v. Alabama, 326 U.S. 501 (1946) (company town); Pruneyard Shopping Center v. Robins, 447 U.S. 74 (1980) (shopping center).

90. The intrinsic difficulty of even imagining a meaningful right of free speech (or of the press) without including within it exclusive use rights in *some* kind of "property" is obvious. As the Supreme Court noted in Lynch v. Household Finance Corp., 405 U.S. 538, 552 (1972), "a fundamental interdependence exists between the personal right to liberty and the personal right in property. Neither could have any meaning without the other." The principal constitutional antecedent for the way in which that proposition has been applied is John Locke's *Of the Ends of Political Society and Government*, in his famous SECOND TREATISE OF CIVIL GOVERNMENT (1690). Still, it is obvious, too, that the proposition cuts both ways; to the extent one lacks one's "property," one lacks a meaningful right in free speech.

One technique for mitigating the difficulty of inequality, in respect to free speech, is by prohibiting more than a specified speech-use of one's own private property, *i.e.*, by "leveling down" speech-rights in respect to property, without necessarily otherwise affecting private property holdings. It is an aspect of what Marx called "crude" communism (*see, e.g.*, his discussion on *Private Property and Communism*, in his ECONOMIC AND PHILOSOPHIC MANUSCRIPTS of 1844). The approach has generally been rejected in the Supreme Court. *See, e.g.*, Citizens Against Rent Control

v. City of Berkeley, 102 S. Ct. 434 (1982); First National Bank of Boston v. Bellotti, 435 U.S. 765 (1978); Buckley v. Valeo, 424 U.S. 1 (1976). It is the object of Kurt Vonnegut's popular parody in *Harrison Bergeron* (1961). *But see* Wright, *Money and the Pollution of Politics: Is the First Amendment an Obstacle to Political Equality?*, 82 Colum. L. Rev. 609 (1982).

A related notion is that of "leveling up" by selective subsidy. The general notion is that to the extent X invokes his property advantage (*e.g.*, private savings, inherited newspaper, or lucky winnings at the track) to express a point of view (as by purchasing "speech-time"), revenue collected via taxation shall be funneled to Y so that Y may spend it to express an opposing point of view, the measure of the disbursement to Y reflecting some wealth difference between X and Y. (Consider also an application for equivalent subsidy to Z and others, namely, persons [or associations?] with less speech-usable property than X but holding views different from those of either X or Y, which they, too, assert they have an equal intensity of desire to express and which the body politic "needs" to hear equally, if the "best" idea is to prevail in the outcome.) Complicated variations are examined and supported in Lowenstein, *Campaign Spending and Ballot Propositions: Recent Experience, Public Choice Theory and the First Amendment*, 29 U.C.L.A. L. Rev. 505 (1982). It is not clear (*see* Rawls and *compare* Mandel *infra*) why most proposals of this genre draw a line respecting private property more or less "external" to oneself. Charisma may be as potent a speech influence as dollars spent on redundant advertisements, as may physical appearance, forensic skill, grateful friends, etc. None of these "properties" are evenly distributed among all persons. Some of them are not more (or less!) earned than indifferent dollars. If their uneven presence is felt to "pollute" or "distort" an "ideal" speech outcome, presumably the case for leveling up, etc., is theoretically as strong as other proposals now afloat. Neither is it obvious that the administrative judgments would be more complicated or odious.

A related approach is that of "forced sharing" of private property, which the Court has appeared to accept (unless, as in *Tornillo*, the private property is peculiarly "speech property" [though that phrase is my own characterization, not the Court's]) and which the text illustrates with references to *Pruneyard* and *Marsh v. Alabama*. But forced sharing of property for speech is nonetheless treated differently than "forced expression," despite the difficulty of discerning the difference in many instances. At one extreme is the forced expression by one's own voice or gestures, of sentiments one disbelieves. *See, e.g.*, West Virginia State Bd. of Education v. Barnette, 319 U.S. 624 (1943). At least in the circumstance where it is the *government*'s choice of utterances that is being compelled, the principle also has been applied in respect to other personal property (Wooley v. Maynard, 430 U.S. 705 (1977) and to compelled money contributions for third-party political activities (Abood v. Detroit Board of Education, 431 U.S. 209 (1977). It is also worth noting, as Paul Freund has done (P. Freund, On Understanding the Supreme Court 20–21 (1949)), that even the early English reformers denigrated as "Levellers" nonetheless resisted the idea of improving conditions for the disfranchised by the particular device of forced sharing of private property. Thus, the 1649 Agreement of the Free People of England, while urging a large number of egalitarian changes, nonetheless stipulated that "it shall not be in the power of any Representative, in any wise, to . . . make all things Common . . . ."

The piecemeal socialization of property resources, with use-rights consequently assigned by some sort of "neutral" parliamentary allocation (*e.g.*, queuing), is a commonplace means of dealing with the problem also, as the text discusses, though Marx regarded this as at best a form of "crude" communism. See the essay cited *supra*, and compare his essay, *On the Jewish Question* (1843).

Taxation and redistribution are the most conventional forms of partial amelioration, consistent with a fundamental private property system, and the subject has received extraordinarily thoughtful attention during the past two decades. *See, e.g.*, J. Rawls, A Theory of Justice (1971) (and especially his presentation of the "the difference principle"), and the very impressive new work by M. Sandel, Liberalism and the Limits of Justice (1982). For other principal writings in the field, see B. Ackerman, Social Justice in the Liberal State (1980); B. Ackerman, Private Property and the Constitution (1977); R. Posner, The Economics of Justice (1981); L. Becker, Property Rights: Philosphic Foundations (1977); R. Nozick, Anarchy, State, and Utopia (1974); R. Dworkin, Taking Rights Seriously (1977). And for excellent reviews in the periodical literature, see Monaghan, *Of "liberty" and "property,"* 62 Cornell L. Rev. 405 (1977); Michelman, *Property, Utility, and Fairness: Comments on the Ethical Foundations of Just Compensation Law*, 80 Harv. L. Rev. 1165 (1967); Coase, *The Problem of Social Cost*, 3 J. Law & Econ. 1 (1960).

Index of Subjects

Index of Persons

Persons mentioned in the text are in italics.

Index of Cases

Cases mentioned in the text are in italics.

William W. Van Alstyne is William R. and Thomas C. Perkins Professor of Law at Duke University. He has served as consultant to numerous U.S. House and Senate committees on constitutional matters involving the first amendment.